For
Grenville Clark.

Herbert John Spiro

Christmas 1960

NOMOS III

RESPONSIBILITY

THE AMERICAN SOCIETY FOR POLITICAL AND LEGAL PHILOSOPHY

The American Society for Political and Legal Philosophy was founded in 1955 by a group of friends in the social sciences, law and philosophy who share an interest in the range of problems traditionally treated within the broad context of political and legal philosophy. The purpose of the Society is to encourage interdisciplinary exploration, treatment and discussion of those issues of political and legal philosophy that are of common interest to these fields. The Society has two major activities: First, an annual meeting of members devoted to the discussion of one particular topic in political and legal philosophy, and second, the publication of a yearbook, NOMOS, in which the results of the discussions are incorporated in a series of articles on the topic discussed by members who have participated formally or informally in the discussions.

NOMOS

YEARBOOK OF THE AMERICAN SOCIETY
OF POLITICAL AND LEGAL PHILOSOPHY

RESPONSIBILITY

Edited by
CARL J. FRIEDRICH

THE LIBERAL ARTS PRESS
NEW YORK

PREFACE

The third volume of *Nomos* has been built on the foundations laid by the papers and discussions of the third annual
meeting of the American Society for Political and Legal Philosophy, held at Chicago after Christmas 1958. This meeting
was held in conjunction with the meeting of the Association
of American Law Schools. Its topic was *Responsibility*. It includes three of the papers presented there, although unfortunately not the key paper by John Austin of Oxford. A serious
illness, culminating in his death on February 8, 1960, prevented him from completing his revisions. The preliminary
outline distributed at the meeting and available to the participants is printed as an appendix to this volume (p. 305).
Because of the unavailability of Austin's paper, Lon Fuller
preferred not to submit his comments. As in previous years,
brief comments at the meeting were elaborated into full
papers; still others were contributed to extend the coverage,
such as "Responsibility and Existence," "The Dilemma of
Administrative Responsibility," and "Responsibility and the
Goal of Survival."

The volume follows the organization of the meeting, dealing respectively with "Responsibility in General," "Criminal
Responsibility," "Responsibility in Modern Government," and
"Responsibility of Citizenship." These are the major areas of
public, as contrasted with private, responsibility, but the papers
certainly do not pretend to exhaust the subject. "Responsibility" is one of the most frequently employed terms in practical and theoretical discussions on public affairs. This volume
brings together a richer and more varied treatment than any
other recent publication on the subject.

The editor was much helped by two fellow members of the
Society, Professor Harry W. Jones and Professor John Ladd,
who more particularly evaluated critically and co-edited the

contributions in their respective fields; this work which they did while under great pressure is gratefully acknowledged, with sincere thanks. We should also like to thank the Twentieth Century Fund for helping us to publish the first three volumes of *Nomos*. We are also grateful to Miss Roberta G. Hill for the continued devoted labors in our behalf.

C. J. F.

CONTENTS

ix

PART ONE

RESPONSIBILITY: DEFINITION AND GENERAL ISSUES

✆❀❙ I ❧❀

THE PROBLEM OF RESPONSIBILITY

J. ROLAND PENNOCK [1]

A BRITISH CIVIL SERVANT, for a consideration, leaks information about the forthcoming Budget to a stockbroker, who proceeds to convert his newly acquired knowledge into a modest fortune. Where does responsibility lie? The appropriate Minister may point to the civil servant; perhaps also to the immediate superior of the erring clerk. Some members of the cabinet may point to the Minister, while others may argue that to give him the sack would be an act of irresponsibility. Parliament, or at least members of the Opposition, may point to the Government. Friends of the civil servant may point to his wife and perhaps also to the stockbroker, while a psychiatrist may fix responsibility on the man's parents, and the family doctor may say, "I believe that the head injury he received in that recent auto accident is responsible for this departure from his usual standard of conduct." The wide variety of responses doubtless reflects differing views of the facts, differing meanings of the word "responsibility," differing standards for the application of a given meaning, and differing theories of causation. If, as the late T. D. Weldon argued, it is the job of political philosophers to clear up linguistic muddles, it would appear that the subject of the present volume of *Nomos* was well chosen.

It might, nevertheless, be argued that the task we have undertaken is impossibly large and that in fact it has only a specious unity. It is possible that, as one member of the pro-

[1] Professors John W. Chapman of the University of Pittsburgh and Charles E. Gilbert of Swarthmore College both put me in their debt by reading and providing helpful suggestions relating to this chapter.

3

gram committee declared, "political responsibility" has in common with moral and legal responsibility nothing more than the use of the same combination of letters. It may be that the term should always be used with an explicit or implicit modifier and that investigations such as this should be confined to some single topic, such as "political responsibility," "administrative responsibility," "criminal responsibility," and the like. Administrative responsibility may be better studied in a context of other aspects of administration than in the context of "responsibility" in the large. But of course these alternatives are not mutually exclusive. Without examining the question carefully, one can not know whether there are sufficient common elements among various uses of the word to make the generalized approach pay off.

The title of this chapter raises the further question whether there is any single "problem" that can properly be called "*the* problem of responsibility," for this goes beyond the matter of definition. It is certainly a word that has come in for increasing use in recent times—use, too, by people who are bothered about "problems" and who are using it to try to express and deal with those problems. Is there a common core not only of meaning, but also of problem, a tension peculiarly characteristic of modern life? The question is certainly worth entertaining. Moreover, it appears initially likely that the search for a common core of meaning might at least produce useful vantage points for analysis of problems and perhaps even uncover a single overriding problem. This is the theory, at any rate, on which the present essay is undertaken.

Let me anticipate my conclusions to this extent. I believe that among various usages (possibly not *all* usages) of the word "responsibility" there *is* a common core of meaning, that part of this core relates to the exercise of discretion, and that herein lies *the* modern problem of responsibility. Looked at historically and sociologically, the problem arises out of the increasing complexity of society and of our failure to solve its problems by neat formulas or simple governmental devices.

From an ethical point of view, the modern emphasis on responsibility represents both a modernization of earlier liberal concepts and a reaction to totalitarian attacks.

When one starts thinking about the general notion of responsibility, certain aspects or categories immediately come to mind. The man in the street may think first of moral responsibility and almost as soon of legal responsibility. A political scientist's thoughts naturally alight first on political or administrative responsibility. (As a matter of fact it appears that the word had its first application in this realm.[2]) He might quickly add judicial responsibility, and after a slight hesitation, electoral responsibility, or the responsibility of citizenship. At this point doubts and questions begin to crowd upon him. Are these different kinds of responsibility, he might ask, or merely, so to speak, separate packages of moral and legal responsibilities as they pertain to particular vocations or situations? The same man will frequently have familial, neighborly, and professional responsibilities. At the same time too, as a holder of public office, he may have political or administrative responsibilities. Are these really all different kinds of responsibility, or are they all reducible to moral and legal responsibilities? Surely a man's responsibility to his family is a moral and also a legal matter, just as is his responsibility for keeping the sidewalk in front of his house in reasonably safe condition. The responsibility of citizenship may likewise be reduced to a matter of simple morality. But

2 Richard McKeon, in his helpful article, "The Development and the Significance of the Concept of Responsibility," *Revue International de Philosophie*, 39 (1957), 3-32, states that "responsibility" was first used in English and French in 1787, and was applied to the operation of political institutions. (*Ibid.*, p. 23.) Presumably he based this statement upon the fact that the earliest example of the use of the word given by the *Oxford English Dictionary* is from Alexander Hamilton, in No. 63 of *The Federalist*, published in 1787. However, it appeared at least eleven years earlier in Bentham's *A Fragment on Government* (1948), p. 94. The *O.E.D.* cites a use of the adjective "responsible" as early as 1643, in a passage referring to the king as "responsible" to Parliament.

what of the responsibility of a government, or of a member of the legislature, or of a member of a regulatory commission? Here the moral and legal categories begin to seem inadequate. Perhaps "political" responsibility, in a broad sense, is after all a separate category.

According to the Oxford English Dictionary "responsibility" is "the state or fact of being responsible"; and "responsible" means "answerable," "accountable (*to* another, *for* something)," "liable to be called to account," "morally accountable for one's actions," and "capable of rational conduct."[3] Webster lists as synonyms, "responsible," "accountable," "amenable," and "liable," saying that they all mean "subject to an authority which may exact redress," but goes on to note that the kind of subjection to authority involved tends to be somewhat specific in the case of each of the terms except "responsible," which is the vaguest and most general.[4] Another clue may be gained from the derivation ("*re*" plus "*spondere*," to promise). This notion is taken up by Crabb (*English Synonyms*), who says that "responsible" and "answerable" convey "the idea of a pledge given in performance of some act, or the fulfillment of some engagement. . . ."

Pretty clearly the notion of accountability is normally central to the concept; yet in certain usages it becomes marginal at best. For example, in certain contexts it must be understood to include accountability to one's conscience. The actor, I, is accountable to the censor, me. Matters of duty and obligation are easily brought within this framework. When I ask, "What is my responsibility for my starving neighbor?" I may mean, "What ought I to do to help him?" or, "What is my duty toward him?" This in turn can easily be expressed in terms of what I am accountable for doing—what I may properly be held to account for by other people or by my own conscience.

But also the question about my responsibility for my starving neighbor may be retrospective rather than prospective, meaning "What have I done or omitted that led to this situa-

3 *Ibid.*
4 *Webster's New Collegiate Dictionary* (2nd ed.; 1953), p. 722.

tion?" It is this usage that leads many writers who have discussed this subject to say that one meaning of "responsibility" must be cast in terms of the concept of causation. I believe this view is generally incorrect. Causation, to be sure, is often relevant to moral or legal duty or obligation, which are in turn part of the notion of "responsibility"; but I doubt that the relationship is any closer than this. Of course if I cause you to fall and injure yourself, as by pushing you, I may be responsible; but this is because I am, under the circumstances, legally liable, or morally accountable, or both. Generally speaking, it may be said that those who cause injury to others are presumptively responsible (answerable) to them for the injury done. But it is only a presumption. If I injure a man in the course of fending off an attack, the fact that I caused his injury does not necessarily mean that I incur responsibility for it. If I say to you, "I am cutting down this tree and it is about to fall: keep away," and nonetheless you come close, saying, "I'll take my chances," I may be said to have caused any injury that you may suffer as a consequence, but certainly not to bear responsibility for it.[5]

As the last example illustrates, responsibility may be transferred. In that case you accepted responsibility for my actions insofar as they might affect you. Here is the element of promise or pledge. To all intents and purposes you promised not to hold me accountable. If you lend me money, normally it is my responsibility to remember to repay you, but if I borrow it saying, "I do this only on condition that you accept the responsibility for reminding me of my debt," and you agree, responsibility has been transferred.

It is pertinent to point out, parenthetically, that there are limits to this process of transferring responsibility, thus suggesting that the word cannot be defined entirely in terms of promises or contracts. Promises that are very unreasonable and that may be thought therefore to have been extorted under duress will not be held to suffice to transfer responsibility—for example, a promise made to a kidnaper. Possibly such an in-

[5] My action was not of course a *sufficient* cause of your injury.

stance might be explained by saying that there was no valid contract. However, my responsibility for taking care of my aged parents clearly flows neither from promise nor from my role as a causal factor.

Returning now to the matter of causation, it is to be noted that I may accept responsibility for events that I do not cause and cannot prevent: legal responsibility as in the case of an insurance company; political responsibility as in the case of the Minister in the example with which this paper opened. But this would not be true of moral responsibility. Here we have an additional argument for holding that causation relates to responsibility only indirectly as it affects duties, moral or legal. Again, to borrow from the late Professor Austin, if, while driving with all due care, I collide with your car deliberately, as the only means of avoiding hitting a child who has just run out into the street, I may cause considerable damage, but surely one would not say that the responsibility for the accident was mine or that I was responsible for it.[6]

Literally, I believe, responsibility encompasses all duties—wherever I have a duty I have a responsibility—but ordinary usage avoids applying it to certain kinds of duties. Consider the following hypothetical case. You hand me what you take

[6] In the case of the adjective, usage sometimes appears to elevate causation to a primary role in the definition. Webster notes, as an Americanism, the use of "responsible for" to mean "answerable as the primary cause, motive, or agent." (*Op. cit.*, p. 722.) The notion of answerability is still present, however. The point being made by the use of the word responsibility is never *simply* a matter of identifying the causal agent; it is doing this for the purpose of establishing a resultant continuing relationship between the agent and the effects of his action or the conditions he created. This relationship, however, need not be one of duty or debt; it may be one of credit. Thus I may say, "*I* am responsible for all of the improvements you see in this house." This extension of meaning seems not to have been carried over to the noun.

In any case, as was indicated above, I am searching for a common core of meaning for most applications of the word "responsibility." If there are occasional or specialized extensions of meaning or even meanings that are independent of the "core" which I believe exists for most uses of the word, my argument is not affected.

to be a dollar bill, in repayment of a debt. I note that in fact it is a ten dollar bill. Probably most people would say it was my "duty" to call attention to your mistake; they would be unlikely to say it was my "responsibility." For my part, I might be tempted to argue (perhaps to myself!) that it was your "responsibility" to be more careful; but I should hardly say it was your "duty." Where what is due is simple and clear cut, we tend to use "duty" or "obligation." On the other hand, where what is due follows from an act within an area of individual freedom, where judgment or discretion is or ought to be exercised, we are more likely to use the word "responsibility." Take the following example. I might say, "It is my responsibility around here to dry the dishes," or I might refer to the drying of the dishes as one of my household "duties." [7] A clearer case for the use of "responsibility" is presented, however, if I refer to my responsibility for taking care of the garden—a matter demanding considerable knowledge and the exercise of discretion.

When we consider political responsibility, it is clear that the area of accountability for choices, decisions, exercises of judgment, is broader than the area of duty. And it is vaguer. What is the responsibility of a congressman to his constituents? He is accountable to them, meaning that they may vote him out of office at the next election because of the way he has conducted himself. The standards they will apply are vague at best. But he has accepted this condition in running for office. He has accepted "responsibility" for pleasing a majority of the voters, knowing that this may prove impossible. But it is at least partly with respect to his exercise of judgment

[7] The latter usage has an idiomatic flavor. I would be less likely to say, "It is my duty around here to dry the dishes." Note that the phrase "around here," in each instance implies that we are talking about a condition of general application. If I were referring to an obligation arising out of a particular circumstance—say, the fact that my wife is very tired— I would be more likely to say "it is my duty to dry the dishes." The application is specific rather than general and the emphasis is on a moral obligation not fraught with significant exercise of discretion in the manner of its discharge.

that they will presumably make their decision. If his fate were to be determined by drawing lots, or by some sort of contest between his supporters and their opponents in which winning was a matter of pure chance or of skill on the part of the players but in which the way the legislator had conducted himself in office had nothing to do with the matter, we would hardly say that this was a situation of responsibility. Here, too, it appears that a person who is in a position of responsibility enjoys a certain freedom of action or area of choice and that he may rightly be held praiseworthy or blameworthy or subject to some form of reward or deprivation (punishment, damages, moral censure, loss of power or position, or the like) by reason of the way in which he exercises his power (freedom to choose or act). It may be further suggested that while the standards to be used in judging his conduct may vary greatly according to the circumstances (including agreements made at the time responsibility is assumed), there are always some standards, however vague, and the responsible person is subject to sanctions if he fails to use sound reasoning, good judgment, and careful deliberation in the application of those standards. At the very least his action should not be arbitrary and should be such that a reasonable man might believe it to be conducive to the attainment of the goal the official is charged with pursuing.

Again, let us examine the term "responsible government." It is easy to get into muddles in connection with this term, simply because we use it, often at the same time, in varying applications. We mean that the government is responsible to the electorate, in the sense discussed above; it is accountable, in some not completely arbitrary fashion, for the exercise of its trust. But we also mean that it is morally responsible; that is, that it acts in a fashion that would be morally approved by disinterested observers (or by ourselves). It holds itself to account to high standards of duty, justice, and public welfare. It may, for instance, refuse to cut taxes when the best opinion of economists is that such action would be bad for the economy, even though it is known that such a step would be electorally popular.

It follows from what has just been said that there would be no inconsistency, under certain circumstances, in charging a government with irresponsibility for following popular opinion. Recognizing the danger of such situations arising, Hamilton, in that number of *The Federalist* (No. 63) to which reference has already been made, argued in favor of the six year term for senators on the ground that this long a period was necessary in order for constituents to be able to form a reasonable judgment on the effects of certain kinds of legislative action, such judgment being necessary, he said, for "effectual responsibility."

At this point it will be useful to consider what is the legitimate meaning, if there is any, behind the claim of fascists that their government is supremely "responsible," that the "Leader" is responsible. There is no electoral accountability, nor is it seriously contended that there is. But it is argued that the Leader holds himself accountable, in his own conscience, to the public welfare or some other respected standard. He might claim that he, as contrasted with a divided and pusillanimous democratic government, had the *power* to act without which there can be no (moral) responsibility,[8] and that he exercised it wisely, with discretion. He might further argue that, under such a centralized government, duties (responsibilities) are clearly allocated (all in one spot) so that there can be no doubt as to who is accountable, and moreover, that their burden will be so overwhelming that they cannot pass unnoticed or be ignored by the bearer, as might happen when governmental responsibility is widely scattered.

Especially in the case of the adjectival form, "responsible,"

---

[8] Even with respect to political responsibility, Hamilton declared "responsibility, in order to be reasonable, must be limited to objects within the power of the responsible party. . . ." Alexander Hamilton, J. Jay and J. Madison, *The Federalist or the New Constitution* (1926), No. LXIII, 321.

there is a further source of confusion. Not that the central meaning is any different, but the adjective may mean either "bearing responsibility" (as in "a man is responsible for his wife's debts") or "fit to bear responsibility" (as in "he is a responsible person"). In the latter usage, we may note, paralleling our finding with respect to "responsibility," that we mean more than "dutiful." A moron might be dutiful, but we would hardly speak of him as a responsible person. He lacks the understanding and ability to exercise discretion that is required for this designation.[9] Where it is will that is the missing element of responsibility, we are likely to use the word "*ir*responsible."

Sometimes "responsibility" also, as was illustrated in the preceding footnote, bears this more emphatic sense, as when we say that X "lacks responsibility" or "a sense of responsibility," not referring to any particular act, but referring rather to an awareness of the considerations that ought in the circumstances to govern one's behavior, the ability to make sound judgments respecting those considerations, and the disposition to act accordingly.

For a further useful example, let us consider what we mean when we say, "X is a responsible citizen." We mean, I suggest, that he is mindful of his civic duties; but also more than this.

---

[9] To be sure, if a moron fails in his duty and thereby causes an accident, we may say that he was responsible for the accident. The difference appears to be one of emphasis. When we say "X is a responsible person," we emphasize the elements of capacity and disposition to act in the light of good judgment and due consideration of obligations and the interests of others. When we say, "X is responsible for the occurrence of Y," we mean that if he had acted as he should have acted Y would not have occurred. In other words, even though X does not have that *degree* of capacity for acting responsibly that would lead us to call him a "responsible person," we would nonetheless say that he was "responsible" for an event that occurred because of his lack of responsibleness (or "responsibility"). But if X was an idiot, although we *might* possibly say his action was responsible for Y, I think we would recognize that we were using the word in a rather attenuated sense, and would tend to say that the "real" responsibility lay with someone who stood in some relationship of guardianship for the idiot.

If a person is so stupid as to be incapable of voting intelligently, we would hardly say he failed in his duty. Perhaps
we would not say he failed in his responsibility either, but we
might well say that he lacked responsibility. Moreover, we
might say that he was not a responsible citizen, while we
would not say that he was not a dutiful citizen. In short, he
lacks responsibility in the sense of fitness for acting responsibly in this context. His weakness is intellectual rather than
moral.

In emphasizing the rational, deliberative aspect of the word,
we are not denying that it is sometimes used in a narrower
sense, substantially equivalent to "duty," but we normally
reserve it for cases where the performance of duty requires
discernment and choice. We might well say to a child, "It is
your responsibility to take care of your room"; but we would
not be likely to say, "It is your responsibility to do as you are
told."

Responsibility, then, has various meanings in different contexts, some of them fairly precise; but if we are seeking a common core for these meanings, we must say that it means more
than duty or dutifulness and more than accountability, although it includes these meanings. The "more than" points
toward the exercise of discretion by deliberate and thoughtful
decision in the light of a sound calculation of probable consequences and a fair evaluation of claims. In the parable of
the talents, the rich man did more than hold his servants
accountable; he held them accountable for acting responsibly.
He put them in a position where they could exercise choice
and then held them accountable for showing judgment, a
consideration for what the master would like, and (therefore)
even imagination and initiative.

In fact, it is fair to say that "responsibility" has two primary meanings, or that what I have called the core of meaning has two facets, (a) accountability and (b) the rational and
moral exercise of discretionary power (or the capacity or disposition for such exercise), and that each of these notions
tends to flavor the other. In any particular application, either

one may be dominant, but the other remains in the background. When we use the word "responsibility" to mean "accountability," it is usually when we have in mind accountability for some proper exercise of discretion. If I lend you a dollar, I speak of your "duty" to repay me; or I may say that I have a "right" that you should repay me. Put in accountability-responsibility terms, I would say that you are accountable for repaying me. But if you ask me how I can expect you to repay the dollar when you have lost it, I may reply, "that is *your* 'responsibility.' " [10] On the other hand, when we use the word "responsibility" to refer to behavior of the "proper-exercise-of-discretion" type or to the disposition to exhibit such behavior, the notion of accountability for such behavior is generally in the background, even if only in the sense of accountability to conscience or high standards.

It was earlier noted that the term "responsibility" appears to have been of relatively modern origin; and it is certainly true that it has quite recently achieved an uncommon vogue. Yet surely the central ideas are not new. This statement is reinforced by Professor Fuller's remark, at the meeting of the Society, that the concept of responsibility gives to the law much of its coherence. It is worth speculating why this is so. Of course the law is always and centrally concerned with duties. Perhaps this fact in itself would be enough to explain his statement. But responsibility and the law seem to have more than this in common. The emphasis on rationality also is reflected in the law's concern with the standard of the reasonable man—the standard used in the law of torts for the determination of responsibility for negligence. Here and else-

[10] A further point: it is of course *possible* that I would reply, "You are nevertheless accountable," but I would never say, "that is your accountability." The noun "accountability" denotes simply that for which one is accountable or possibly the condition of being accountable (for some particular thing, series of things, or act or series of acts). Unlike "responsibility" it is not used where there is room for considerable discretion in discharging the account.

where in the law what is used is essentially the notion of a responsible (as contrasted with irresponsible) person. At least in part its value would seem to flow from its flexibility, allowing both for application to a multitude of situations and for change in accordance with changing conditions and standards. It will be observed that the test of the reasonable man is individualistic in that its content is based on the standards of behavior of the normal individual. In the same way the concept of responsibility, on what I call its rationality or discretionary side, has an individualistic reference.

It is worth noting that the development of law (in particular, Anglo-American law) relating to liability for injury to others manifests three stages.[11] In medieval times there appears to have been no law of negligence and therefore no standard of the ordinary, prudent man. There were rules of strict liability for doing damage in specified situations, as for example, damage done by straying cattle. Gradually, however, the ideas developed of a more general liability and also of the defense that the defendant had taken due care (such care as a normal, reasonable, prudent man would take in the circumstances) to prevent damaging events. Although the latter principle appears not to have been formally laid down until 1837,[12] it had, in fact, pervaded the developing law of torts long previously.

No sooner had this second stage of the law, in which the subjective concept of the prudent or responsible man played such an important role, reached its maturity than it began to give way in the face of new conditions and considerations.

[11] The material relating to legal history has been drawn from the following sources: W. S. Holdsworth, *A History of English Law* (1925), VIII, 450; XI, 606; XIII, 552; Percy H. Winfield, "Negligence," *Encyclopaedia of the Social Sciences* (1933), XI, 329-331; Sir Frederick Pollock and Frederic William Maitland, *The History of English Law Before the Times of Edward I* (2d ed.; 1903), II, 475, 528; and Charles O. Gregory, "Trespass to Negligence to Absolute Liability," *Virginia Law Review*, XXXVII (1951), 359-97.

[12] *Vaughan v. Menlove*, 3 Bing. N. C. 468, cited in Holdsworth, *op. cit.*, VIII, 450.

Certain things were inherently so dangerous that the standard of due care seemed inadequate for the protection of others. The focus shifts now from consideration of fairness to the individual who was, after all, acting responsibly, to that of concern for the protection of society. There is no need here to detail the steps or the extent to which the doctrine of strict liability has replaced the prudent man standard in the law of torts. It is sufficient to note the fact and direction of the development. Sometimes legislatures rather than courts have been the instruments of this trend, as in the case of workman's compensation acts; here also the collectivized solution no longer leans on the concept of individual responsibility.[13]

The general movement toward administrative regulation sometimes represents simply a transfer to the state of functions previously performed by the market or not performed at all; but often it is more than this. The Securities and Exchange Commission, for example, seeks by detailed requirements of disclosure to accomplish what was previously left up to the general law of fraud, imposing on the individual seller of securities the responsibility to avoid intentionally misleading buyers to their detriment. Under the new dispensation the individual is not relieved of responsibility, but the public is less dependent upon his responsibility for its protection. The jurisdiction of the Federal Trade Commission over unfair trade practices is closely parallel. Administrative regulations of many sorts seek to lay down in advance detailed regulations that will protect the public interest rather than relying upon more generalized standards interpreted in the first instance by the responsible individual to whom they apply.

---

[13] In the course of development sketchily outlined above, two distinct things were happening: (1) the idea of legal liability depending upon negligence as contrasted with the sound discretion of a reasonable man ("due care") was tending to give way to that of absolute or, better, strict liability; and (2) in some cases the law directly collectivized the liability. Of course, the first type of development tended to lead to collectivization in effect, by way of insurance.

We have noted that the concept of responsibility, wherever it appears, tends to inject a subjective element into the situation. This is because the term implies deliberation and rationality as well as liability. There is always a certain tension between subjective tests and the constitutional ideal of the rule of law. As long, however, as the test is that of the reasonable man (or the ordinary, prudent man) in a fairly simple society, courts could apply it with a minimum of arbitrariness. In a dynamic and complicated society, however, both the old test and the old institutions often seemed inadequate. Railroads, factories, and the like, involved ever new hazards to the safety of employees and others. In this situation the ordinary, prudent man's ideas of what care he should take to prevent injury to others did not keep pace with the needs of society. Consequently, the more elastic but vaguer test of "public interest" was often substituted for that of rationality. At the same time administrative agencies, unencumbered with common law doctrines of responsibility, were widely substituted for courts as the agencies for applying the new test. As a protection against the arbitrary invasion of the legal rights of the individual, made easier by the vagueness of the new test, maximum reliance was placed upon detailed, prospective regulation in lieu of after-the-fact adjudication. In many situations, however, this device is not feasible, and the net result is to give to administrative officers and commissions considerable latitude in determining what individual rights will be recognized. With this increase of administrative discretion the focus of interest in responsibility shifts from the private individual to the government official. Of this I shall have more to say.

In totalitarian societies, the subjective element reaches its apogee. The standard is social rather than individual, and correspondingly vague, and the mode of its application one that encourages arbitrariness rather than rule of law. Much of the development of recent democratic thought in this area is to be understood in terms of a reaction against totalitarian abuses while giving recognition to those needs of modern society to which totalitarianism represents an exaggerated accommodation. Modern individualism reasserts the claims of the individual—to liberty, to privacy, and so on—but at the same time it recognizes that they must be more flexible than was true of private rights in the past, and also that they must be conditioned upon "responsible" individual conduct. This is the significance to be attributed to the vicissitudes of the clear-and-present-danger test and generally to the increasing recognition that First Amendment and other freedoms are relative and yet that they are of vital importance and must not be eroded. "Rugged" individualism stressed rights; the reaction against this philosophy emphasized duties; we may today, I believe, be seeing the emergence of a new individualism in which responsibility is the central theme. The individual, as in all liberal thought, continues to be the center of value; but he is not an isolated or self-sufficient unit. The new individualism, starting with the individual and his rightful claims, looks outward and considers his claims in relation to the rightful claims of others upon him, in other words in terms of his responsibility to others. This more organic individualism combines the ideas of individual value and individual debt, and includes both a concept of freedom that is neither anarchistic nor self-centered and a reference to rationalism that does not demand the impossible, while at the same time it calls for the creative use of the imagination and initiative rather than conformity to a preordained pattern. Even in some Existentialist thought we may see a rather exaggerated form of the new individualism—in its assertion that the individual is free and therefore responsible.

Somewhat the same forces have been at work, and the same lines of development may be noted, in the field of criminal law, especially as it pertains to punishment. The concepts "guilty" and "not guilty," like "rights" and "duties," now seem inadequate. Granted that an individual has committed a crime, it would be argued in many quarters today that his responsibility is a matter of degree, to be determined by reference to the circumstances. Society must share his responsibility.

Insofar as this notion of social responsibility is admitted, the retributive element in punishment tends to be qualified, and utilitarian considerations play a larger role. It is notable that none of the contributors to this volume who deal with this question espouse a purely retributive theory of punishment. It is worthy of comment, too, that among the utilitarian considerations bearing on punishment, the desirability of rehabilitating the criminal in the direction of making him a responsible individual ranks high in importance.

"Responsibility," then, is a term for use in a complicated, dynamic, quasi-organic society. In criminal law and in morals, increased attention to this notion reflects a growing belief that relations between "individual" and "society" are too complicated and involve too much dynamic reciprocity or "feedback" to be dealt with adequately by the concept of "rights" and "duties," "guilt" and "innocence." In politics, too, the term "responsibility" is useful for a period when simple concepts like "will of the people" are recognized as inadequate, and when "responsible" government is distinguished from "responsive" government and even from public accountability, although it includes the latter.[14]

Turning now from definition and history, let us look at the tasks of the political scientist (in his capacity as adviser on matters of governmental organization) as they appear in the perspective of matters of "responsibility." They may be thought of as falling in one of two categories: the allocation of responsibility and the provision of conditions favorable for eliciting responsible behavior on the part of those to whom responsibility has been allocated.[15]

[14] See the writer's "Responsiveness, Responsibility, and Majority Rule," in *The American Political Science Review*, XLVI (1952), 790-807.

[15] It must be recognized that this division, like any such categorization, is somewhat arbitrary. To a certain extent, the allocation of responsibility necessitates, indeed involves, the allocation of power as well. Beyond this, provision for the effective exercise of power may be thought of as a condition favorable for eliciting (and essential for) responsible behavior. The

Both tasks require knowledge of the prerequisites for the exercise and growth of effective responsibility. One consequence of the nature of responsibility is that it is something that can develop. In this instance, moreover, it may be developed by exercise. This at least is the faith of the democrat. It is also the basis of Mr. Justice Frankfurter's great reliance on the proposition that "responsibility is the great developer of men." The point here relates to the difference between external and internal accountability. If we make a man responsible for something—that is, give him power, discretion in the matter, and tell him he will be held accountable for the results—we appeal to his pride and consequently he will exert greater effort and hold himself to higher standards than if he is given little choice of means—such at least is the theory.

Of course, the growth of effective responsibility on the part either of government or citizens depends upon more than opportunities for choice, for selection of means and weighing of values. The situation must be such that the persons in question, whether citizens or officials, can comprehend the probable consequences of the options before them. Here is probably the most crucial problem facing all governments of industrialized states today. Peter Drucker has recently argued that American government is breaking down because of the inability of any President to control the vast and endlessly complicated operations for which he is presumably responsible.[16] From the point of view of democracy the even more serious question is whether citizens can possibly have the knowledge and understanding essential for the responsible exercise of the power that is committed to them. Perhaps the burden of responsibility is too great. Perhaps we are seeking to make both citizens and governors carry a greater freight of

two categories certainly must not be thought of as successive stages, for the proper allocation of responsibility will depend in part upon a consideration of, and perhaps some experimentation with, possible institutions for developing responsible behavior.

[16] Peter F. Drucker, "The Breakdown of Governments," *Harpers Magazine*, 218 (January, 1959), 35-40, especially 35-6.

responsibility than they can bear. This too is a possibility the political scientist must take into consideration.

Scarcely anyone would think it feasible or desirable to locate full power and responsibility for all of society's concerns in one spot. The problem of the allocation of responsibility for the affairs of society is consequently a matter of degree; but it is no less vital for being so. Although it *is* a matter of degree, it is not simply a question of how widely responsibilities should be dispersed. It is a question of the types of agencies to which it should be committed. Even within the governmental area, the issue takes two forms. It may be a matter of whether we need different kinds of governmental institutions for bearing different responsibilities. Again nearly everyone would give an affirmative answer to the question as posed. A tax collector should not be responsible for social work, a court for milk inspection, or the legislature for adjudication. But other cases are more controversial. Moreover, how independent and separate governmental institutions should be from each other and from any common superior, what provision should be made for reallocation of their responsibilities, and many similar questions, are exceedingly controversial and difficult. To speak of parcelling out different responsibilities to different organs may obscure the fact that these different responsibilities are all parts of the single responsibility for good government, public welfare, common good, or whatever phrase one prefers. Divided responsibility then becomes shared responsibility. The gains of expertise, division of labor, and up to a point, greater power, eventually are balanced by losses from attenuation and frustration of power and lost scope of vision.

The extent to which the "single responsibility for good government" should be recognized as such by placing it in a single organ or branch of government has been a classic subject for debate. Many people, indeed many political scientists, have thought that the British governmental system, because of its great concentration of power in the cabinet, reduced the problem of electoral responsibility to the simplest and therefore most efficient proportions. For this reason this form of government is often referred to by the honorific title "responsible government." This is not the place to argue the case for and against cabinet government, English style; but it is pertinent to note the applicability to this issue of a remark made earlier. It is possible that the very concentration of power that gives the English system its simplicity, which makes it easy for the voter to see where responsibility rests for any given Governmental action or inaction, defeats its own purpose. Under this system the citizen who disapproves of his Government's action in Nyasaland and with respect to Suez but who approves of the bulk of its domestic policy is in a predicament. Too many powers must be exercised by a single act to make discriminating action possible. Yet discrimination is of the essence of responsibility. So we arrive at the point where responsible Government may defeat responsible citizenship. The American, who can insert a measure of such discrimination into his exercise of political power in casting ballots for President, Senator, and Representative may, in this respect, be somewhat better off.

The problem under discussion is not just a matter of allocation of responsibility among organs of government. It is also a question of how much responsibility can be borne by government and by its citizens. At some stage the point may be reached where no amount of refinement of institutional adjustment nor of improvement in selection and conditioning of personnel will achieve satisfactory results. Then the search may turn to other agencies of society, such as Big Unions, Big Business, or, to take an example from the other end of the spectrum, the family. There will also be cases—and here the need for further research and reflection is great—where no agency can be found that can or will effectively accept responsibility for certain ends, and where those ends will be better secured as a bi-product of behaviors directed to different ends, related to different responsibilities, operating, from the point of view of the ends in question, blindly, without "overview," like the mechanism of the market.[17] In such a case the term "responsibility" can be applied only metaphorically.

Most of what has just been said about "responsibilities" might be cast, and often has been, in terms of "powers." The point here, however, is to stress the fact that in distributing powers it is important, perhaps crucial, to consider the whole problem from the aspect of responsibility—of that blend of rationality, accountability, imagination, and concern for public welfare that that term involves.

Turning to the subject of conditions favorable for eliciting responsible behavior, none is more important than knowledge and power. Although in themselves quite different, they are so closely linked in the present context that they may be treated together. Whether we speak of citizen, legislator, President, or any person charged with a responsibility, one cannot be justly held responsible for something unless he has some power to affect it. Nor will allocating responsibility to someone have the desired result unless that person has power commensurate with his responsibility. Moreover, legal power may not be enough. The possessor of authority may lack the knowledge to put it to effective use. His legal powers may be so vast that he cannot, within the limits of time available, exercise them so as to accomplish his purposes. Likewise, especially when it is a question of the responsibility of citizens, a feeling of impotence may lead to apathy. Men who are so baffled by the policy issues before them that they lack the understanding of how to use their political power to any good end are likely to withdraw from participation in politics, or to participate only in the most ritualistic fashion. (Sometimes, in the case of certain Existentialist thought, the reaction is in the opposite direction: toward a strident and irrational *assertion* of responsibility in the absence of effective power.)

[17] For a stimulating statement of this notion, see Charles E. Lindblom, "The Science of 'Muddling Through,' " *Public Administration Review*, 19 (Spring, 1959), 79-88.

One can do no more here than point to the problem. It is at least worth suggesting, however, that electronic brains may hold an important key to its solution or at least its amelioration. Where it is a matter of weighing values, men must decide. But when it is a question of calculating the impact of many different factors on a complex equation, the computor may come to our rescue. It should be possible to work out problems, sometimes in game-theory fashion, trying various hypothetical weights or values for different products and bi-products of policy.

Responsibility requires will as well as power. It must be accepted; people must be under the weight of it. This consideration could take us right back to the problem of apathy. One of the most cheering suggestions along this line, although advanced very tentatively, is to be found in Professor Long's contribution to this volume. He offers us at least a glimmer of hope that megalopolis may carry with it the cure for its own distemper, possibly even with a modest remainder. Perhaps in the great cities of today and tomorrow we may have a unit of policy problems that fits the mean we have been seeking— the mean, that is, between problems so vast and complicated as to be beyond the comprehending powers of the voter and those so petty as to be incapable of arousing his interest and holding his attention, of inspiring him to responsible political behavior.

As a last item under the heading of the provision of favorable conditions for the eliciting of responsible behavior, we have the whole matter of sanctions. There will be no attempt here to do more than show where these questions fit into the framework we have been depicting. Here one deals with institutions for enforcing accountability.[18] The supporters of centralized power and responsibility do battle with those who find in a greater or less degree of dispersion of both a more

---

[18] It may seem to be stretching a point to include this topic under the heading of conditions for "eliciting" responsible behavior, but as is pointed out below, the line between "eliciting" and "enforcing" often becomes tenuous.

likely path to that over-all goal of responsible government, or to that still more inclusive (and vague) goal of the good society. Partly within the area of that controversy and partly outside of it, one must face the issue, time and again, of what might be called external accountability *versus* internal accountability. Democratic government rests on the assumption that no government that is not accountable to the people will long remain responsible. But that is not to deny that people, even people who are entrusted with governmental authority, may be responsible to their own consciences, to internalized standards. No government can afford to neglect this important sanction for responsible behavior. Accountability to the people is indispensable; at the very least it is the club in the closet; but at best it is a crude and blunt instrument, to be supplemented wherever possible by a keen sense of personal or professional responsibility on the part of officials provided with standards and measurements for evaluating their success in doing their jobs. This sense of professional responsibility brings to the support of high standards both pride in craftsmanship and dedication to a particular form of public service, each reinforced by the knowledge that the product will be subjected to the critical judgment of professional colleagues both within and without the sphere of government.[19]

Finally, one must note that there are innumerable devices for external control of administrative action in addition to that of accountability to the people.[20] These run the gamut of governmental checks and balances, including judicial review, administrative review, and quasi-judicialized administrative procedures. It is sometimes argued that all such devices interfere with the operation of responsibility—with accountability either to the people or to internal standards. With respect to

[19] The classical statement of this argument has been set forth by the editor of this volume. See Carl J. Friedrich, "Public Policy and the Nature of Administrative Responsibility," in Carl J. Friedrich and Edward S. Mason (eds.), *Public Policy*, (1940), I, 3 ff.

[20] For an excellent discussion of this subject, see Charles E. Gilbert, "The Framework of Administrative Responsibility," *Journal of Politics*, XXI (1959), 373-407.

internal responsibility, this is the essence of the Frankfurter argument—that administrators must have effective power if they are to wield it conscientiously. On the side of external controls, David Spitz, for example, argues that a government, like ours, that tries to combine accountability to voters with a system of checks "is characterized by an ambivalence or political schizophrenia in which the majority is both directed to rule and is restrained or prevented from doing so." [21] But surely all human experience runs to the contrary: the combination of responsibility and checks—assuming of course that the latter are not overdone—provide the best control of human behavior. In this fashion we seek to guide and limit the conduct of our children; and by combining penalties with educational programs designed to appeal to the driver's sense of responsibility we strive to diminish the accident toll on our highways. Checks, whether procedural or of the separated-powers variety, foster responsible exercise of power, in the large interstices left by popular accountability, in two ways. Most obviously, they may stop or reverse arbitrary or otherwise irresponsible action once it has been initiated. But also they may encourage the development and observance of internal controls. The Frankfurter argument is valid only within a rather narrow range. It is of course true that an official whose actions are normally thoroughly revised may cease to have much concern for how he performs them. But if he knows he has a substantial area of discretion and that it is only if he steps outside of that area or disregards certain known standards of conduct that his actions will be revised, the situation is quite different. Now he is challenged to responsible action. And if, as is likely, he develops standards of professional conduct in this situation it would be a wise man indeed who could tell whether his observance of them was dictated from within or without, by pride or fear. No one, I suppose, would doubt that a physician or lawyer often is governed by the ethical standards of his own profession, without thought of sanction. Yet who would wish to do away with

21 David Spitz, *Democracy and the Challenge of Power* (1958), p. 72.

the possibility of sanctions imposed by the proper professional association or doubt that in certain cases professional conduct is influenced by fear of such action?

What conclusions emerge from this bird's eye view of the subject of responsibility? Without trying either to review or to summarize what was said with respect to definition, I should like to recur at this point to part of what I call its core of meaning—the notion of the exercise of judgment and discretion in the light of careful analysis and conscientious weighing of values. The crucial problem of responsibility today is the question of how to provide the most favorable conditions, in all sorts of contexts, for maximizing this kind of behavior. In ethics, the weakening of tradition, of respect for old rules just because they are old, has brought this problem to the fore. In politics, the increased complexity of society, the tremendous expansion in the role of government, and the development of democracy itself has given it greater scope, while the modern concept of individualism enhances its importance in general estimation. At the same time the ever-increasing complexity of the issues on which the citizen must pass judgment chronically threatens to deprive him of one of the necessary conditions of effective responsibility—understanding. In law, as well as in politics, the rule-defying complexity of modern society and its attendant ever-increasing pressure for giving greater discretionary powers to administrators, administrative tribunals, courts, parole boards, and the like, has made the problem one of utmost importance. The liberal concept of the rule of law must be given more and more sophisticated interpretations to hold on to its central location in a liberal philosophy. Students of man and society are being increasingly driven to explore the safe limits of reliance upon discretion and the means for enlarging those limits. This, as I see it, is *the* problem of responsibility, or at least one of its major dimensions. Even the problem of citizen impotence is in large measure but the reverse side of the same coin.

✦ II ✦

RESPONSIBILITY—DEFINITIONS, DISTINC-
TIONS, AND APPLICATIONS IN
VARIOUS CONTEXTS

LUDWIG FREUND

THE CONCEPT OF RESPONSIBILITY has a *variety* of meanings. There are several definitions and a patently end-
less number of applications. An analysis like Professor
Austin's of such terms as "intention," "purpose," "deliberate,"
"undeliberate," may be helpful in clearing up some of the
juridical or *general* attitudinal implications of the concept of
responsibility, but they do not define it. At best, it may be said
that a semantic inquiry into those terms aims in the general
direction of *one* particular meaning of responsibility—namely,
that of responsibility in the sense of "personal accountability,"
a meaning of special interest to judges and lawyers in criminal
law.

Now, I submit that there are several possible definitions of
responsibility, one of which is the aforementioned, that of
personal accountability. This is largely supplemented and supported by, yet by no means synonymous or interchangeable
with, a series of other, really autonomous concepts such as, for
instance, "intention," "purpose," or "deliberation." This particular meaning of responsibility may occasionally and actually be more closely related to "authority" than it is to either
of these latter terms. To give an example: A person entrusted
with the supervision of a collective task or enterprise will be
held accountable, i.e., responsible, for its success or failure, regardless of what his "intention," "purpose," "deliberation," or
lack of it may be. If he fails to satisfy the trust placed in him,
or if he falls short in exercising the "just or competent au-

thority" vested in him, he probably and logically will be called to "account" for his failure by whatever superior authority or power there be.

Most legal, social, and political philosophers will agree, I think, that there is a significant gap here between mere *subjective* categories of an "accountability" largely circumscribed by Professor Austin and usually accepted by legal minds, and the *objective* type of personal accountability, closely related to the functions of outward "authority," which is simply a well-known and quasi-automatic, yet no less significant, concomitant of responsibility within a certain, narrowly defined limit of this latter term. They also will agree, I believe, that there are at least *two more* possible and relevant definitions of "responsibility" quite often alluded to in the literature of social and political theory: 1) responsibility as a sense, or an acknowledgment, of obligation; 2) responsibility as a consideration of the consequences of one's action.

These three meanings of responsibility are subtly interlinked, of course, but should nevertheless be very carefully distinguished from each other both for methodological reasons and for purposes of common understanding. To illustrate again: A person of "authority" is normally, though not necessarily, equipped with a "sense of obligation" toward the "responsible" job he is doing or toward the community or institution in his charge. But even if a sense of obligation should fail him, the very first meaning of responsibility, i.e., in the sense of "personal accountability," still will apply to him. Conversely, a person not in charge of any "responsible" (leadership) function, therefore neither "authoritative" in this respect nor logically to be held "accountable" because of it, may have a "sense of obligation" toward the community of which he is a simple member, and may faithfully fulfil the duties of his humble position. In this sense, then, he too is to be predicated as "responsible" in a very definite but separate meaning of the word.

Quite distinct from these cases may be another, where a person, again assumed to be "in charge" of a collective purpose, has a sense of "obligation" but lacks the ability, patience, or will to consider the detailed "consequences" of his actions. He is "responsible" in one sense, but not in the other. Or, lacking a sense of obligation toward his charges, he may still be "smart" enough to consider those consequences which, if realized, would reveal him as irresponsible. Hence, he will strive to appear as a responsible individual by avoiding actions whose visible consequences would quite evidently bear witness to his faulty loyalty. All of us know that such politicians and officials exist. One suspects that they often occupy positions of responsibility and leadership in certain public and private associations, but this is very difficult to prove because they so carefully disguise the "evidence."

Therefore, consideration of the consequences of one's actions may imply all the varied degrees of reasoning or awareness which are linked with such subjective acts or notions as "intent," "purpose," "deliberation," but may go much further and to infinitely more portentous lengths than are envisaged in a mere juridical or semantic consideration of these terms. In fact, Thomas Hill Green's and Max Weber's political essays were written in vain if the three basic meanings of *responsibility as such* are not accepted in the full dramatic import suggested, though not entirely explained, in their writings. To be sure, the pragmatic views of Max Weber and the idealistic anti-utilitarian views of T. H. Green were at opposite ends. But to us the important fact is that the latter emphasized the ethical obligations, the former the practical consideration of consequences of politically responsible action. And both of them stressed the accountability of government, or of any authority, for its acts or omissions. Green even went further and believed in the right to "restrain" those citizens "in whom civic sense is lacking." [1] In other words, he widened the circle of what I have called "personal accountability" to include all the members of a free society, even those not in a position of "authority," charging them with an "obligation" toward the

[1] "Lectures on the Principles of Political Obligation," *Works of Thomas Hill Green* (1885-8), II, 432.

"common good." [2] In fact, and in all fairness, the very pertinent question may be raised as to how far the citizens of a
"free society," in their collective function as an electorate
holding their elected leaders "responsible" for their actions,
can themselves do so in a "responsible" manner unless some of
Green's allegedly "idealistic" notions regarding this matter are
realized. An irresponsible electorate not feeling an "obligation
toward the common good" is liable to tolerate and produce a
representative government which is equally unconcerned with
"the common good." All this is quite apart from the very difficult problem, which does not concern us directly in this specific context, of the analytical search for the "common good"
and what really constitutes it.

Concentrating a little further on the problem of authoritative or leadership obligation, a topic of special significance
even within a democratically organized society, we cannot
help being baffled by some of its inescapable complexities. A
person in an authoritative position and endowed with a sense
of obligation toward his charges and his community will, we
should think, consider the consequences of his actions for his
community. However, at this point precisely *begins* the dilemma of "leadership" in a democratic society. A whole series
of questions spring to mind: What consequences is the chosen
representative or "leader" of a democratically constituted society to consider? Who are his "charges," and what is the
"community" in his care? Is he to consider the interests of his
constituency in his home district? Of those who elected him?
Of the wider community, the state, the nation? Which?

We shall return to these questions but wish to round out
the problem by pointing to Max Weber's summary conclusion
that politics requires an "ethic of responsibility" which consists in considering and carefully weighing the more distant as
well as immediate consequences of political actions.[3] He noted

[2] This is one of T. H. Green's main themes. See, for instance, "Lecture
on Liberal Legislation and Freedom of Contract," *op. cit.*, III, pp. 371ff.

[3] *"Politik als Beruf,"* in *Gesammelte politische Schriften* (1921), transl.
as "Politics as a Vocation," by H. H. Gerth and C. Wright Mills; *Max*

that the choice might be cumbersome and problematic, and indeed it is. For here, again, we are confronted with the question: Which of the numerous, often contradictory and seemingly equally important consequences is the statesman to consider? The material, the moral, the military, the economic, the particular party-group or class-related ones, the world-wide—which?

Life, in particular political life, is not simple and does not smoothly conform to generalities. The statesman or politician with a sense of obligation will be precisely the one who is haunted by the torment of choice between alternatives, the competing claims of which may sound equally justified to him, but among which he must make a decisive selection. The total consequences of his decision he cannot predict with certainty, even if he is an expert in such a variety of fields as fiscal policies, diplomacy, strategy, agrarian, industrial, and labor conditions, and many more which he is called upon to judge. To cite a few examples of his dilemma in terms of "considering consequences": Is the financial soundness and stability of the United States a consequence more seriously to be considered than the friendship and security of states whose benevolent attitudes as well as inner stability depend upon further financial commitments on the part of the United States? Are economic necessities to be subordinated to political and diplomatic expediencies, or, conversely, public policies and diplomacy to economic necessities (two equally distasteful choices at times)? Are domestic and individual standards of liberty and security to be sacrificed to the needs of a more efficient body politic at a time of international insecurity and "existential crisis," or are individual liberties and domestic satisfactions values which a democratic society must uphold as long as it is humanly possible? And when is the

---

Weber: Essays in Sociology (1946), pp. 119-127. Among modern writing of a quite different style, but with similar perspective, see particularly Wayne A. R. Leys, *Ethics for Policy Decisions: The Art of Asking Deliberative Questions* (1952).

point reached, in a responsible statesman's judgment, where it is no longer "humanly possible"?

The questions sometimes have an even more urgent and specific ring. For instance: If there is a possibility, entertained by some experts, that Red China, along with Soviet Russia, will succeed in developing—as they claim they will in the foreseeable future—their vast resources to a point which may exceed the productive capacity of the United States, must the United States, in the interest of survival, not seek to develop the economic potentialities of all the Americas at utmost speed, without consideration of fiscal consequences and the threat of raising to the South of us potent competitors in some fields? If, on the other hand, the estimate of the potential strength of Red China and Soviet Russia in comparison with that of the U.S. ultimately should prove to be exaggerated, how "responsible," then, would appear the "hasty" conclusions drawn from this estimate? Likewise, if the Russian leadership—as some indications seem to bear out—is becoming increasingly wary of the growing power and independence of Red China, should the diplomatic potentialities of this situation not be more forcefully and cleverly exploited than the U.S. State Department seems to have done up to now? But suppose the two communist countries remain firmly allied, while one of them succeeds in goading the U.S. into making vital concessions for its own benefit—what then?

I really do not believe that a theorist or theory has the immanent capacity for charting a *responsible* statesman's course of action with regard to such or similar calamities, or for counselling him on his concrete choice at all decisive junctures. For theory is circumspect and, if it is realistic, must consider *all* sides and possibilities and consequences of a relevant situation. The thoughtful statesman may consult theory in order to be certain of the total scope of the problems he faces. But the politician's or statesman's individual choice must of necessity be one-sided: he cannot remain—as the theorist must —contemplative, objective, and detached. Quite often, though not always, he is constrained to favor one valid claim and reject another. Not infrequently must he be content with just hoping that his final choice represents the least of a number of possible risks. He may "balance the account," if history and the political constellation permit, by shifting favors later, if only for reasons of political justice, but at any one given time he cannot satisfy rivaling and opposing interests and opinions by granting full or even equal recognition and consideration to both antagonistic sides at once. He might wish to do so, but the array of political forces and pressures rarely allows him this pleasure. At other times, the very nature of the competing interests, their diametrically opposite principles and substance (for instance, moral vs. material claims), forbid it.

If we return at this point to the previous question of the *locus* of interests which the responsible statesman or politician is to consider—district, state, nation, party, etc.—it is equally obvious that this question can and will not be easily answered to the "responsible" politician's liking. The numerous textbooks on politics, parties, and pressure groups fully explain this. What interests us at this point is a delicate question, which is intimately interwoven with this total situation. Few people will quarrel with the statement that, in a democratically constituted society, the politician is supposed to render service to publicly relevant interests.[4] But what does "publicly relevant" mean, and what does "interests" mean? "Public" or "publicly relevant" may be anything that concerns a large enough number, or an important enough segment, of the people to warrant attention by government or by those who attempt to influence or direct government. A "politically relevant interest" in this sense may be defined as anything that is needed, wanted, or desired by a publicly relevant group and, since the men who are responsible for government

4 Ludwig Freund, "Power and the Democratic Process," *Social Research*, 15 (September 1948), pp. 341ff.

action certainly constitute a very important group in the sense of this definition, by government itself. It will be noted that our definition tends to be merely descriptive and seeks to avoid involvement in such disputes or generalities as are easily brought about by normative definitions of, e.g., "the Common Good" [5] or "common necessities." [6]

The problem of responsible leadership in a democracy begins here with the seemingly subtle, in reality rather definite distinctions between wants, desires, and needs as synonyms of interests. A public "want" may be defined as a *necessity*, the satisfaction of which is demanded or consciously striven for by a publicly important (business, military, religious, etc.) or numerous (labor, farming, veterans, etc.) group. A public "desire" would be the longing or striving of the group, or an important section thereof, for an object or a situation the realization of which would *not* constitute a vital necessity for the specific group or total community. A public "need," in contrast to the two former, would then constitute—according to normal linguistic usage—a *necessity* imposed by circumstances and pertinent facts. Its satisfaction is vital to the group or to an important section of it, *regardless* of whether the members of the group are aware of its urgency or not. Without consideration of this "need" the well-being, the survival perhaps, of an essential group within the body politic, or of the total community, may be endangered. It can easily be seen that "wants," "needs," and "desires" become confused in political debates. It seems also obvious that it is one of the most difficult responsibilities and problems of the statesman to distinguish between them. The difficulty, of course, arises not infrequently from the individual's inability to *predict* future contingencies or to overlook the sum total of interests and *consequences* involved in the pursuit of satisfying one particular want or need.

[5] T. H. Green, *op. cit.* Also: G. A. Schubert, "The Public Interest in Administrative Decision Making," *American Political Science Review,* LI (1957), 346ff.

[6] Herbert Schneider, *Three Dimensions of Public Morality* (1956), chap. 4.

Moreover, the normal juxtaposition and opposition of various public wants, needs, and desires (as different versions or levels of the "public interest"), the usual clamor of the political dispute, blur judgment with reference to the distinction between what is "needed" and what is "wanted." One of the paramount, yet almost insoluble, problems amidst this confusion and debate is whether politicians and statesmen of a democratic state ought to represent only the interests, stated as "wants" or "desires," of their respective constituencies, or whether they should, *on occasion,* rise above them and strive for the satisfaction of certain necessities which they recognize as such, although the majority of their electorate do not recognize these necessities. More bluntly, are democratic politicians supposed to serve their community by acknowledging public "needs" in the sense defined above? Still more directly, are they justified in satisfying such needs, even if the people do not seem to want this satisfaction, or are not sufficiently enlightened or not "disinterested" enough to see its long-range advantage for the community as a whole? [7] Also, can "needs" of a budgetary soundness, for instance, be ignored for very long periods in favor of such "desires" as, for example, are constantly and increasingly expressed by the highly articulate and powerful veterans' lobbies with their fatuous show of "patriotism"?

Questions like these clearly aim at the heart of the democratic process and the intrinsic problem of responsible leadership in a democracy. I can well imagine that they may have caused many a responsible man in the White House and on Capitol Hill not a few heartaches and possibly sleepless nights. On the other hand, I cannot discover essentially helpful hints on the subject on the part of those prominent political figures

[7] This is not the same problem which Walter Lippmann stated in his *The Public Philosophy* (1955). I believe it is more specific than Lippmann's sweeping and essentially anti-democratic notions. But it comes close to John S. Mill's distinctions between popular *inability* or *unwillingness* and government *duty* to act responsibly (*Representative Government* (1860), p. 193), although his argument is quite differently and optimistically stated, unaffected by the agony of an industrial age such as ours.

who have ventured to write on it. Even a U.S. Senator, formerly Dean and Professor of Law, who was supposed to enlighten an academic audience with regard to this crucial matter in the form of a prepared, and later published, speech, was—perhaps understandably—vague and self-contradictory on this touchy subject, touchy particularly in the United States with its extremely sensitive organs for the "rights of the people."

Nevertheless, it may safely be stated that neither President F. D. Roosevelt with his decision to push toward selective service in this country prior to its being drawn into the war, nor President Truman with his decision to enter the war in Korea, waited for the outcome of a popularity test of their respective actions in these matters. And at the risk of sounding slightly heretical or unprincipled, we may venture the additional statement that any *responsible* statesman, or politician, with a sense of obligation toward his country, or toward an even wider community, and with sufficient intelligence to foresee certain drastic consequences of inaction or of a false direction in public affairs, due to his superior insights or information not available to the general public, may at times act in a similarly self-reliant fashion. At the least, this is a hope. Yet, as has been borne out by the two experiences cited above, once a popular statesman makes a decision—and for as long as he *remains popular*—the majority of the people will usually and at length sustain his action, even if it seemed unpopular and risky at first glance. One of the most pitiful sights in politics perhaps is the "popular statesman" who never dares a risk, even where such risks are called for in a situation.

In a wider political sense, responsibility is a correlate of both authority and freedom. Authority and freedom may be linked, but they are not inseparable from each other. It may be said, however, that responsibility in the political realm always presupposes a state of freedom on the part of the "responsible agent." One cannot act responsibly and one cannot be held responsible for actions if one is not free either to commit or to omit them. This patently undeniable fact, while

largely acknowledged in the case of communist-controlled
peoples, has been denied by scores of writers, even some political scientists, in regard to Nazi Germany. This may have its
reason partly in the perturbingly high popularity ratings
which the Nazi party received in the last free elections preceding the ascendancy of Hitler. Nonetheless, the state of total
political nonfreedom, which afterwards descended upon the
German nation, invites doubts at least as to a reliable estimate
of the people's endorsement and "accountability" for *all* of
Hitler's and his party leaders' actions. In a tyrannical political
order only the few persons "in authority" are free to act and
hence are "responsible." Under the modern totalitarian forms
of government even "passive resistance" has become all but
impossible, so totally has freedom become eclipsed. In a directly proportionate measure in which they are deprived of
freedom, people cannot be held morally, politically, or
juridically responsible for actions of the men in authority over
them, although it is true that in the case of Germany a shock-
ingly large number of people favored Hitler when they were
still free to reject him. The question whether they were politically too immature to anticipate all the moral, political,
and physical consequences of this attitude, and whether a
much lesser number of the German voters (who, incidentally,
never produced a *majority* for the Nazis during free elections)
would have supported him, had it been possible for them to
realize in advance these consequences, is an idle one, since the
truth about this problem can never be established in scientifically reliable terms. At any rate, it seems certain that, while
the German people, or at least a very considerable portion of
them, might have been held responsible for finally making
Hitler's party the strongest among the many political parties
of the Weimar era, it is difficult to see how some writers could,
with claims upon scientific method, wish to see a whole nation punished for the ensuing excesses of its despotic rulers,
without confusing all concepts of "responsibility."

Beyond this, the whole problem of political responsibility is
intimately interwoven with problems of psychological dimen-

sions relating to the roles of power and social institutions and conventions. They can be demonstrated as imposing limitations of special kinds upon individual and collective freedoms and, to the identical degree in which they succeed in doing so, also upon the responsibility, i.e., "accountability," of those subject to their effectiveness. To deal appropriately with these aspects would require a separate paper.

Nor is it possible to delve into a detailed description of many more of the vast number of distinctions and applications of the term. A few final and rather sketchy remarks may conclude our analytical attempt. They may indicate some of the enormous difficulties stemming from the crossing and overlapping of life's varied obligations and interests. There is, to start close to home, the whole wide area of "intellectual," or, to be perhaps more precise, "scholarly" responsibility.[8] To make a long story short in relation to this uneasy subject: Scholarly responsibility will permit substantial judgments only after thorough, methodical, and conscientious study and comprehensive appraisal, checking and rechecking, of a given subject matter.

His "intellectual honesty" (which is merely another word for scholarly integrity or responsibility) will furthermore bind the ideal scholarly person to the unadulterated *truth as he finds it.* The unavoidable question here is not so much the well-known metaphysical or epistemological one: How can truth be established? We are not concerned with this question here. It is rather the question: What are the "human frailty" barriers necessarily or quite understandably limiting the uninhibited search for truth? We do not necessarily refer to the well-publicized qualms and the less advertised acts of renunciation of atomic scientists, which led a man like Carl von

---

[8] There are many intellectuals, but relatively few scholars, among these. A journalist, for instance, may be an intellectual, but it is often more than doubtful that the above cited criteria of the scholar will apply to his trade. Similar reservations may apply to a good number of the teaching profession, even on the college level.

Weizsäcker, for instance, to surrender his chair in physics at
the University of Göttingen and turn to philosophy. This represents quite another type of dilemma, making scholars wish
to stop the further pursuit of truths which have been exploited for destructive purposes. Such moral pangs are not
signs of human frailty; not at all.

Here we wish to call attention to a more common phenomenon, applicable more frequently to the work of the social, in
particular the political, scientist and philosopher than to that
of the natural scientist. If the ideal scholar's responsibility
is exclusively to the "truth as he finds it," then it should follow that he cannot be overly concerned with how the "truth"
may affect his personal life, his career (if it is an unpopular
truth), his private likes, dislikes, interests, and prejudices.
What, however, if the truth, or its applications, clash with
other of his loyalties: with religious or moral responsibilities
as in the now classic case of the atomic scientists? More to the
point with respect to *social science* researchers is the reminder
that at certain historical points or junctures, or under extraordinary circumstances, the truth as found by a scholar may
be harmful to his society. Here is the point of friction between his scholarly and civic responsibilities. Who would dare
resolve this conflict for any person but himself?

Many persons, of course, not faced themselves with this conflict, will tend to present hasty and simple solutions. "Of
course," they will say, "his obligation to society comes first,"
if they are members of the same society to which they feel he
owes an allegiance. Just as unquestioningly will the same persons probably take the opposite stand if the troubled scholar's
doubts and loyalty relate to a society which is foreign or antithetical to their own. These paradoxical attitudes merely reflect the self-righteousness and the double standards so typical
of the average man, but the answers do not help toward
counseling the individual who is torn by a conflict between
"responsible scholarship" and "responsible citizenship." The
latter concept should not be confused with "responsibility
toward one's government," although it may normally include

it. Nevertheless, citizenship responsibility is much wider than this. It may include the obligation to resist government, if the latter breaks down values upon which civic virtue and dignity rest, and insofar as effective powers of resistance are left to members of society. But precisely because civic or citizenship obligations exceed obligation to government, it is not easy to leave them out of account and to remain apathetic with regard to the possible consequences of an opposition to the government which may affect the whole of society, either in terms of retaliation or in terms of other types of sufferings. The valiant but vain and, in the outcome, tragic uprising in Hungary of 1956 may be a case in point. The frictions between "scholarly" and "civic" responsibilities, of course, are much subtler and usually harder to resolve than these instances.

Another, yet intimately related, feature of this aspect of scholarly responsibility is a not unusual distortion occasionally associated with the work of the social scientist stemming from the quite natural tendency to remain socially acceptable. No objection could be voiced against this normal inclination, if it did not at times mislead a scholar into adapting some possibly true, even socially useful or desirable, but unpopular or unwanted finding or insight to the predilections of his social environment. If carried too far, this accommodation may result in what the philosopher Nicolai Hartmann called the "pseudo-ethic of striving toward a good reputation" (*Scheinethos des guten Rufes*). This is a temptation dangerously prone to blunt a scholar's incorruptible judgment if he allows himself to be too strongly motivated by it.

To be sure, nobody is more aware of the importance of certain types and degrees of "conformity" for the wholesome functioning of the body politic than is the political and social philosopher. The question nevertheless is to the point, whether the spontaneous, often half-conscious, maybe even unconscious, yielding to certain invisible pressures, even within a relatively free society, if it is carried beyond given limits— as it occasionally seems to be—does not only impair responsi-

ble scholarship, but may go so far as to stifle completely origi-
nality of thought in philosophical and social science fields
where these informal and conventional pressures and adapta-
tions make themselves too often felt. The most farsighted
thought is often a non-conforming or inconvenient one. This
certainly should not be mistaken to mean that every odd or
extreme idea has a right to present itself as farsighted, simply
because it is non-conforming. But it is to be kept firmly in
mind that the scholar, in his very pursuit of scholarly objectives, is the person least to be forced into shallow conformi-
ties of opinions and ideas. The truly responsible scholar will
be constantly on his guard against discrete pressures and
temptations of this kind, if and as they arise.

RESPONSIBILITY AND EXISTENCE

GEORGE A. SCHRADER

JOHN DEWEY has stated that liability is the beginning of responsibility. Dewey's statement is surely correct, though it might have been put more strongly. Liability is not merely the "beginning" of responsibility but responsibility itself. The English term "responsibility" means, when taken literally, the liability for making a response. We cannot rely too heavily upon the received meaning of the term for an understanding of the concept expressed. But the etymology of the term offers a beginning point, at least, for an understanding of its philosophical meaning. If, for example, responsibility is a generic term which refers to those situations in which a person is required to make a response to someone or something, we might obtain a suitable understanding of the concept by considering the human condition. In what respects, for example, is man liable for making a response, to whom, and for what? Is this liability dependent upon his choices, or is it in part or in whole due to factors over which he has no control? If we can answer these questions we may succeed in achieving a fuller understanding of the nature of human responsibility.

In certain philosophical circles, particularly English and American, the appeal is made to language for answering questions about the meaning of ethical concepts. Thus, it is maintained, if we wish to know what such a term as "responsibility" means, we must look to linguistic usage. It is possible to understand the meaning of an ethical term, we are told, only when we know how it is used. The analysis of ethical language has led to the discovery that ethical terms have

unique meaning in that they serve to commend and to recommend. This result should not have been particularly surprising to anyone acquainted with the passion of moralists of
all times. And it need not be disturbing unless the claim is
made, either tacitly or explicitly, that it is the only sort of
meaning that ethical terms have or can have. Surely it is possible for linguistic expressions to convey more than one type
of meaning. The barest factual statement may be designed to
evoke an aesthetic response or an immoral action. Only a mad
man would bother to utter true statements about the world
with no regard for the interests of his hearers. Kierkegaard relates the doubtless apocryphal story of the man who sought
to demonstrate his sanity by the repeated proclamation that
"the world is round." It is extremely doubtful if pure theoretical interest is anything more than a limiting case. But
factual statements apart, we cannot rule out the possibility
a priori that ethical utterances perform more than one linguistic function. The fact that they *commend* or *recommend*
does not in itself entail that they do only that. It is completely
arbitrary to conclude that ethical statements have no cognitive meaning from the mere fact that they perform non-cogni-
tive functions.

It is quite likely that some proponents of the non-cognitivist
theory of ethical language are reinforced in their view by the
conviction that there is no cognitive function for ethical language to perform. There are, in other words, no ethical facts
to be expressed by language; hence, language cannot function
cognitively. It is evident, I believe, that this issue cannot be
settled by appeal to language alone. To understand a language we must have some grasp of what the language is attempting to express. Unless we take the most extreme idealist
interpretation of language which holds that language constitutes the reality to which it refers, the extra-linguistic situation must be taken into account. To understand the language
of love, for example, we must know something of the facts
and experience of love. We may then find the language of
love meaningful, and be in a position to determine its ade-

quacy. We need not argue that language and the concepts it expresses add nothing to experience in order to insist that experience is essential. To understand the language of ethics we must have some experiential grasp of the ethical predicament of man. Comprehending this situation, we may then assess the function of ethical language and determine to what degree, if at all, it is descriptive. Ethical language is necessarily limited to an emotive function only if there are no ethical facts to express. And this is surely not a question of language but of metaphysics. The term "responsibility" suggests a *descriptive* meaning of the concept. I propose to inquire if any basis for the hypothesis that it has a descriptive meaning can be found in human experience.

If to be responsible is to be liable for responding to someone, to state that man is a responsible being might be simply to state a *fact*—albeit a metaphysical fact. Moreover, to indicate the ways in which man is liable by specifying to whom he is liable and for what, might be only to describe further the general features of the human situation. It is important, then, to inquire whether there are in fact certain liabilities attached to the human situation as such and, further, whether responsibility in its various forms can be accounted for in terms of these liabilities.

To begin with the most basic factor in human experience, namely existence itself, we can easily see that *to exist is to be liable*. Man is, as Heidegger describes it, "projected into the world" and responsible for his existence. The resultant "care" which derives from the original fact of his "being-in-the-world" permeates every aspect of his existence. He is, Heidegger argues, responsible for himself and to himself. And this is an ontological fact! The voice of conscience is nothing more than the call issuing from his being for the individual to acknowledge responsibility for his existence. Moral responsibility, instead of being original and ultimate, as some moralists have thought, is rooted in and derived from man's *ontological responsibility*. Man's original liability is not simply that he exists, but that he "has to be." He confronts his existence from the first moment of his awareness as a problem and an object of concern. Man does not exist in the way that a stick or a stone exists but, as Heidegger expresses it, he "ex-sists," that is, he transcends himself in a reflexive relationship.

Self-consciousness is generally conceded by philosophers to be a reflexive relationship, involving a relation of the human subject to itself. But too often self-consciousness is treated as if it were an epi-phenomenal affair. If, as Sartre argues, "the being of self-consciousness is the self-consciousness of being" and, conversely, "the self-consciousness of being is the being of self-consciousness," self-consciousness is constitutive of human existence. The point is not novel with Sartre, since both Hegel and Kierkegaard before him had insisted upon the constitutive character of self-consciousness. As Kierkegaard puts it, "the more consciousness of self, the more self."

To be a self is, in other words, to be a *subject,* and to be a subject is to be self-related and, further, conscious of the relatedness. This reflexivity of the self constitutes its uniquely human character, distinguishing it from the mode of existence of other organic entities. To state this is not to argue that only man is self-related, but rather that only man is conscious of his self-relatedness. When a being is conscious of being related to itself, the reflexivity takes on a new meaning and is constituted as subjectivity. Consciousness of one's relatedness to oneself is a necessary condition for the existence of a subject. Thus it is not a matter simply of the human subject's being conscious of a relatedness which is altogether independent of his consciousness, but that in being self-conscious a unique mode of reflexivity is constituted. If self-consciousness were epi-phenomenal, the difference between man and other organic beings would be relatively insignificant. They would not differ in their basic mode of existence, but only in their mode of awareness. The unique self-awareness enjoyed by man conditions his reflexivity in all of its aspects and, thus, endows his existence with special ontological characteristics. To be a man is to be a self, and to be a self is to be a subject.

The peculiar reflexivity exhibited by subjectivity is the ultimate point of reference for all aspects of human existence.

In thinking of self-consciousness it is important not to identify it, as is too often done, with the passivity of intuition. Very frequently we conceive of consciousness on the model of seeing, as if it were an evanescent quantity. On this view, consciousness is dissociated from active processes and regarded as if it were contentless. We need to remind ourselves that feeling, thought, volition, and even physical action are, for the human subject, phenomena of consciousness. We are most intensely conscious of our world when we are most actively engaged with it, and most acutely self-conscious in those moments when we are most involved with ourselves. Neither consciousness nor self-consciousness is a passive and contentless mode of intuition. Intuition is at most one factor in consciousness and always a derivative factor. Anxiety, for example, is a phenomenon of self-consciousness though it is not and has not generally been regarded as a mode of intuition. Even Immanuel Kant, who placed so much stress upon the role of intuition in knowledge, insisted that intuition is possible only through what he termed "self-affection." Philosophers have too often been misled by their own abstractions and nowhere more than in the case of consciousness. Because it is possible to distinguish a content or a process from the awareness of the content, they have sometimes concluded that the awareness is separable from its content. Actually consciousness is never a mere awareness of a content. A necessary condition for my awareness of an object is the multiple determination of myself in relation to the object. Similarly, my self-consciousness requires and is constituted by the various ways in which I determine myself. Each new level of self-awareness involves a new type of self-determination, the complexity of self-consciousness is no less and no greater than the complexity of the self.

The point I have tried to make is that it is not only self-consciousness that is reflexive but the self as a being. We must

not lose sight of the double truth that self-consciousness constitutes the reflexivity of the self even as it is constituted by it.
To affirm only the one or the other of these propositions is to
bifurcate self and self-consciousness and to misunderstand the
nature of conscious awareness by identifying it with the passivity of intuition. The relation of the reflexivity of the self
to the reflexivity of self-consciousness is reciprocal and necessary. To allow the reflexivity of self-consciousness is necessarily
to acknowledge the fundamental reflexivity of the self.

If to be a man is to be a subject and to be a subject is to be
reflexively related to oneself, we have found an ultimate
ontological basis for human responsibility. Man is responsible,
in the first instance, because he is burdened with the ontological necessity of responding to himself in the sense of having to answer to himself for what he is and does. The first as
well as the last problem man encounters is his own existence.
To be is not simply to be liable; it is the original human liability. It is not so much death or even freedom that we dread
and seek to escape, but our responsibility to ourselves. We
must answer to ourselves not only for what we do but for
what we are. Whatever may have been the ultimate origin of
our existence, we find that it is now in our own "care" (Sorge).
It is something to be cared for and to be cared about. This
"care," which Heidegger regards as the most basic feature of
human existence, is not psychological or moral but ontological. No man can escape it, since the only way to avoid it
would be to make oneself not to be—a power which man as a
finite being does not possess. As Kierkegaard pointed out, instead of providing an escape from responsibility, suicide requires a man to take supreme responsibility for himself. Even
if it were the final end of his being, which remains problematic, suicide would remain an expression of man's ultimate
concern about himself. Only highly intensified concern about
oneself could drive a man to attempt his own destruction.

To be a man, then, is to be responsible to oneself for oneself. To state this is in no wise to recommend what a man
ought to be in some ideal sense, but simply to state what he

is and *must be.* This reflexive relation founds an ought, a moral ought, but does not in itself constitute a normative ought. The original necessity involved in man's ontological responsibility is more accurately expressed by a *must* than by an *ought.* To be concerned about oneself is not a matter of choice but of fate. It is not a resultant of choice but a condition of choice. In its original ontological mode, responsibility is the *necessity of caring for oneself,* of *answering to oneself for what one is and does.* All other modes of responsibility reflect and express this basic ontological accountability of the self to itself.

It may seem that to make this claim is either to state an altogether trivial point with no significant consequences, or else to smuggle concepts into the analysis which are pregnant with normative meaning. I admit straightaway that the point is obvious enough if one only looks at the human situation, and not only obvious but undeniable. I cannot imagine how anyone could deny it or even consider it without exhibiting responsibility for himself. If, however, the point is obvious, the claim must be innocent of concealed normative implications. In stating that a man *must* care for his existence in the sense of presiding over his own destiny, we are not claiming or even suggesting that he *should* be concerned about himself. At this stage of the analysis there are no explicit or implicit norms involved. To ask whether or not man ought to be responsible for his existence is to ask whether or not he should have been created as he is. I do not propose to ask this kind of normative ontological question, for I see no way of answering it.

If, then, man's ontological concern for his existence does not in itself constitute moral responsibility, how does it found such responsibility? To answer this question it is necessary to consider the problematic features of man's reflexivity. Human existence is, as we have noted above, problematic. Although there are certain factual conditions of his existence which the individual is fated to live with, he must determine what he is to do with and about them. There is no single aspect of man's empirical nature which is not problematic. No matter what his endowments may be, a man may respond to them in a variety of possible ways. And these possibilities can never be finally catalogued until the last human subject has ceased to exist. The individual determines himself as a self in the way that he responds to his own facticity. The fact that he has physical appetites does not in itself determine what sort of person he is to be, for he must decide whether they are to be expressed and if so, how. The most significant fact about man is not that he has sexual appetites, for example, but what he does with them. He must respond to his factual nature, do something with and about it. The fact that he can and must respond to himself in this fashion constitutes his original freedom. *A self is what it chooses to be.* It can be a self only by freely taking over responsibility for itself. Choices, once made, become part of the individual's facticity and, hence, further materials for decision and response.

Insofar as it is reflexive and problematic to itself it is evident that the self exhibits a fundamental negativity. Sartre has expressed this negativity in a deliberately paradoxical way by stating that "the self (*pour-soi*) is what it is not, and is not what it is." In stating it this way Sartre plays on the ambiguity of the "is" involved in the two parts of the assertion. It is clear from the context of his discussion that even for Sartre the self is and must be identical with itself and, hence, must include both terms of the negation. I am the self that I am not, for only in being it can I not be it. If this seems paradoxical, it is only because the negation is of a *particular mode* of my existence and not of myself as a *totality*. What Sartre wishes to express is that I am not simply identical with myself in the way that a stone is self-identical. My body is mine and constitutive of my existence; yet, I transcend my body in being related to it at all. It is perfectly proper for me to say that I *have* a body while denying that I *am* a body. To affirm the latter would be falsely to reduce myself to a body.

But, we may ask, what does this negativity have to do with

responsibility? The negation, we have seen, requires a positive relation of the self to itself and, thus, expresses one feature of the basic ambiguity of human existence. I am and I am not myself at one and the same time in clearly definable ways. Again, this is a condition of volition rather than a result of it. At any time when I choose or make a decision it is on the basis of this fundamental ambiguity. I must respond to myself in the mode of my facticity and the way in which I respond determines what I am to be. But this is a free response which allows wide choice. Through my volition the ambiguity of my situation is made determinate, but it is my volition and action alone which make the determination necessary.

To see how an ought may be founded by man's ontological responsibility, we can ask first: how is an imperative possible for man? Suppose, for example, that I regard it as morally necessary to care for my own body in the sense of securing its health and well-being. The "ought" here is of a different order from the original necessity pertaining to existence, for it may express that which I do not do rather than what I do. I may neglect or abuse my body instead of taking care of it. The "ought" then expresses the discrepancy between what I actually do and what I should do. This is, in fact, most generally the case with ought statements. We think of an imperative only when there is either an actual or a possible discrepancy between what we are doing and what we should do. We would never, I think, use an ought statement where a state of affairs followed naturally and necessarily. As the linguistic analysts have claimed, ought statements are always used to recommend either to ourselves or to others. And it makes sense to recommend an action only if there is some question as to whether or not the action will transpire.

To state that I ought to care for my body in the sense of nurturing it leaves the question open as to whether or not I do care for it in this sense. I may take care of it and thus do what I ought to do, but, if so, it is because I choose to care for it and might have chosen otherwise. The "ought" expressed in the statement is, then, a normative ought. But we must be careful not to conclude too hastily that it is a pure normative statement with only a contingent connection with the facts of existence. We have noted earlier that every man does and must care for and about his body in so far as it is an integral part of his existence. For him to be able not to care for his body in this ontological sense it would be necessary for it not to be his body—which is obviously impossible. It cannot both be and not be his body, and since it is his body it constitutes an object of his concern. We have, then, at least two senses of "care" here, namely caring for and about in an ontological sense and caring for and about in a normative sense. If our analysis is correct, the first is unconditionally necessary in allowing no options, whereas the second is ontologically contingent. Moralists would ordinarily distinguish between the two types of necessity as metaphysical/ontological and moral. And they would usually regard it as a mistake to attempt to derive a moral necessity from an ontological necessity, or normative statements from descriptive statements. Since we have admitted that the affirmation of man's original concern about his existence is a pure descriptive statement, how can it provide a foundation for the imperative of moral obligation? In other words, what has man's inescapable *ontological liability* to do with an alleged *moral liability* to care for one's body in a normative sense?

In spite of the striking difference between the two imperatives, if we may call them that, they have certain equally apparent similarities. In the first place, they both represent modes of liability which require a reflexive relationship of the self to itself. Moreover, both express a particular type of liability, namely concern for one's body. If we look more closely at the "ought" statement, we find that it reflects and presupposes the descriptive statement. If I tell myself that I ought to take care of my body I surely presuppose that it is my body and, further, that it is an object of concern to myself. As a matter of fact, every ought statement assumes this. Ought statements do not in themselves *found* a concern but only *determine* it. To state that I should nurture my body is not

to establish concern for my body but rather to specify how
I should respond to this concern. My care for my body is, in
the ontological sense, ambiguous and problematic. The ought
statement prescribes the way in which I should determine this
problematic relationship. What I do in the ought statement
is to acknowledge the claim which my body makes upon me
by being my body. If the ought statement is valid, it can do
nothing more than this. Either the fact that I have a body in
itself establishes a claim upon me such that I should nurture
and affirm it as a vehicle for the realization of my existence,
or the moral *ought* commanding this is arbitrary. The moral
imperative expresses and must express a *de facto* relationship
of the self to itself. So far is it from being a pure normative
statement prescribing an ideal, that it actually expresses the
ontological condition of the self. Implicit in the statement: I
ought to care for my body, is the proposition: I do care for
my body. The normative statement is possible only because I
can both care and not care for my body. I *must* care in the
ontological sense, and the imperative expresses this care even
when I do not follow it. But I can *not* care in the sense that
I may act contrary to the imperative. I may, in short, act irresponsibly, which means that I may act as if my body were
not an object of my care.

The morally conscientious man simply *accepts* his responsibility and acts in conformity with it. The normative ought
does not constitute his responsibility simply by laying down
an ideal, but only expresses his responsibility. It commands
him to care for the body which is in fact an inescapable object
of his concern. An *irresponsible* man is clearly a man who is
responsible but negates his responsibility. To be *irresponsible*
is not to be *non-responsible,* and we commonly recognize this
fact, even as we recognize that to be irrational is not the
same as to be non-rational. Human beings may be irrational
but they cannot be non-rational. Similarly they may be irresponsible but they cannot be non-responsible.

Kierkegaard has described despair as a "disrelationship"
within a relationship. We might borrow his term and describe

irresponsibility as a disrelationship within a relationship. A man who does not care for himself in the way that he ought to is a person who is disrelated to himself. Such a disrelationship is a form of self-alienation. The ought statement expresses either the actuality or the possibility of this alienation and recommends that it be surmounted. It represents the claim of the self upon itself to acknowledge and affirm itself in the fullness of its being. The call of conscience issues from the depths of the self and thus expresses man's original ontological responsibility. A man can be disrelated to himself only because he is related to himself. The original relatedness founds the possibility of the disrelationship and, hence, of the norm. I have a body which is an integral part of my existence, but I may act as if it were not mine, as if it were simply a thing or an object in the world. To act on the latter assumption is to deny that I am what I am and, hence, implicitly to affirm a falsehood. To assume my responsibility for myself and make it the principle of my action is to exist in the "truth"; to refuse it is to exist in "error." Truth may not be, as Kierkegaard claimed, subjectivity, but truth is surely possible in the mode of subjectivity. To take responsibility for oneself is an essential condition of the "truth" of subjective existence. Truth and moral value are not so disparate as philosophers have sometimes believed.

We have discovered thus far that man is liable in two fundamental ways, namely ontologically and normatively, and, further, that the two modes of responsibility are closely related. The first mode of liability posed no serious problems since no claim was made for its normative status. It was seen to be unconditionally necessary but non-normative. The second mode appears to be just the opposite, namely, normative but wholly contingent. We have not yet seen how the one may found the other. Why does the fact that I am ontologically concerned about my body entail that I ought to take care of it? The answer is, I think, that the normative ought expresses the ontological necessity of care for one's body in the light of one's freedom to disregard and abuse it. Although the normative ought is not a mere reiteration of the original concern for one's body, it is based upon and expresses this fundamental concern. Moreover, it depends for its validity entirely upon the ontological liability. This situation need not be puzzling if we take into account the fact that the normative ought only expresses the necessity of responding to one's facticity, only states the claim which this facticity makes upon one's freedom. No matter how I act I am accountable to myself for the way in which I respond to the claims made upon me by the facts of my existence. If I disregard these claims, my action establishes a "disrelationship" or "alienation" in myself which manifests itself in the form of *guilt*. All guilt is based upon a disrelationshp and, hence, is provided by the ultimate reflexivity of the self. Guilt is the awareness of a claim which is not acknowledged. The fact that we feel guilt at all is possible only because our existence continues to make claims upon us even when we refuse to acknowledge them.

A normative claim in the form of an obligation may be first in the order of our awareness, so much so that we may wonder if it has anything to do with the facts of our existence. It may seem to us that we are engaged exclusively in attempting to pursue an ideal. The truth is, however, that the ideal appears to us as an ideal only because of our freedom. The normative ought expresses a relationship of the self to itself as the possibility for a disrelationship. Since the relationship is always prior and derives from our existence, it is never abrogated by the disrelationship. The norm has a binding power upon us even when we act irresponsibly, precisely because we never cease to be responsible for and to ourselves. In other words, moral irresponsibility is possible only because of our ontological responsibility. Kant saw this point with admirable clarity in insisting that the imperative of morality is categorical and unconditional. He saw, further, that it is and must be rooted in the very being of the self. He was mistaken in attributing the force of the imperative to our rational nature. But his insight went deeper than this, for in the formulations of the imperative he made it clear that moral responsibility is ultimately the liability of the self to itself as a subject or, in his terms, as a person. Reason discovers and promulgates the law of morality, but it does not constitute it. One is always tempted to ask of Kant: why should I be rational? Kant recognized that an argument is required to show that to be responsible is to be rational in one's conduct. The argument can be supplied only if appeal is made to the facts of self-existence. I cannot escape the imperative of morality only because I cannot escape myself. Even if we were to affirm the synthetic proposition that responsibility entails rationality we would still need criteria of rationality. And such criteria can be supplied only by appeal to the conditions of human existence.

The ontological liability of the self founds moral responsibility for the reason that the ontological conditions of our existence are, also, conditions of our freedom. My moral obligation to myself is a constitutive characteristic of my existence and, in a broader sense, ontological in character. The ought of morality expresses a relation of obligation of the self to itself. If the obligation did not obtain as a real liability, the ought would be an illusion. It is either categorical or no moral responsibility at all. The larger and more inclusive concern of the self includes moral concern. Man is as much a responsible being as he is a rational being. The possibility that the moral ought can appear only as an ideal or that it can appear as an ideal at all depends upon the fact that it may not be fully constitutive of my existence. In other words, it may found a disrelationship or alienation within the self. In the latter instance there is a discrepancy between a claim made upon me and the way in which I act. Action and principle do not conform in that I act as if the principle were not binding upon me. But the discrepancy is a discrepancy within the self in two of its modes. The ought continues to express a basic feature of my existence even when I disregard it. In expressing an actual claim of the self upon itself, the ought is constitutive of my existence. In being repudiated, it continues to be constitutive in that the claim continues to be valid and, even more important, to found the resultant disrelationship and guilt. But in the latter case the ought is constitutive in a deficient mode. The ought is then the measure of my disrelationship to myself.

For purposes of simplicity we have limited ourselves thus far to the analysis of self-responsibility, though responsibility is by no means limited to the reflexivity of the self. In fact, the self would not be a self if it did not exist in a world with other selves. Hence our discussion has offered a somewhat artificial representation of the self as an isolated being. We need not, I think, give up anything that has been said, but it is important to consider the situation of man vis-à-vis the world in order to understand adequately even his responsibility to himself.

In the case of self-responsibility I have maintained that the ultimate condition is the reflexivity of self-existence. I have interpreted responsibility in this context as itself a mode of relatedness of the self to itself. If we enlarge the context to include other beings, we might expect the same fundamental conditions to obtain. And this is indeed the case. If to exist at all is to be responsible, to exist before other beings and together with them in a world is to be liable to them. To state that we must reckon with other beings in our world is to state the most obvious fact imaginable and, yet, a fact of the greatest importance for an analysis of responsibility. *To have a world at all is, like existing, a liability.* If we sometimes desire to be rid of ourselves, at other times we desire to be rid of the world. Both of these fundamental human desires manifest themselves in everyday life and in psychoses. Some individuals try to rid themselves of their world by withdrawing from it, depriving it of all meaning, attempting to cancel it out. They live as if they had no world at all. In exaggerated form they express a normal human concern about the world and, above all, the liability which it poses for man. Responsibility for living in the world may become so dreadful that it is too much for an individual to cross the street, to ride in a train, to confront another human being. Surely no argument is required to show that to live in the world is a liability and a responsibility. And, like our original self-responsibility, it is ontological. We are all concerned about our world even though we may express our concern in different ways. The world makes demands upon us by the mere fact of its being there before and around us. I am concerned that the stars should not fall in, the sun cool off, the automobile run me down, in short that the world be orderly and meaningful. I am oriented toward my world both in general and specific ways. My world-orientation is inseparable from the organization of my subjectivity. If I am mad I can have only a mad world and, if my world is mad, I can only reflect this madness in my subjective existence. A self without a world would be no self at all. As Heidegger describes it, the self is a "being-in-the-world."

That the world is something to be reckoned with, no one would deny. Our plans and aspirations are contingent upon the course of the world. The farmer is most aware of this contingency as it pertains to weather and climate, the financier as it pertains to markets and business cycles. Every man in his own way calculates the probable course of events and adjusts his plans accordingly. But insofar as it is merely this sort of reckoning that is involved in our responsibility as a being-in-the-world, we have discovered no claims made upon us by other beings. Or have we? We have, at least, been forced to reckon with the world and this means to take into account the course of world events. To reckon with the world means not merely to make such calculations but, further, to make appropriate adjustments in the light of them. It would be foolish for a New England farmer to plant his crops in mid-January. If he persisted in actions of this type we would have no hesitation whatever in declaring him irresponsible. And he would be correctly judged irresponsible for the simple reason that he had failed to take into account the world in which he lives.

In using the term "appropriate" with respect to the farmer's action, a double reference is involved. There is, on the one hand, the process of nature which determines climate and, on the other hand, the plans of the farmer. For his action to be appropriate it must exhibit a proper response to both factors. He is no less irresponsible if he fails to consider his own needs and desires than if he ignores the weather. A claim is made upon the farmer by natural processes even though it is qualified by his own plans. As such, the claim is only hypothetical: mind the weather if you would harvest your crops! If he were not a farmer but the pilot of a space-ship, he would reckon with the heavens in a different way. Because of his changed objectives, nature would make different demands upon him. In each case his purposes would determine which natural factors were relevant for his calculations. Human objectives are highly variable and man's orientation toward the world is largely pragmatic. What constitutes appropriate and responsible action in the concrete case is a function of these variables. Yet some objectives one must have and, thus, in one way or another one must respond to the surrounding environment. Appropriateness of response is necessarily a function of the world one confronts. Every man must exist in the world and, thus, contend with it. And he cannot do this entirely on his own terms. He is responsible for acknowledging the other beings in his world, in the first place, and, in the second place, for knowing what they are. Knowledge is essential for responsible action, since it is through knowledge alone that man can hope to relate himself appropriately to the objects in his world.

The will to truth is based upon the will to acknowledge what is. The possibility of knowledge presupposes both that there is a world to know and that man is related to this world. Being and the relation to being are prior to truth in all of its modes. To be in a state of objective error is to *mistake* the world, to *mis-appropriate* it. Viewed objectively, error is a type of disrelation to objects in the world. It is for this reason that error and ignorance are of serious import. I am related to the objects in my world and as they are. This relatedness, again, is a constitutive feature of my existence. I am liable both for acknowledging the objects to which I am as a matter of fact related and, further, for recognizing the nature of my relationship to them.

There is, then, a mode of ontological responsibility toward objects in the world which is constitutive of the human condition. Even as my own existence constitutes a liability, so, too, does the existence of objects in my world. Whatever I do, I cannot evade this basic responsibility. As in the case of self-responsibility, this original relatedness grounds the possibility of an objective irresponsibility. I can act toward objects in ways that either ignore their existence altogether or misrepresent them. If I act deliberately in this fashion, my action is irresponsible in that it is not appropriate to the nature of the objects involved. To treat a dog, for example, as if it were incapable of feeling pain is to regard it as if it were like a stone. We ordinarily recognize that it is irrational and intellectually irresponsible to assert that a dog is a stone, but we do not always recognize that an action which entails such a false proposition can be equally mistaken and irresponsible. In my assertion I am cognitively disrelated to my world; my assertion is false because it misrepresents what is and, hence, puts me in a false relation to it. By the same token my action is in error because it is not consonant with the world of actuality. The action implies that dogs have no capacity for feelings. If, to justify my action and thus render it responsible, I need to represent dogs as other than they are, my action is without warrant and hence morally wrong. It is evident, I think, that cognitive error and moral error are not so unrelated as is often maintained. Both involve misrepresentation of objects and both involve a relation toward objects which is inappropriate. Objects are what they are initially in full independence of our actions and beliefs. We are originally related to them as they are and can never alter this basic ontological relation. It is this original relation that provides a measure for inappropriate and appropriate action toward objects.

Because of its humanism, the Western philosophical tradition in ethics tends to neglect man's responsibility toward natural objects. We assume all too easily that such objects are present in our world only to be used as we see fit. Regarding man as the supreme end of creation, we feel justified in our action so long as the use we make of natural objects affords us pleasure and satisfaction. I do not intend to pursue the very complex question here as to human responsibility toward creatures of the natural world. But it is evident, I think, that if we are to justify our conduct as responsible in the normative sense, we must evaluate it in the light of the objects in our natural world and our original relation to them within nature. Whether we acknowledge it or not we are liable toward the natural world both ontologically and morally.

In the second formulation of the Categorical Imperative, Kant states that we ought to treat others as ends in themselves and not merely as means. Kant means that we should treat others as morally responsible subjects like ourselves. This formulation is intended to express the pure ought of moral obligation. But if I ask: Why should I treat others as ends-in-themselves? the answer must be: Because they are ends-in-themselves. Kant's ethics has and requires a metaphysical foundation, as he well knew. We cannot understand how we should treat either ourselves or other persons until we understand what it means to be a person. The ought expresses, as I have indicated earlier, an ontological reflexivity in the subject and, secondly, an ontological relation to other men. If I ask: How should I treat another man? the answer Kant gives is: As a man. This is only a formula, to be sure, and a highly abstract formula at that. But it affirms the fundamental requirement of morally responsible action toward other human subjects. We might state the matter even more formally in this fashion: so act toward others that your action is appropriate to the existence of the other. Surely this is both an absolutely necessary condition of responsible action toward others and an instructive principle for determining action. Discrimination on the basis of race is immoral and irresponsible for the reason that it misrepresents the members of another race. It is precisely for this reason that racial discrimination is inevitably accompanied by such elaborate rationalization. For the practice of discrimination to be justified the facts need to be different from what they are. No more eloquent testimony of the awareness of human responsibility can be found than in the urge to rationalize one's conduct. Rationalization is, after all, but a deficient mode of justification. If legitimate reasons cannot be given, the best one can do is to offer pseudo-reasons.

As with ourselves, we are liable to others both morally and ontologically, and the former liability is founded by the latter. I could have no moral responsibility to another man if he did not exist and, further, if I were not related to him. I am in fact related to him as father or brother, neighbor or employer, stranger or friend. We are never related to other human beings simply in the abstract. It is always to some individual that we are related and the particularity of his existence is a factual determinant of the situation. The other makes a claim upon me not only by confronting me as a person but as this particular person. There is, in other words, a facticity with respect to other persons, a concrete determinateness, which is as important as my own facticity. I had nothing at all to do with the fact that I was born of human parents or of these particular parents. Yet from the first moment of my existence the parent-child relationship is constitutive of my existence in its social dimension; it establishes a problem for me so long as we both exist.

It is doubtful if even in a culture whole-heartedly devoted to progressive education any single child has managed to remain completely unaware of the liability of child to parent. Parents have a way of asserting their claims upon their children and of making these claims directly felt. The child is quite literally answerable to the parent for its conduct; it must give an account of itself. But this accounting does not consist solely in the child's measuring his action by the parent's yardstick. The child learns very early to justify his aberrant behavior by reasoning with his father. He is quick in

detecting *arbitrary* demands made upon him and in counter-
ing them with what he regards as appropriate standards. In
challenging the parent the child is asking that the parent
justify his demands. With what right, he asks, are these claims
made? To act responsibly toward a parent does not entail
doing everything that is specifically demanded, since unjustifiable claims may be made upon the child. The child appeals
in its challenge to the father as a father and quite properly
assumes that the father is a responsible agent. In questioning
a specific demand, the child is not necessarily questioning the
authority of the father or denying that it has a responsibility
toward the father as a parent. It may, of course, persuade itself that it is in no way accountable to the father, but, in the
latter case, it will not feel required to justify or to discuss its
action with its father. The situation is complicated by the
fact that, as with all social relations, responsibility is shared.
Justice requires that both parent and child recognize and
abide by their responsibilities. Freud has said that the death
of his father is the most important single event in a man's life.
This may overstate the case, but it hardly exaggerates the importance of the role of the parent in the life of an individual.
The problem of the father-relation which has become so prominent in psychoanalysis is not merely a psychological problem.
It has, also, moral and ontological dimensions. A sense of dis-
relatedness to the father is often at the core of psychic distress.
The psychical disturbance has both moral and ontological
roots in that it reflects both an awareness of the constitutive
character of the parent-child relationship and the requirements it imposes for appropriate action. The initial task is
that of clarification, which may require what is termed "depth-
analysis." The individual is required not only to recollect the
decisive events of his relation to the parent, but to grasp the
significance of the relationship itself. His recollection must
recover the meaning of his own being in relation to that of
the father so that he can make a new beginning in understanding and interpreting the relationship. The fact that the
problem first appears as an inner conflict is in no way sur-

prising, since to be disrelated to another person is inevitably to be disrelated to oneself. Analysis must reveal the true source and scope of the conflict. It is important to note, however, that clarification is not, in itself, enough to eradicate the disturbance. At most clarification can place the individual in a position to determine freely and responsibly what the father-child relationship is to mean to himself. The decision is all the more serious in that it determines in part, also, what the relationship can mean to the father. No one of us can unilaterally determine the meaning of our relationships with others. If we could, life would be far simpler and our responsibility far less demanding.

Other persons make claims upon us and thus make us liable to them by existing in our world. In the most general terms they demand that we acknowledge them and treat them as persons. This is a demand, incidentally, which no man can forfeit by his own volition. No man can, for example, by selling himself as a slave make himself not to be a person. The relationship of master and slave which assumes this to be possible is founded upon a double deception. The slave fools himself no less than he fools the master; both fool themselves as well as each other. A man remains a man no matter what his condition in the world. He may not demand in any verbal way that he be treated as a man; in fact, he may even recommend that his humanity be disregarded. But the fact that he continues to exist as a man entails that his claim upon us as a human subject has not been removed. We are responsible for acting toward him not only in terms of what he says he is but in terms of what he in fact is. I can no more escape my responsibility toward the other because he regards himself as a slave than I can escape my responsibility toward myself by looking upon myself as a slave. A slave is, by definition, a human subject who is *made to be* simply a tool for the service of others. But no man can actually make himself or another to be merely a slave; he can only make him play the role of a slave. It is not difficult to exhibit the deception and bad faith involved in such a relationship. The other must be treated as a man in order to be kept in the position of slavery, and this fact alone reveals the deception.

It is crucially important to take account of the full dimension of human existence in analyzing our responsibility to others. If, for example, we were to accept the cultural situation as exhaustively determinative of human beings, we would be perfectly justified in treating some men merely as slaves. Culturally viewed, such men might be said to be only slaves. Hence, responsible action would require only that I treat any one of them in a way appropriate to his station in life. A slave would be only a slave, a criminal a criminal, and an aristocrat an aristocrat. To live responsibly would be, as some people actually regard it, to treat each man in a way befitting his cultural situation. And this is, in fact, what conventional morality sanctions. It is, on this view, justifiable to abuse criminals, to exploit slaves, and to defer to the gentry. If we take into account only explicit or voiced claims, conventional morality is more or less satisfactory. But if we refuse to identify the *existence* of a man with the *role* he plays and refuse to deny that he is capable of transcending his appearance as a cultural object, we cannot be content with conventional morality. No man can be identical with his appearance in the way that a stone is simply a stone. To transcend oneself is an a priori characteristic of all human subjects. However wicked a man is, he cannot be simply the embodiment of wickedness in concrete form. The reason is that he has always the possibility of repentance. Curiously enough, those who are most ready to make an absolute judgment upon the wicked man are the first to rejoice at his reform.

We are responsible toward others, then, not simply in terms of their empirical nature but, also, their existence. We are related to others in this twofold way and must take both factors into account if we are to act responsibly toward them. We are accountable to them even as we are accountable to ourselves. Initially as well as continuously it is the fact of their existence which constitutes our liability. But it is, also, their response to us. Other people are continuously presenting us with the necessity for responding to their overtures. They invite our friendship or elicit our scorn. All human relationships have a contractual foundation insofar as they are based upon a reciprocity of response. If another person invites my friendship he makes me liable toward him in a special way. Whether or not I accept his invitation, I am obliged to take account of it in my response to him. I may, of course, be insensitive and not perceive the meaning of his gesture. But if I do perceive it, it makes a claim upon me—not to offer my friendship in return, necessarily, but at least to respond to him as one who has exhibited friendliness toward me. If, however, I do accept his invitation, our relationship has been constituted as a friendship. We are now related to each other within the context of this implicit contract. That we have become friends is a factual characteristic of our mutual situation. For either of us to act toward the other as if this were not the case would be to act irresponsibly.

The social contract theory of the state has recognized the contractual nature of human relations but has too often stressed the formal and political side of it. Marriage is a formal contractual relationship between two people in our society, sanctioned by both state and church. But it represents also a moral contract. The recognition of common-law marriage, for example, acknowledges that more basic contractual relationship involved. Contracts may be broken off on grounds which are valid both legally and morally. But it is one thing to sever a contract for cause and another to pretend that none exists. We do not need to appeal to special moral intuitions in order to know that promises ought to be kept. Such an intuitionist theory as that of Sir David Ross treats ethical norms as if they were divorced from factual situations. It is the fact that one has entered into a contractual relationship with another person which makes it mandatory that promises be honored. To understand what a promise is, is to know to what one has obligated oneself. No special moral intuition is required to understand the commitment involved in promise making. Legal contracts are simply more formally and meticulously defined commitments sanctioned by the laws and authority of the state.

The possibility of a political order depends upon the fact that man is a social being. The establishment of an explicit political order simply formalizes and institutionalizes the reciprocal relatedness of members of a community. For the most part, the individual is born into a fairly developed political order. He has probably had no part in constituting it or in determining its laws and institutions. This fact makes it difficult for some men to understand why they are responsible to this order. They fail to understand what Socrates knew full well, namely that to be born into and develop within a civilized society is to participate in the contractual relationship of the political community. One need not be a Hegelian advocate of an organic and monistic state to recognize this point. One need only take note of the fact that the political order is as fundamental for him as the familial and social order. His original political responsibility is based upon his participation in a community of civilized men. He may choose to be exiled and renounce his citizenship but, as Socrates saw with great clarity, to do so is a responsible political action which must be carefully weighed. It was simply a fact for Socrates that he was a citizen of Athens, as much a fact and as important a fact as that he was a teacher. He could not justify his action simply by an appeal to an abstract norm. Could he have done that, his problem would have been easy and his conscience untroubled. In his analysis of the situation Socrates appealed both to the social and political community of which he was a member and to the explicit demands being made upon him by its official representatives. He defended himself in terms of what they ought to expect of him in their capacity as responsible members of the community. He did not take their pronouncements as the last word in specifying his responsibility as a citizen, but appealed to the contractual foundation of the state in rejecting their claims. Socrates regarded himself as a loyal citizen of Athens even in disobeying its orders, and rightly so. But even in his disobedience he did not fully reject the authority of the political order, for he accepted his imprisonment, and, to the distress of his friends, drank the hemlock. It might be argued, of course, that Socrates would have been fully justified in choosing exile. But, whatever may be said on that point, the fact remains that the evaluation of his action would require consideration of his participation in the Athenian state.

It is impossible to assess political responsibility adequately without an understanding of the nature and origin of the state. It is necessary to understand not only the authority of specific laws but the source from which this authority itself is derived. There are both bad laws and unwritten laws, and politically responsible behavior requires that both be taken into account. We see easily enough that the fact that something is prescribed by law does not make it *morally* right but not so easily that it does not necessarily make it *politically* right. Moral norms have a certain priority over political norms in that they are concerned with the responsibility of men as men. But there are, also, political norms which derive their authority not simply from the constitution of particular states but from the nature of the political community as such.

We have seen that in the case of all of our relations with others, be it as individuals or as members of an organized community, explicit demands are made upon us which are frequently accompanied by sanctions. If we do not hand over our purse to the thief we may be shot, and if we do not obey the speed limit we may be deprived of our license. These are concrete demands upon us and constitute recognizable hazards. But they do not constitute the whole or even the most important part of our responsibility. We may seek to outwit the thief and disarm him, but we are liable for the way in which we treat him. We are not justified in shooting him on the spot in retribution, nor in subjecting him to punishment without due process of law. The important fact is, however, that the law itself is but a rough and approximate statement of our responsibility toward the other. Fortunately, the greater part of our conduct does not require explicit legislation but follows of itself, else the task of making and enforcing laws would be an impossible undertaking. The other person has political rights which may or may not be stated in a constitutional document. These rights are nothing more than the claims which he makes upon us simply by participating with us in a political order. *They are a priori and unconditioned in that they would necessarily be asserted in any political order whatever.* Ultimately these rights follow from the humanity of the citizen. To deny them is in effect to deny that the community is a community of men. No change in explicit rules can erase these claims and absolve us from the responsibility to honor them. No man can be deprived of his rights as a human being, though he may be treated as if he made no such claims upon us. *To state the requirements of a just political order is but to affirm those conditions which lie at the foundation of any political order.* The normative ought derives from the contractual relatedness, both original and historically developed, of men. The ought is not here, any more than in the case of personal morality, simply expressive of an ideal, but is definitional of a situation which factually obtains. *It characterizes our liability and, hence, the condition of our political freedom.*

Throughout this exposition I have stressed the ontological and factual basis of responsibility, insisting that responsibility in the normative sense is founded upon responsibility in the ontological sense. Our liability is initially a *condition* rather than a *consequence* of our decisions. Insofar as we respond to our initial situation we constitute for ourselves further determinate contexts which qualify our liabilities in new ways. In our dealings with others the responses take the form of more or less formal contractual relations. As such, they are factual determinants of our social and political existence. It is mistaken, I believe, to divorce moral responsibility from political responsibility or to divorce either, normatively conceived, from factual liabilities. To understand human responsibility in all of its aspects it is necessary to consider man's total involvement with himself and others in the world. We may, for certain purposes, concentrate on some one aspect of his involvement but never without a certain measure of artificiality. The ultimate responsibility is existence itself. To exist means to be in a world, and in a social as well as a natural world. *Man is a responsible being, personally, naturally, socially, politically.* He may live irresponsibly in any or all of these contexts, but he cannot live non-responsibly. To be in a position to assess the explicit claims which are made upon him, he must understand the basic structure on which these demands are predicated. He must, in other words, have an ontological as well as an empirical understanding of himself, of nature, and of the social and political order.

ঙ IV ঙ

PLATONIC, PRAGMATIC, AND POLITICAL RESPONSIBILITY

WAYNE A. R. LEYS

IN THIS ESSAY I wish to examine contrary reasons that have been advanced for attributing "irresponsibility" to Plato and the Pragmatists. Do these polemics throw any light on the meaning of "political responsibility"? And do they tell us anything about a philosophical approach to law and politics?

Plato has been much criticized as an apologist for "irresponsible government." His critics remind us that the ideal rulers of *The Republic* are bound by no constitutional law and that they are accountable to no one but themselves. In *The Statesman* and *The Laws* there is a grudging admission of law (in the absence of perfectly virtuous governors), but there is no effective provision for making the office-holders accountable. This Platonic indifference to the problem of accountability, coupled with a penchant for master-minding, has been interpreted as an endorsement of dictatorship.[1]

A second line of attack upon Plato is Dewey's contention that all abstract idealisms give encouragement to political irresponsibility. According to Dewey, the Idealists expound a way of life that is so perfect and so far beyond existing practice that it is obviously impractical. This is said to justify a "dualism," a separation of theory and practice; and thus irresponsible practice is made to appear right because it is unavoidable.[2]

[1] This contention is found in Karl Popper, *The Open Society and Its Enemies* (1950); and it is also the tendency of Warner Fite's *The Platonic Legend* (1934), and R. H. S. Crossman's *Plato Today* (1937).

[2] See Dewey's *German Philosophy and Politics* (1915), *Reconstruction in Philosophy* (1920), and *Human Nature and Conduct* (1922). See also G. R.

The defenders of Plato have argued that Idealism, through-out occidental history, has been opposed to subjectivism, relativism, and the irresponsibility of men who recognize no objective standards by which they might be judged. Plato is thus pictured as one of the founders of the natural law tradi-tion, a tradition that has certainly resisted the exercise of arbitrary power on numerous occasions.[3]

As I read Plato, he is neither an exponent of irresponsible government, nor a friend of responsible government. Even though he talks about "the State," he is not advocating any *government* at all. Plato is anti-political. *The Republic,* is, for the most part, the description of a society without conflict: hence, it describes a society that does not need government, law, or political activity.

Although the later dialogues recognize the need for law in a second-best society, they never find a useful function for sophists, politicians, barristers, propagandists, and negotiators.[4] Advocates continue to be represented as having no capacity except to make the worse reason appear the better. Plato is still thinking about a society in which every decision is on the merits. He has little, if anything, to suggest for the settlement of disputes in which there is a persistent disagreement on the merits.

Turning now to the Pragmatists, we notice that they, too, are accused of promoting irresponsibility. Because the Prag-matists acknowledge no fixed standard and because they urge open-minded, problem-solving inquiry, they are said to have undermined the public order. They are pictured as promoting the kind of irresponsibility that was proclaimed by Nietzsche. Without a super-personal standard, it is alleged, men can be

Geiger, *Philosophy and the Social Order* (on MacLeish's "Irresponsibles"), (1947), p. 380.

[3] The contention is that of John Wild in *Plato's Modern Enemies and the Theory of Natural Law* (1953). See also Ronald Levinson, *In Defense of Plato* (1953).

[4] *The Statesman* (1957), sec. 291, pp. 61-2. Plato never softens his de-nunciations (in the *Gorgias*) of politicians as flatterers.

nothing more than undependable adventurers and oppor-tunists.[5]

The defenders of pragmatism assert that the very absence of belief in an independent standard makes a man recognize, for the first time, that he alone is responsible for his own actions.[6] Responsibility is not given in the nature of things; it is achieved. It begins when a man is held liable by his fellows, but responsibility soon develops beyond mere liability:

One is held responsible in order that he may *become* responsible, that is, responsive to the needs and claims of others, to the obligations implicit in his position.[7]

With such a psychogenetic explanation of responsibility in mind, the Pragmatists commented on the development of re-sponsible attitudes when intelligent persons are elected to office or placed in situations where others depend upon them. James contrasted the pragmatic problem-solver with the in-tellectualists whose ready-made universe (moral and physical) was an excuse for a "moral holiday." [8]

5 W. Y. Elliott, *The Pragmatic Revolt in Politics* (1928); Walter Lipp-mann, *A Preface to Morals* (1929), and *The Public Philosophy* (1955); Lewis Mumford, "The Pragmatic Acquiescence" in *The Golden Day* (1926), M. J. Adler, "God and the Professors" in *Science, Philosophy and Religion* (1941); Bertrand Russell has called pragmatism a "police theory of truth" and a theory that determines truth by "the arbitrament of the big battalions," in *The Impact of Science on Society* (1951), p. 49.

6 William James regarded every choice as unique (sec. 4 of "The Moral Philosopher and the Moral Life"); hence, not prescribed by any abstract and general philosophy; hence, determined by the chooser. He believed that "the deepest question that is ever asked admits of no reply but the dumb turning of the will and tightening of our heart-strings as we say, 'Yes, I will even have it so!!' " (*Psychology*, chapter on "The Will"). And James perceived this ultimate arbitrariness as a call to heroism and re-sponsibility: "The world thus finds in the heroic man its worthy match and mate; and the effort which he is able to put forth to hold himself erect and keep his heart unshaken is the direct measure of his worth and function in the game of human life." (*Ibid.*)

7 Dewey and Tufts, *Ethics* (1932), pp. 338-9.

8 James, *Pragmatism* (1907), p. 74.

Dewey conceived of himself as an advocate of responsible participation in social life:

The blunt assertion that every moral situation is a unique situation having its own irreplaceable good may seem not merely blunt but preposterous . . . Then it surprisingly turns out that the primary significance of the unique and morally ultimate character of the concrete situation is to transfer the weight and burden of morality to intelligence. It does not destroy responsibility; it only locates it.[9]

As I read the early Pragmatic literature, I am not impressed by the support which James and Dewey gave to any system of law and politics, responsible or irresponsible.[10] The outstanding characteristic of the Pragmatic *philosophers* was their zest for solving problems and their impatience with institutions that were not geared to problem-solving.

James and Dewey, unlike Plato, never tried to escape from social conflicts; but their approach to conflicts was the very one which is rarely possible in government: a "scientific" or "intelligent" or "problem-solving" approach. Their typical reference to politicians is a slurring one. The most gratifying applications of pragmatic doctrines have occurred when it was possible to get away from contentious debating and litigating.[11] The Pragmatists have tried to dissolve formalities,

---

[9] Dewey, *Reconstruction in Philosophy* (1950), pp. 132-3.

[10] I am not saying that James and Dewey did not support constitutional government when they had occasion to say something on the subject. See James's approval of Cavour for refusing to proclaim martial law (*Talks to Teachers* (1904), p. 180, and Dewey's rejection of revolutionary tactics, *Liberalism and Social Action* (1935).

[11] Cf. M. P. Follett, *The New State* (1918), and *Creative Experience* (1930). See also Leys, "Pragmatic Policy Making by Labor Unions and Management" in *Ethics for Policy Decisions* (1952). For expressions of impatience with "unscientific" action, see Dewey, "The Future of Liberalism," *The Journal of Philosophy* 32: 228 (April 25, 1935). "Experimental method is not just messing around nor doing a little of this and a little of that in the hope that things will improve. Just as in the physical sciences, it implies a coherent body of ideas, a theory, that gives direction to effort."

formal procedures, and the rigid oppositions that insist on formality.

The pragmatic conception of responsibility is awareness of the consequences of one's action and the choice of alternatives that promise problem-solving consequences. If I look around for opportunities for responsible work in this sense, should I not stay out of courts, legislatures, administrative agencies of government, and the top managerial positions in large private organizations?

It was, perhaps, a contribution to political philosophy to suggest, as the Pragmatists did, that non-political and extra-legal solutions are sometimes feasible, even though the issues have landed in courts or in politics. But that suggestion did not constitute a political or legal philosophy. They did not provide a rationale for action in the presence of persistent conflict of interest and opinion.[12]

The quarrel between the Platonists and the Pragmatists is a family quarrel. Both of these groups define responsibility as responsiveness to a good (an unchanging good, according to Plato; a changing good, according to the Pragmatists). Both are opposed to philosophies that assume that government is the institution that cannot achieve the good because it is the institution that settles disputes about the good.

To find a conception of responsibility that is radically different from either Platonic or Pragmatic "responsibility," we must turn to Machiavelli, Hobbes, Burke, Hegel, Mosca, Michels, Bentley, and other modern writers who are concerned with responsibility in the sense of "dependability in controlling conflict situations." For some of these writers, at

---

[12] We need to remind ourselves that Dewey's first application of his insight was in Education. For the teacher, whose purpose is to help the pupil to learn and develop, Dewey's faith in the possibility of intelligent problem-solving is an admirable encouragement to eschew the use of coercion. The teacher may fail but it is clear that he cannot succeed by destroying the pupil's opportunity to think and learn. The question we are raising is whether a teacher's commitment provides a model for what we call legal and political activity.

least, the objective of government is the avoidance of evil (chaos and destruction) rather than a positive good.[13] The responsible man is the man who preserves the decision-making machinery and secures the survival of people and agencies.

In the most extremely anti-Platonic writers we encounter what might be called a purely political conception of responsibility. It is implied in the criticism of "irresponsible" leaders and governments, e.g.:

1. A government is irresponsible if it embarks on a program which it is unable to carry out. A government that is forced to default on debt payments or goes down in revolution, trying to implement a program, is irresponsible.

2. An official is irresponsible if he loses his temper, gets drunk, or for other reasons makes public statements that can be used by the opposition to wreck or hamper his agency or his agency's program. He will also be adjudged irresponsible if he neglects the amenities that are necessary for good "public relations."

3. A member of a political party may be adjudged irresponsible if he forgets about "party regularity," particularly if he takes part in a schism that results in the loss of an election. A responsible party member does not have to be a blind partisan, asking only "What is our party line?" [14] But

[13] For such writers it is unrealistic to speak of health, prosperity, education, etc. as proper aims of government. The primary task is to prevent or to settle conflicts, to keep the service functions of government from generating conflicts that destroy or weaken the established order. The most important question about any decision is whether it can be made to stick and whether it will undermine the government's ability to make future decisions stick. Political scientists (especially authors of books on parties and pressure groups) describe at great length the evidence available for calculating the effect of policies on political strength. The descriptions may claim to be "value-free," but only a person who is going to be controlled by survival value would spend so much time trying to ascertain it.

[14] I have in mind the kind of partisanship described by Silone in *The God that Failed* (1950), where Kolarov is quoted as saying that he had not read Trotsky's document but that Kolarov was going along with the condemnation of the document because "we are in the thick of a strug-

when he questions or deviates from his party's position, he is careful not to give aid and comfort to the opposition.

4. A citizen is said to be irresponsible if he claims to speak for a bloc of voters or the whole electorate, but actually cannot deliver their votes.[15]

5. A citizen or an official is irresponsible if he takes measures that undermine the established order.[16]

All of these references to political responsibility are references to the power situation. Someone is acting without sufficient consideration of political feasibility and the survival value of his actions. Someone is risking "political suicide" for himself, for his party, or for his governmental institutions.[17]

Is this political conception of responsibility reconcilable with such philosophical conceptions as we find in Plato and

---

gle for power between two rival groups of the Russian Central Directorate" and the leader with whom Kolarov was allied was using the document as a pretext for condemning Trotsky.

[15] See S. Alinsky, *Reveille for Radicals* (1946), p. 91, where a professor is ridiculed for speaking on behalf of the city. One is reminded of Sam Rayburn's advice to Mr. Forrestal: "If you want to be a statesman, you have to get yourself elected."

[16] For example, see Charles A. Gulick, *Austria from Habsburg to Hitler* (1948). The author obviously believes that party leaders in Austria, by their bitter and uncompromising opposition during the late '20's, paved the way for the end of free government.

[17] For a description of an administrator who kept thinking about the merits of his program rather than the political situation, see D. Hulburd, *This Happened in Pasadena* (1951). For an interpretation of F. D. Roosevelt as counting the political cost of a program, see Summer Welles' account of the decision not to make a bold move against the Axis on November 11, 1937, in *Seven Decisions that Shaped History* (1951), pp. 7-8. Roosevelt apparently judged that his "court-packing" effort had stirred up all the opponents he could handle at the moment. Equally interesting in this period was the behavior of Justice Hughes as he modified his decisions in an effort "to save the court." Less momentous, but of the same kind, are the kind of "tactics" which Louis Brownlow employed in dealing with the D.A.R. in Petersburg, Virginia, and other oppositions encountered during his career as a city manager. See Brownlow, *A Passion for Anonymity* (1958), p. 124, etc.

Dewey? Can a man or a party satisfy both the demand for stability and the demand for good works? Or are we here confronted with an ultimate, undebatable difference in values?

As the first part of my essay implies, I believe that some men hate litigation and/or politicking. Those who have disliked and disapproved of these forms of conflict include many philosophical and religious leaders, men as diverse (in other respects) as Plato and Dewey, Epicurus and St. Paul. On the other hand, I believe, there are some men who tolerate, if they do not thoroughly enjoy, litigation and politics. Among intellectuals there are those who love stories of ritualized conflict, whether or not they have a stomach for the real thing. Here I would mention such writers as Jefferson, Madison, and Judge Holmes (not merely the "Machiavellians").

It would be false to assert that there are only two creedal families among writers on the subject of government. Those who have an appreciative attitude toward the conflict-mediating institutions disagree sharply on the kind of game that should be played and the purpose of the playing. Some, like Hobbes, are asking only for biological survival. Others, like Edmund Burke, insist that what survives shall be "due process." Still others, like Mosca, seem to be carried away by the love of game-playing.

My point in arraying the legal and political game-players against the game-haters is to suggest that the two kinds of responsibility (previously described) are sometimes opposed to one another as an undebatable difference in preferences. Responsibility as a seeking of good program objectives and responsibility as regard for survival may be incidental to the commitments of men who have determined to live, so far as possible, outside the courts and the political arena—as opposed to the men who have decided that they are going to be participants in the arbitration and persuasion machinery of society. To the extent that these commitments become fixed prejudices, it is futile to try to reconcile the two conceptions of responsibility.

I shall now propose a reconciliation of the political and the non-political conceptions of responsibility, with no hope for its acceptance unless the pro-political and anti-political predilections are to some extent overruled by the persons who possess them. This means that a man who dearly loves to "solve problems" by good staff work and ingenious technical studies must be willing to put up with the "fuddyduddy-ism" of lawmen and the "nonsense" of politicians on suitable occasions. It also means that the man who dearly loves to play games in court or in the lobbies must be willing to restrain his game-playing proclivities at times.[18]

Let me try to state several conditional propositions that Plato, Dewey, the lawyers, and the politicians (thus restraining their preferences) might all accept:

1. If men can agree on the merits of a policy, it is better for them to think and act on the merits than to let the policy be determined on the basis of power that is not related to the merits.

2. If men cannot agree on the merits of a policy, it is better for them to employ "legitimate" political and legal methods (even though these methods ultimately rest on power) than to resort to disorderly violence and non-co-operation.

3. If men resort to political or legal methods to reach a decision, it is better to employ methods that take as much notice of evidence as possible (concerning the merits of a policy) than to use methods that are completely irrelevant to the merits.

[18] It is difficult to avoid the impression that some men come to find an instrinsic value in game-playing and in a particular game. Officials in regulatory agencies, for example, soften their regulations so that the regulated persons or industry will not be driven into a campaign to liquidate the agency or cut its appropriations. They may be so carried away by this consideration that they forget about the factions that originally demanded the regulation. An opportunistic line of thought, originally motivated by the desire to survive, acquires intrinsic value.

These three propositions, it seems to me, should be acceptable to anyone who does not have a fixed prejudice for or against litigation and the political processes. Taken together, they assume that the decision-making machinery of society has several gears. In high gear, when there is substantial agreement on the ends of action, the non-political conception of responsibility is relevant. In second gear, when there is disagreement on the ends to be achieved but agreement on procedure, the legal conception of responsibility (respect for due process) is appropriate. In low gear, when there is disagreement on the ends and no clear agreement on procedure (beyond the avoidance of civil war), the political conception of responsibility takes over.

In judging whether we must "shift gears," whether we are warranted in compromising on the merits, whether we should acquiesce in some kind of arbitration, our judgment has two kinds of components: (a) a factual component, an estimate of the extent of opposition; and (b) a value component. The value component is not simple in that it includes (1) definable goods (the ends and goals of specific programs), and (2) the complex of vested interests that are conserved by the order-maintaining institutions of society.

When a political theory closes inquiry into the factual question (how much disagreement exists or is likely to develop), one of the value components may acquire the status of an absolute directive instead of being regarded as one of several tests or criteria. The result is the elaboration of rival political "philosophies" between which it is difficult to define any resolvable issues.[19]

19 In *Philosophy and the Public Interest* (published by the Committee to Advance Original Work in Philosophy, American Philosophical Association, Western Division, 1959) Professor Charmer Perry and I reported an extensive correspondence with economists, political scientists and lawyers, in which many of our correspondents conceived of the public interest as an aggregate of goods, and many others as the preservation of certain procedures. It seemed to us that the discussion was not characterized by *vague,* emotive phrases, but by such radical differences in definite con-

If, on the contrary, goodness and power remain standards of judgment (rather than absolute directives), the maxims of political life impose only *prima facie* obligations; real obligations can only be determined after reflection on the rival claims *in situ*.[20]

Curiously, Dewey agreed with this view in principle. In his *Theory of Valuation,* he said it is improper to identify as "values" the objects of sheer likes and dislikes or any *given* approval. "Value," he contended, is the object of approval *after* deliberation.[21] In spite of this general theory, Dewey apparently could not bring himself to a real open-mindedness with respect to legal and political game-playing. When he was backed into a corner by those who insisted that popular agreement on the merits of policies is impossible, Dewey would beg the question. Thus confronted by the inability of most human beings even to understand some of the complicated policy issues, Dewey diverted the discussion to the question whether, if society were reorganized, the low I.Q. citizens might not turn out to be quite intelligent.[22]

Much the same point can be made with regard to Machiavelli. Machiavelli recognized that governments are not all in the same predicament. Some governments rest upon "the favor of the people," whereas others depend upon "the favor of the nobles." "The good will of the people may be secured in various ways, unnecessary here to specify," he writes, whereas the nobles can be controlled only by power politics.[23] Despite this admission, Machiavelli goes on,[24] to assert: "Princes ought,

cepts that each group experienced difficulty in taking the other group seriously.

20 I am borrowing the phraseology of W. D. Ross. (See his *The Right and the Good,* 1930.) I agree with the recent British intuitionists that not all duties can be reduced to a calculation of the means of securing maximum happiness.

21 *Theory of Valuation* (1939).

22 *The Public and Its Problems* (1927), p. 209.

23 *The Prince,* chap. IX.

24 *Ibid.,* chap. XIV.

therefore, to make the art of war their sole study and occupation, for it is peculiarly the science of those who govern." This preoccupation with the power of friend and foe has, of course, become the identifying characteristic of "Machiavellians," in spite of Machiavelli's passing recognition of conditions under which it should not be the exclusive consideration.

To summarize the argument, Plato's responsible man was responsible for the common good but not accountable to any part of society that might oppose him. Dewey's responsible man was responsible for maximizing shared goods, but his accountability to the opposition was limited by a profound prejudice against contentious debate and propaganda. Machiavelli's responsible man was responsible for dealing with all actual and potential oppositions, but tended to be indifferent to the merits of the particular policies through which he could deal with his opposition and survive. Each of these philosophies treat a criterion as an imperative.

To generalize on the relative importance of program-goal responsibility as compared with political or survival responsibility seems futile, as futile as trying to generalize in answering the question: Is a navigator acting responsibly when he keeps his attention on his destination or when he keeps his attention on the winds and shoals that may wreck his ship? What is general is the two questions, not the answers. The relative importance of the two conceptions of responsibility cannot be determined in general, for the simple reason that no one knows for sure how much disagreement and conflict will be generated tomorrow. An adequate philosophy of government will provide norms for both clear weather and foul.

To raise the question of political responsibility, to *ask* about the chances of survival, is not the same as asserting that, under all conditions, survival must be preferred to program objectives.

To raise the question of responsibility for good is not to say that, under all conditions, program objectives must be preferred to survival and political success.

There may be a reasonable expectation that the production of useful goods will tend to vary according to the severity of political storms. But we should be exaggerating human wisdom if we expected a general theory to eliminate choice by the decision-makers at the scene of action.[25] General theory may make suggestions to the decision-makers, reminding them of some of the possibilities that should be explored and standards (tests) that should be applied.

To those who are familiar with Dewey's writings, it should be obvious that I have agreed with his dictum that there are no problems-in-general. I disagree with Dewey to the extent that he tried to deny that there are general questions, i.e., standards, criteria, or tests of wide relevance. I disagree with Dewey, further, in his reluctance to consider the survival question. But such disagreement does not necessitate a Machiavellian obsession with the friend-and-foe aspect of our situation.

[25] What, for example, can be generally asserted about the relative importance of responsibility-for-the-production-of-goods and responsibility-for-survival, that will be equally applicable in 1960 to weak governments (such as Cuba and Indonesia) and strong governments (such as the U.S.S.R. and the United States)?

PART TWO

CRIMINAL RESPONSIBILITY

IS PUNISHMENT OBSOLETE?

EDGAR BODENHEIMER

WHEN THE VOTARIES of a branch of knowledge which in the eyes of many is concerned with esoteric, otherworldly, and transcendental subjects venture to descend into the arena of the practical and propose to talk about matters which various groups of experts such as criminal lawyers, criminologists, and psychologists regard as their proper preserve, a brief word of explanation seems apposite. In my opinion, there is little need to expatiate on the fact that the question of human responsibility, i.e., the question whether human beings are the true authors of their doings and may be held morally accountable for them, is one which involves the whole structure of the human personality and its relation to the outside world. Few will disagree on this point. It has, on the other hand, been asserted by competent scholars that the broad and fundamental philosophical and psychological issues incident to a discussion of human responsibility have little relevance for the practical administration of the criminal law. It has been suggested that criminal liability and the punishment of offenders are matters of pragmatic and utilitarian import which can be solved without an immersion in the difficult theoretical problems with which the philosopher or student of jurisprudence concerns himself.

I find myself unable to share this last-mentioned viewpoint. It seems to me that in a field of law which is fraught with such central significance for the well-being of society as that of criminal law we are obliged to take a close look at some very troublesome philosophical and moral issues which have agitated human beings for centuries. Should we come to the conclusion that some of these problems are not capable of being solved by human perception, this will entitle us to make certain assumptions or form certain hypotheses if necessary in order to gain a starting point for our attempts to settle matters of more concrete character. To proceed, on the other hand, from the platform of basic assumptions which have not been validated by philosophical or scientific thinking in its most advanced stage is dangerous and may have social consequences of a deleterious character. I hope I shall be able to clarify this statement in the course of my argument.

I propose to approach the problem of human responsibility from the vantage point of the theory of criminal punishment. "Is Punishment Obsolete?" is the title I have selected for my paper. A layman hearing this title would perhaps be deeply puzzled and perturbed by it because it might suggest to him that an assembly of lawyers and scholars would seriously wish to launch a debate into the question whether punishment should be abolished as a legal sanction and criminals be permitted henceforth to remain at large and roam around freely in society after having committed their misdeeds. I hardly have to explain that the theme I am going to discuss is not the alternative between punishment and community forgiveness of crime. It is an alternative of a different character, namely between "punishment" in a specific and restricted sense and other measures for fighting crime which may entail deprivations quite similar to those which punishment involves. The term "punishment" will be used to designate an unpleasant act which society, through specially appointed organs, imposes upon an offender as a requital for a wrong committed by him. Punishment, in this sense, cannot be entirely dissociated from the notion of moral disapproval.[1] The assumption is made that a person has committed an irresponsible and

---

[1] The notion that criminal sanctions properly conceived are imposed for conduct which incurs the moral condemnation of the community is developed by Henry M. Hart, "The Aims of the Criminal Law," *Law and Contemporary Problems,* 23 (1958), 404-05.

blameworthy act, and that he deserves to suffer disagreeable consequences for this act. Punishment, under this conception, is brought into a direct relationship with the criminal act which preceded and caused it; it is thought of as a reaction by organized society to this act. The penalty is inflicted upon the wrongdoer because he has without justification and excuse transgressed against the laws of society. It would seem that this view of the essential nature of punishment is quite in keeping with the popular notion of the term as it is held by most laymen.

As soon as we assign this restricted meaning to the term "punishment," the usefulness and appropriateness of this conception of punishment within the framework of a modern enlightened penal system will be questioned by the representatives of certain schools of thought. These schools of thought have in common the conviction that crime and criminality present no moral issues but must be looked upon as biological, psychiatric, or social phenomena. According to this viewpoint, the criminal is an unfortunate product of hereditary defects or adverse environmental conditions; the true causes of his crime must be sought in external factors and influences which were instrumental in shaping the offender's character and personality, rather than in a morally reprehensible decision on his part to prefer wrong to right. The actions of the criminal are held to be produced by forces over which he had no control, and he cannot therefore be treated as a free agent who deserves moral blame for his delinquency.

I think that it is safe to say that the opponents of the "requital for wrong" notion of punishment all agree in taking a strictly deterministic view of criminal behavior. But their ways may part when they are called upon to pass judgment upon the aims and functions of a criminal law which has been stripped of any vestiges of a retributive conception of punishment. Some will define the goal of the criminal law to be the protection of society and the deterrence of potential wrongdoers. From this point of view, the term "punishment" might appropriately be replaced by the phrase "measure of social defense," a term which was advocated by the positivistic Italian criminologist Enrico Ferri [2] and was used for some time in the Soviet Union and in Cuba. Others will seek the aim of the criminal law in the rehabilitation, reformation, and re-education of offenders, in which case the phrase "treatment of offenders" would be preferable to punishment. It is also possible and quite common to combine these two approaches and declare both societal protection and reformation of the criminal to be legitimate objectives of the criminal law. From all of these viewpoints, which have often been called the positivistic theories of criminal justice, the notion of punishment conceived as a requital for a wrong would appear to be obsolete.

This brings us face to face with our central problem. It can hardly be questioned that in the mind of the common man the punishment of a delinquent carries with it an overtone of disapproval and condemnation of the criminal deed. According to certain versions of deterministic psychology, this overtone of disapproval and condemnation is irrational and out of place. The criminal was a victim of his physical or psychological make-up, or of his upbringing, and could not help doing what he did. In the words of Robert Fearey, a radical protagonist of this position,

while no man in his right mind would think of blaming a ten-year-old car for bad performance, an adult criminal is everywhere considered responsible for his crimes, with only a partial bow toward the inherited, environmental and other passively acquired characteristics which, together with a possible soul, in fact entirely account for his waywardness. Man's variegated character and wide capacities have blinded us to the fact that he is in fact as passive to his creation and development, and hence as unaccountable for his actions, as an inanimate machine.[3]

[2] Enrico Ferri, *Criminal Sociology* (1917), p. 352, trans. J. I. Kelly and J. Lisle.

[3] Robert A. Fearey, "Concept of Responsibility," *Journal of Criminal Law, Criminology and Police Science*, 45 (1954), 24.

If this is the only scientifically tenable view of human behavior in the light of the most up-to-date evidence, then we must conclude that an almost unbridgeable gulf exists between the popular view of criminality and the scientific position toward the criminal act. The public expresses strong disapproval of crime and demands that the punishment should fit the crime. The criminologist holding the view just outlined replies that the criminal act flowed from the character of the perpetrator and was unavoidable, and that the purpose of punishment must be something quite different from the idea of inflicting pain upon a person as a reparation for a culpable act. In the light of certain psychiatric views which are widely held today, such a gap in attitudes is certainly no figment of the imagination. How can the common man and the scientifically oriented criminologist understand each other under these circumstances?

Those who believe that there exists in fact an irreconcilable antithesis between the public's reaction to crime and a scientific analysis of the phenomenon have proposed two alternative means for narrowing the gulf or bridging it. One of these alternatives was suggested by Alexander, a psychiatrist, and Staub, a lawyer, in a book translated from the German and entitled *The Criminal, the Judge, and the Public*.[4] Alexander and Staub maintain that the public's demand for atonement and reparation for crime is so strong and irrepressible that scientific criminology must come to terms with this urge of human beings and to some extent yield to its force. This urge, they maintain, is an almost insuperable obstacle to the creation of a purely rational criminal law based on a deterministic psychology. "Scientific insight will sooner be thrown overboard than the gratification of an emotional drive," so conclude these two authors in a note of pronounced pessimism. The upshot of the proposal is that truth and rational analysis must of necessity make a compromise with irrationality and popular misconception.

[4] Franz Alexander and Hermann Staub, *The Criminal, the Judge, and the Public* (rev. ed., 1956), p. 212.

The second alternative is to launch a systematic campaign of education to convince the public that indignation at crime and moral condemnation of the criminal constitute an attitude and reaction which is outworn and not worthy of a civilized human being. What we must do, according to this viewpoint, is to understand the criminal and the causes for his departure from socially approved conduct. We must protect ourselves against the transgressor as long as he remains dangerous and apt to relapse into crime and, above all, we must do our best to treat, cure, and re-educate him. What we must avoid at all costs is to view punishment in any sense as a retribution for the past offense, because retribution smacks of vengeance, an attitude characteristic of primitive mentality which should have no place in a modern enlightened community.[5]

The second proposal appears to me to be more honest, straightforward, and commendable than the alternative I mentioned earlier. At the same time, it is perhaps the more dangerous avenue upon which to proceed. By endeavoring to eliminate the element of moral indignation and condemnation in the reaction to criminality, this solution may have a tendency indirectly to weaken the collective sense of right and wrong, the moral conscience of mankind, or, to use a term more acceptable to modern psychologists and psychiatrists, the Freudian super-ego.[6] It is not easy to preserve the moral sentiment of mankind if it is argued, as a generalized and universal proposition, that the criminal is an impulse-ridden man who could not help committing his crime, just as he could not help contracting tuberculosis.

I believe that the conflict between popular attitude and scientific truth is not nearly as serious, sharp, and pointed as is often alleged, and that scientific method does not compel us

[5] This appears to be the approach advocated by Henry Weihofen, *The Urge to Punish* (1956).

[6] This point was made by Robert Waelder in his article on "Psychiatry and the Problem of Criminal Responsibility," *University of Pennsylvania Law Review*, 101 (1955), 387.

to reject completely the assumptions of common-sense morality. This is not to suggest, however, that common-sense morality does not sometimes oversimplify the perplexing problems which we have to face.

One of the difficulties which stands in the way of an easy and clear-cut solution must, of course, be sought in a problem which has been debated back and forth and with great intensity and fervor ever since mankind became interested in philosophical analysis and speculation. This is the troublesome problem of freedom of the will. It has been said by some legal scholars that this problem has no place in modern criminal theory, and that it can be safely excised from the curriculum of worthwhile and relevant subjects for discussion in this branch of the law. This is true if we look at the criminal law and the theory of punishment from the vantage point of the positivistic theories which regard either deterrence, or reformation, or both combined, as the functional goals of penology. As soon as we inject the issue of moral responsibility into the debate, i.e., as soon as we ask ourselves whether a criminal should be punished because he has deserved punishment, we cannot evade the problem of free will. In the words of Sir Walter Moberly, "a man is morally responsible for his action in proportion as he is their originating cause." [7] If, as the representatives of a radical determinism declare, the will of the delinquent is in no sense the originating cause of the criminal act, there is no occasion for fastening moral responsibility upon an offender.

The claim is sometimes made by modern psychologists and psychiatrists that the free will issue is today foreclosed and no longer in need of being seriously debated. It is maintained that in the free will versus determinism battle one side has emerged as the clear and indisputable victor, and that that side is determinism. If the word determinism is used in a broad sense, namely as a synonym for universal or nearly universal causality, the claim is to some extent justified, I

[7] Sir Walter Moberly, *Responsibility* (1951), p. 5.

believe. There are few serious philosophers today who uphold
the view that the human will is an uncaused cause, or, differently expressed, that human beings make their decisions
arbitrarily and without being influenced by reasons and
motivations. I think that modern psychology has convincingly
demonstrated that human choices and the actions based on
them are, in the majority of instances, not a matter of random
chance, but subject to the laws of causality. Otherwise it
could never be predicted what a person will do under certain
circumstances.

But if modern psychology believes that by establishing this
fact it has proved to everybody's satisfaction that human
choices are unfree, it must be retorted that this is a philosophical *non sequitur.* According to the natural and commonly
accepted meaning of the term "free," an act is free if it is
uncoerced, not if it is uncaused.[8]

If a man who for several years looked in vain for a job
decides to join a criminal gang in order to make a living, the
decision is caused by a strong economic motive. There may be
subconscious motivations supporting the conscious ones. But
it does not follow that the decision was impelled with the in-
exorable necessity of a natural event, such as an earthquake.
It is possible that in a particular case the balance of biological,
psychological, economic, and social factors was weighted so
heavily and overwhelmingly against the triumph of the law-
abiding instinct that the decision to become a criminal was
practically "coerced" by a battery of powerful determinants.
But it would be very difficult to prove that this is true in every
case in which a person decides to depart from the path of
law observance.

These considerations suggest that a distinction should be
made in our criminal law between causality and determinism.
Professor Northrop has shown that the distinction performs a

8 See Sterling McMurrin and Hardin Branch, *Is There Freedom of the
Will?* (1956), pp. 33-34, 36, 41-42; cf. also Georg Jellinek, *Die Sozialethische
Bedeutung von Recht, Unrecht und Strafe* (1878), p. 64.

useful service in the natural sciences,[9] and I believe that it is also profitable to use it in the social sciences. Northrop points out that there are different types of causes, strong ones and weak ones, decisive and non-decisive ones, and he identifies determinism with "the strongest possible causality." [10] Human actions lend themselves to explanation and interpretation by this yardstick. Some acts of human beings are produced by a cause or combination of causes of such sweeping and controlling force that the result is felt to be inevitable and irresistible. In other actions or decisions, although one motive or group of motives finally gains the upper hand, the actor as well as the outside observer feels that, prior to the decision, the outcome was in the balance and could have been different from what it actually turned out to be. The mere fact that a motive or combination of motives finally became dominant in producing the decision does not stamp the character of objective, unconditional, and ineluctable natural necessity upon the decision. A controlling motive is not per se a coercive one.

I believe that the most thorough and profound recent disquisition on freedom of the will is found in the work on ethics by the German philosopher Nicolai Hartmann. In this work Hartmann points out that in the decision-making processes of human beings, causation is usually not monistic and one-dimensional, but multiple and complex.[11] Various layers of causality are usually discernible, manifesting themselves in heterogeneous and conflicting inclinations and impulses. What Hartmann calls mechanical causality, i.e., the impact and push of forces that have formed the personality of the actor in the past, may enter into a battle with motivations and impulsions of a teleological character, such as the desire to avoid an encounter with the criminal law, to remain a respected member of the community, to act in conformity with the moral law.

[9] F. S. C. Northrop, Introduction to Heisenberg, *Physics and Philosophy* (1958), pp. 11-16.
[10] Northrop, *op. cit.*, p. 15.
[11] Nicolai Hartmann, *Ethics* (1932), III, chaps. 5 and 6, trans. S. Coit.

Experience seems to teach us that a man may move against the stream of past causality and, within circumscribed limits, resist and overcome inherited and acquired traits, or the influence of the environment.[12] Freedom consists in the possibility or potentiality that in a welter of different and often conflicting determinations of the human will, the human choice, although it is clearly the product of a number of causes which together are sufficient to bring about the choice, adds a new element to the complicated web of causation regressing back into an indefinite past.[13] Differently stated, the human decision represents the effect of a number of past causes, but may at the same time be viewed as setting a new cause which is not contained in the antecedent causal nexus. Such a statement may seem paradoxical to the logical purist, but reality unfortunately does not lend itself to explanation by the methods of a simplified logic.

The validity of this interpretation is denied by those who consider the human will as a purely passive playball of blind forces that exert their mechanical pressure upon it from the outside. Responsible for the act of the delinquent, it is argued, are the faults of his parents and teachers, the bad influence of his friends, the slum environment in which he was born, innate predispositions. Many people and events have contributed to the crime, but the active personality of the criminal contributes nothing to it. While there may be cases in which such a conclusion would be justified, a general and convincing proof to the effect that no amount of self-determination on the part of the human personality is psychologically possible has never been furnished.

However, the fact that such proof has never been made does

[12] Demosthenes, handicapped by a serious speech defect, through persistent effort maintained against all odds, managed to become one of the most powerful orators in history.

[13] See Luis Recaséns-Siches, "Human Life, Society, and Law" in *Latin-American Legal Philosophy* (1948), p. 38; Raymond Saleilles, *The Individualization of Punishment* (1911), p. 178, trans. R. S. Jastrow; W. D. Lamont, *The Principles of Judgement* (1946), p. 202.

not mean that the doctrine of freedom of the will can today be elevated to the rank of an ironclad philosophical truth. It would be highly pretentious to make such a claim. The ultimate existence of freedom of the will is a metaphysical problem which is probably incapable of being solved with any degree of final assurance and certainty. Is the structure of the world such that at any crossroad of choices made by human beings there existed several possibilities before the decision was made, or is the world completely and rigidly determined in the sense that choice exists only from a subjective but never from an objective perspective? This question points to one of the great riddles of the universe, the answer to which may be forever hidden from our perception.

A widespread belief prevails that, from a purely empirical viewpoint, determinism is the more serviceable doctrine as compared with the assumption of some form of free will. It has been said that the doctrine of free will is based on assumptions of a metaphysical nature, whereas the deterministic view of human behavior is anti-metaphysical.[14] This, I submit, is an erroneous conclusion. Whether the world is open-textured, leaving room for alternative courses of human volition, or whether it is a closed world in which everything that happens is predestined to happen is a metaphysical problem and a matter of human belief or religious conviction.[15] The empirical evidence, however, is strongly in favor of some degree of human freedom. Let us take a brief look at this empirical evidence.

There is, first and foremost, the subjective sense of freedom; most actions by human beings are accompanied by a feeling that they were the product of choice and not thrust upon the person by compelling and irresistible external factors. That this subjective sense of freedom is deeply ingrained in the whole texture of the human psyche and not merely the result

[14] See Jos. Andenaes, "Determinism and Criminal Law," *Journal of Criminal Law, Criminology & Police Science,* 47 (1956), p. 409.

[15] See on this problem William James, "The Dilemma of Determinism," in *Essays on Faith and Morals* (1943), pp. 145 ff.

of education and teaching is obvious. It does not prove freedom of the will, for it may be a subjective illusion, but it furnishes an empirical argument in favor of it.

Secondly, there is the fact that normal and sane persons are perfectly willing to bear the burden of responsibility for their acts—even though some determinists tell them that this burden is an unreal and illusory one. The burden of responsibility, as Nicolai Hartmann has pointed out, is contrary to natural impulse, and it is to our self-interest to reduce the loads and encumbrances of life.[16] Why do we have the willingness and capacity for submitting to the heavy strain and severe onus of moral responsibility unless the sense of responsibility is anchored in the reality of the human psyche? Is nature perpetrating a huge fraud upon us by giving us a feeling of freedom as well as a sense of responsibility? Perhaps this may be so, but as lawyers we should in fairness take the position that nature is presumed to be innocent until it is proved guilty.

Thirdly, I wish to make reference to a fact which modern psychoanalysis has brought into sharp focus. It has been observed that many people who have offended against the moral or legal order have a pronounced desire to be punished for their acts, and that their sense of guilt is not relieved until punishment has actually been visited upon them.[17] This is another empirical factor which it is hard to reconcile with the theory that we are not the authors of our acts. True, the objection may be made to this argument that the urge to be punished is merely the result of century-long moral and religious teaching about sin, conscience, guilt, and atonement, and that there is no ontological basis whatsoever in human nature to account for the phenomenon. We shall probably never find out whether the objection is valid, because this could be accomplished only by a campaign which in all

[16] Nicolai Hartmann, op. cit., 11, pp. 154-57.

[17] J. C. Flugel, Man, Morals, and Society (1945), pp. 145-46; Alexander and Staub, op. cit., p. 54; Frederick Wertham, "The Psychiatry of Criminal Guilt," Social Meaning of Legal Concepts (1950), II, 162-63.

probability will never be undertaken, namely, a concerted effort to eradicate the moral sentiment from the human mind and put an end to the super-ego. Whatever the truth may be, the urge to be punished remains a reality according to recent psychoanalytic theory, notwithstanding the fact that deterministic interpretations of human conduct have gained a rather wide currency today.

I think we have the right to draw the conclusion from these observations that the rigid opponent of free will who denies any possibility of self-determination by mentally sound persons is a metaphysician who owes us the concrete evidence necessary to corroborate his thesis. The person, on the other hand, who believes that human beings are in principle (subject to various conditioning and limiting factors) capable of making choices, can point for support to a number of empirically validated phenomena.

What is the relevance of these considerations for our problem of criminal responsibility and justification of punishment? If what I have said is tenable and supportable, it means that the common man's moralistic approach toward crime is not necessarily devoid of a rational and philosophical foundation. There is a core of plausibility in the retributive theory which is sufficiently great to permit us to retain the term "punishment" and the connotations normally associated with the term in our system of criminal law. There is also merit in the conviction incident to this approach that a great deal of attention should be paid to the nature and gravity of the offense itself and the degree of subjective guilt accompanying its commission.[18] It is felt that there should be at least a rough proportionality between the deed and the punishment. The general sense of justice of humanity would, at least in principle, support the idea that the intensity of the penalty should be proportioned to the severity of the crime. I may remind you here of the indignation which was aroused in many

[18] Under the other theories of penal justice mentioned above, the deed itself is of decidedly secondary importance as compared to the primary objectives of deterrence or reformation.

parts of the world by a death sentence imposed by a court for a robbery involving $1.95. In view of the strength and persistency of this sense of proportionality it is desirable that the legislator should make a deliberate attempt to assess the gravity of various types of crimes and to fix at least maximum and minimum limits of punishment. This task cannot be left to the judges, although it may be necessary to develop judicial or administrative procedures designed to alleviate the potential rigors of a legislative system of punishment in appropriate cases. In the words of Jerome Hall, there should be "stable and workable classifications permitting consistency of treatment appropriately tempered to the needs of individual cases . . . (and) effective application of these classifications through rules that can be understood and employed by the agencies of justice, the judge and the jury." [19]

By conceding a place to certain facets and postulates of the retributive theory in a modern penal system, I do not wish to be understood as advocating a full or almost complete return to this theory of punishment. I am well aware that it has serious shortcomings which make it inadvisable to use it as the exclusive or even predominant rationalization of punishment. These shortcomings become very conspicuous in those frequent borderline cases in which the perpetrator of a criminal act is not insane but impulse-ridden and predisposed toward anti-social conduct to such an extent that all the odds are stacked against the prevalence of reason and moral will in this particular individual. Where this state of facts is attributable to a life history with which an unkind fate has saddled the offender, moral blameworthiness may be slight, but social dangerousness may be at a maximum. In this case, utilitarian considerations may demand a solution which would be preferable to the results which the doctrine of proportionality between guilt and punishment would suggest.

At the other extreme we may take the case of an individual whose reasoning faculties are largely unimpaired, but who,

[19] Jerome Hall, "Psychiatry and Criminal Responsibility," *Yale Law Journal*, 65 (1956), 773.

after a thorough evaluation of the factors speaking for and against the contemplated act, commits a murder under very unusual circumstances, a murder which he perhaps considers justifiable under his personal ethical code. Here the act may be as free as human action can be from the point of view of imputing moral responsibility for it to the agent. Yet, there may, under the circumstances, be every reason to believe that this man would never again become a menace to society and that his rehabilitation would present no major difficulties. There is some doubt whether, in judging such a case, the deed alone as abstracted from the personality of the doer, together with the extent of volitional freedom accompanying its commission, should form the sole foundations of judgment. The retributive theory, because of a certain rigidity inherent in it, is not too well adapted to an appraisal of personality factors which may have to condition and qualify the application of generalized standards of punishment.[20]

Even in cases not on the borderline as are the examples which I have given, the "requital for wrong" theory of punishment is open to certain objections and reservations. It is well to bear in mind that, although some freedom to act or not to act may be assumed to exist in the normal individual, the actual scope and extent of this freedom is always problematical and uncertain. Freedom is hardly ever complete; [21] it is limited by external factors, and the actual proportion between self-determination and extraneous determination in human actions often remains hidden from our searching eyes. Suppose we admit that a particular criminal had a chance to resist the onslaught of conscious or unconscious impulses of an antisocial and destructive nature. How strong and real was the chance

[20] See John Dewey, *Human Nature and Conduct* (1922), p. 17: "The abstract theory of justice which demands the 'vindication' of law irrespective of instruction and reform of the wrong-doer is as much a refusal to recognize responsibility as is the sentimental gush which makes a suffering victim out of a criminal."

[21] See Hartmann, *op. cit.*, p. 252: "The free will is always only in part free, that is, there is in it only one independent determinant amidst many that come from outside and are heteronomous."

in the light of the character deficiencies which he had developed due to circumstances over which he had only a partial control? How large a share of the blame must be assigned to others, or to society in general, for creating the conditions which made this crime and this criminal possible? [22] There are infinite gradations of responsibility which we can assess only with great difficulty. If we want to stay clear of pharisaical self-righteousness, we must impose upon ourselves some restraint in appraising the degree of moral guilt of persons whose psychological constitution does not lend itself to vivisection or autopsy. This is another reason why we cannot rely upon retributive notions of punishment to the exclusion of other pertinent considerations.[23]

The utilitarian theory of punishment, on the other hand, which places deterrence of potential offenders in the center of its system, and the humanitarian view, which favors reeducation or curative treatment of the offender, also have intrinsic shortcomings and drawbacks which render them inadequate as single and exclusive pillars of penology. The utilitarian position, in its unmitigated form, has a tendency to play down the claims of justice and the rights of the individual in its attempt to achieve maximum deterrence from crime. Unless it is tempered by non-utilitarian considerations, it may lead to unnecessary harshness and severity in the treatment of offenders. Even a progressive utilitarian like Professor Herbert Hart of Oxford University is willing to make far-reaching concessions to collective expediency under certain circumstances. He writes in a recent article: "(The) recognition of the individual's claim not to be sacrificed to society except where he has broken its laws is not itself absolute. Given enough misery to be avoided by the sacrifice of an innocent person, there may be situations where it might be thought morally permissible to take this step. . . . We would

22 See Dewey, *op. cit.*, p. 18.

23 On the necessity of using "multivalued rather than . . . single-valued thinking" in determining the aims of the criminal law see Hart, *op. cit.*, p. 401.

then sacrifice the principle of fairness designed to protect the individual from society to the principle that an overwhelming advantage to society should be secured at any cost." [24] I find this thought entirely unacceptable; but it is a logical corollary of the deterrence principle conceived of as an absolute.[25]

The rehabilitative theory likewise contains its dangers as a monolithic philosophy of punishment. If it focuses its attention exclusively on the individual offender, viewing him in every case either as an unfortunate victim of circumstances or as a diseased object of medical or psychiatric care, it may lead to a sentimentalism which jeopardizes society's interest in crime prevention,[26] and it may also have a tendency to impair the moral fiber of society. It should be emphasized, however, that this observation is not meant to detract from the supreme importance which should be assigned to an intelligently and humanely administered curative treatment of convicted offenders in accomplishing the aims of the criminal law.

The drawbacks of the two extreme positions suggest that a balance must be struck, an equilibrium be found, between the concerns of society in the repression of crime and the delinquent's interest in being readmitted into the fold of the community at the earliest possible opportunity. If an attempt is made to reconcile both aims in the actual practice of the criminal law, we arrive at the Aristotelian mean as the guiding rationale of penal policy. The goal of justice in its particular application to the criminal law would be the endeavor to assist the convicted criminal in readjusting himself again to society, but in carrying out this policy the public good and the

[24] Herbert L. A. Hart, "Murder and the Principles of Punishment," *Northwestern Law Review*, 52 (1957), 453.

[25] The utilitarian test would seem to permit the extermination of insane persons on the ground that they are a useless burden to the community and a potential danger to society, since they may escape and commit another crime.

[26] From an unqualifiedly individualistic point of view, every presumption of non-recidivism would have to be indulged in in favor of the offender, and society would have to take every chance with him. The deterrence theory would logically adopt the opposite presumption.

need for general prevention of crime must not be sacrificed. Thus, our approach will be governed by the idea of proportionality between the general and the individual interest.

We found that the idea of proportionality is also one of the guiding polar stars of the retributive theory of punishment. The thought which I would like to offer at this point is that a non-retributive philosophy of punishment which regards protection of society and rehabilitation of offenders as equally important goals of criminal justice may often lead to the adoption of fundamental policies quite similar to those which an intelligently conceived and refined retributive theory of punishment would postulate. This latter philosophy, too, has its collectivistic as well as its individualistic ingredients. It demands that society's indignation at crime be reflected in a punishment which effectively conveys to the offender the expression of public disapproval to an extent commensurate with the act. At the same time, unlike the utilitarian position, it insists that the measure of punishment must not exceed the degree of moral guilt implicit in the crime. No penalty is justified under this theory which for reasons of expediency is more severe than is demanded by the nature of the crime and its gravity. This is the reason why a philosopher of freedom and humanitarianism like Immanuel Kant favored the retributive view.[27]

I do not deny that divergences and discrepancies in the treatment of criminals may arise depending upon whether a refined retributive position or a combination of the more positivistic principles of deterrence and correction is made the basis of approach.[28] I have already mentioned some of the

[27] Immanuel Kant, *The Philosophy of Law* (1887), p. 195, trans. W. Hastie.

[28] The balancing-of-interests approach would permit more flexibility in the adjustment of individual and societal interests in particular situations than the retributive view. For instance, where society is threatened by an upsurge or wave of certain kinds of derelictions, such as dope peddling or serious traffic offenses, a policy of deterrence exceeding perhaps the proportionate measure of punishment might be defensible as a *temporary* expedient under the balancing-of-interests test.

possible discrepancies. But such disparities will occur in special cases only and will not cause an unbridgeable gulf to exist between the more traditional and the more recent attitudes toward the problem of crime. The traditional view would say, "Justice requires that the punishment must fit the crime." According to the best modern viewpoint, justice demands that the rights and interests of the individual as well as those of society must be safeguarded by the criminal law. Both standpoints would insist that we must not err grievously either on the side of sternness and severity nor on the side of overleniency and sentimentality in penal policy. While the retributive view is moralistic in outlook whereas the balancing-of-interests approach has a more pragmatic color, both philosophies have in common the conviction that the requirements of justice must take precedence over pure expediency in the administration of the criminal law.

THE CONDITIONS OF CRIMINAL
RESPONSIBILITY

RICHARD B. BRANDT

HAT ARE the conditions of criminal responsibility? I take this question to mean the following: What general principles should be followed in framing laws and administrative policies relevant to the imposition of fines or imprisonment for crimes? One answer to this question is: just one principle—the utilitarian principle, interpreted in one way or another. I think this is the right answer and I shall revert to it briefly at the close of my comments. However, I shall direct my remarks in very large part to a different answer, which we may call the "retributive principle." I wish first to explain this principle and then to state some objections to it.

The central idea of the retributive theory of punishment is the following: "Anyone who commits a morally objectionable offense which affects the community—a 'public harm'—should be caused pain or loss corresponding with the moral gravity of his offense." There are, however, three distinct statuses one may claim for this principle. Some writers have given it exclusive status, in the sense that it is the *only* principle, they think, which should regulate the treatment of criminals. This view was held by Kant, but not by Bodenheimer, who thinks that utilitarian considerations should also play a role. Alternatively, one may say that the principle is one principle, but not the only one, which should be followed in framing laws and policies for criminal procedure. We should try to punish moral offenders according to the gravity of their offense; but utilitarian considerations, such as deterrence and reform, are also important points or values to be taken into account. Third, one may rewrite the principle slightly so that it has only permissive status. One may reformulate it thus: "Anyone who commits a morally objectionable offense (etc.) may be caused pain or loss up to a degree corresponding with the moral gravity of his offense." It may be held that this principle is the sole or at least the main source of our right to punish an individual for his offense, but that utilitarian considerations should determine the extent to which we should avail ourselves of the right to punish.

Which of these variants of the retributive theory does Professor Bodenheimer defend? Clearly not the first. He seems to accept the third, since he says that punishment for utilitarian reasons may never exceed the amount permitted by the retributive principle. But I think he does not accept only the third view; he seems also to defend the second. As I understand him, he would say that we have no right to punish a person to a degree exceeding that of the moral gravity of his offense, and that punishment of moral offenders to an extent corresponding with the gravity of their offense is one thing we should aim at, if not the principal goal of criminal law. This compound thesis is the one I shall have in mind in the remainder of my remarks.

Before we can discuss the retributive theory helpfully, however, there is another point of interpretation we must decide. The theory speaks of punishment corresponding with the "moral gravity" of the offense. But exactly what do we mean by "moral gravity"? There are at least two possible meanings this phrase might bear. First, we may construe "moral gravity" to mean *moral blameworthiness,* or moral reprehensibility, in what I take to be the usual sense of these terms in layman's discourse. In this sense of "moral gravity" all of a person's motives are relevant to assessing the gravity of his deed—as is everything about an action which reflects the character of the agent. In this sense of "moral gravity," it is relevant to the gravity of an embezzler's crime whether he committed it because he loved his wife and she was pressing him for gifts. Let us call this the "moral reprehensibility" sense of "moral gravity." There is a second possible sense of this term which we may call the *lex talionis* sense. Taken crudely, this is an eye-for-an-eye theory of "moral gravity." It was defended, apparently, by Immanuel Kant roughly as the thesis that moral gravity—that with which punishment must correspond—coincides with the amount of harm a criminal has done his victim. Such a crude view is untenable, for obvious reasons. But we may define a more defensible *lex talionis* sense as follows. We might think of various acts a person might perform as ranged in an order of seriousness, the order determined by the strength of one's moral obligation not to perform the act in the total circumstances. A person's act, then, will be said to be immoral at all only if he intentionally performed an act he was morally obligated not to perform; and the "gravity" of his doing so is fixed by the strength of his moral obligation not to perform the act in question. On this view, a person's act might be morally culpable although blameless in the "moral reprehensibility" sense; for instance, on this view a conscientious objector who refused to register for the draft would be culpable if he is really obligated to register, whereas on the "moral reprehensibility" view presumably he is not culpable, if his moral thinking has been sincere, however mistaken may be his conclusions.

Now, is Professor Bodenheimer concerned with the "moral reprehensibility" sense of "moral gravity"? Or the *lex talionis* sense? I believe he has the former in mind. We can therefore state his total view as follows. First, he is saying that a person may not be caused pain or loss for a morally objectionable offense except to a degree corresponding with its moral gravity; and also that the law should have, as one of its principal aims, the causing of pain or loss to offenders to a degree corresponding with the moral gravity of the offense—"moral gravity" being interpreted as meaning "moral reprehensibility" in the ordinary sense.

Are there good reasons for rejecting this view?

Many writers have thought this principle must be rejected

if human conduct is causally determined; they have thought one must defend indeterminism in order consistently to support the retributive principle. Does Professor Bodenheimer agree with this? I am not quite sure. Sometimes he suggests that it is consistent to hold the retributive theory even if we are determinists, provided we think human choices are not always "coerced," or not always *felt* to be inevitable." But in the end he seems to me to conclude that indeterminism is required: that there must be an "open-texture" in the course of human events, that human choices must not be entirely predictable. In the end, then, he thinks that the retributive principle presupposes the incomplete predictability of human choices—indeterminism. Now I should like to point out that Professor Bodenheimer has not offered conclusive reasons for his view. Why does he think the retributive principle presupposes indeterminism? As I understand his reasoning, he thinks that, if determinism is true, then criminal acts are not morally reprehensible at all, and therefore, if determinism is true, the retributive theory implies that criminals should not be punished at all. But why does he think that, if an action is determined, there is no "moral gravity" or "reprehensibility"? The answer is that he assumes, I believe, that a person's moral guilt for a given act is a function of two factors: the undesirability of what he did, and the extent to which he was the originating cause. Now, he argues, if determinism is true, a man is not the originating cause of any of his actions, because his deed was predictable. Predictability implies the criminal is not the originating cause; his not being the originating cause implies that there is no blameworthiness or guilt. But is Bodenheimer justified in his assumption that a man is not morally to blame, morally reprehensible, for a deed if he was not its originating cause in a sense incompatible with determinism? This assumption seems to me highly doubtful. Clearly it is not true by definition; what we mean by "morally reprehensible" does not logically imply "could not have been predicted." Why, then, should we adopt this principle? We do not generally temper our evaluative judgments by reflections on the genesis of the thing being appraised: we do not think John Stuart Mill less great a philosopher because he inherited his genius from his father, or because his father gave him an extraordinary education. Why, then, should we think nothing of a man's self-sacrifice or conscientiousness because we must trace it to his early training? And why should we regard a deed as not morally reprehensible just because in theory it could have been predicted? It is true that we do not condemn a deed if it was not done freely—if it was physically coerced, or done because of imminent threat to life. We do not condemn such deeds, because they show little or nothing of the character of the agent; in these cases the criminal would not have refrained from his deed even if he had an excellent character. But if a deed was done freely—if the criminal would have abstained if he had wanted to or had had a better character—then it is not clear why this act is not reprehensible, why there is no moral guilt.

Incidentally, if we did have to assess the extent to which a person was the originating cause of a deed, in order to decide the gravity of his offense, our task would be in principle incapable of being performed. How should we carry out such an investigation? Must we first decide the extent to which his failure lay in his education, the extent to which it lay with his father's bad example, the extent to which failure was a result of innate constitution? Must we, then, find a share in a man's failure which is *not* attributable to any assignable source of this kind, and which may, therefore, be ascribed to the "free choice" of the agent? If this is what we must do, then assessments of moral guilt must be purely speculative.

My conclusion is that moral guilt does not require "free choice" in the sense of unpredictable, uncaused behavior. If this is correct, then Professor Bodenheimer can, I think, accept the retributive theory without undertaking the defense of metaphysical indeterminism. Determinism is, then, not necessarily incompatible with the retributive theory.[1]

<hr>

[1] I do not mean to suggest that determinism poses no real puzzles for an advocate of the retributive theory, but only that there has not been

But there are still good and sufficient reasons for declining to adopt the retributive principle.

My chief objection to the theory is that, according to it, there ought to be *no* punishment where there is no demonstrable moral guilt. It is difficult to accept this implication. Suppose a man assassinates a public official, with the thought that he is performing a moral duty, or with patriotic motives. Morally, he may be blameless. On this theory, such a man ought not to be punished. Or suppose, again, someone in the Department of Defense convinces himself, after honest moral reasoning, that he should turn over military secrets to Russia; such a person need not be morally reprehensible. Again, on this theory we ought not to punish him. Suppose, again, a Mormon is convinced of his moral right to have several wives; or a Christain Scientist is convinced he ought not to call a doctor to examine his ailing child. These men may be morally

---

stated any clear reasoning demonstrating an incompatibility of the two views. Let me mention two examples of what strike me as real puzzles for the determinist who accepts the retributive theory. First, suppose he thinks circumstances of a criminal's childhood—such as poverty, a broken home, a tyrannical father—reduce the moral reprehensibility of a criminal act and therefore are considerations properly regarded as mitigating, as calling for a mild or even suspended sentence. Must the determinist, then, regard every crime as calling for a mild sentence, since *some* unfavorable factors in the criminal's past must have made him the kind of person who is willing to commit a crime? There is also a puzzle about the line to be drawn between culpable and nonculpable acts, in view of the sanity of the agent. The courst held in *Durham v. United States* that "Our traditions also require that where such acts stem from and are the product of a mental disease or defect as those terms are used herein, moral blame shall not attach, and hence there will not be criminal responsibility." The determinist will presumably view any antisocial act as a symptom of instability or maladjustment, and will view the difference between "mental disease or defect" and such emotional immaturity or instability as a matter only of degree. The drawing of a line between the approximately normal and the clearly abnormal, for the purposes of criminal law, is clearly justified on utilitarian grounds, but it is not so clearly justified otherwise—although there is not any strict inconsistency simply in holding that normal persons are morally reprehensible and others are not.

blameless; again, the theory tells us we may not punish them. In general, the theory does not permit the law to set a standard of behavior with which some may not agree, and require them to live by it. Along somewhat the same line, we may add that the theory is inconsistent with strict liability, although to say this is perhaps to raise no serious objection, since strict liability is open to criticism. But we should be clear the two are incompatible. The theory is, furthermore, inconsistent with the doctrine that "ignorance of the law is no excuse." On this view, a person's performance of any act which he blamelessly thinks is right would not be subject to punishment. These are serious difficulties. Accepting the implications of such a theory would defeat major purposes of the law.

There is a further difficulty of the theory, of a different sort. This consists in its implications for the punishment of *attempted* crimes. From a moral point of view, the act of a person who attempts a crime but fails on account of circumstances beyond his control is exactly as blameworthy as a person who succeeds in crime. The person who attempts a crime acts in a way expected to result in the commission of a crime; his intent and motivation are identical with those of the successful criminal. What follows on this theory? That we ought to punish the two alike, or at least that we have a *right* to punish them alike if to do so serves a purpose. But this consequence is difficult to accept.

A defender of the theory might argue that these charges against the retributive theory are unfair, that I am overlooking the fact that I have been claiming to criticize a theory which is a combination of the retributive and the utilitarian theory, not a pure retributive theory. The charges, however, are not unfair if a combination-type theory retains what I have called the "permissive" form of the theory—that retributive considerations set the upper limit to which punishment is permissible on utilitarian grounds. If, however, a defender of the theory dropped this element, and *merely* held that it is one good thing, along with others, to punish people for their wrong-doing according to the gravity of their deed, then the theory does not have the consequences to which I have been objecting. But in this case it is not clear that the theory has *any* consequences of any importance, and its defender must make clear what is the advantage to be had from adopting it. This leads me to my final criticism.

This theory is an unnecessary complication in one's theory of criminal justice. Professor Bodenheimer agrees that no sensible theory of punishment will omit a utilitarian principle of some sort. Why not, then, adopt a straightforward utilitarian theory as the foundation of criminal justice? This would be simpler, and Professor Bodenheimer agrees that a utilitarian theory would lead to policies "quite similar" to those of an "intelligently conceived and refined" retributive theory. Actually, I think, a utilitarian theory can do better still: it can be so framed as to lead to policies we can accept in our reflective moments, and not lead to the unacceptable theorems to which we are committed by even the most carefully stated retributive theories.

It may be helpful, in conclusion, to glance briefly at the utilitarian theory. The term "utilitarian" unfortunately comprehends various rather different views, but we can confine our attention to the proposal that there is only one basic rule defining right and wrong conduct, as follows: "It is obligatory for an agent to perform an act *A* if and only if the prescription that it be performed ['Do *A!*'] follows logically from a complete description of the agent's situation plus ideal prescriptions for his community; and ideal prescriptions for his community are that set of universal imperatives [of the form 'Do *A* in circumstances *C!*'] which contains no proper names, is complete in the sense that it does not fail to supply direction for any decision one may have to make, and is such that a conscientious effort to obey it, by everyone in the agent's community, would have greater net expectable utility [2] than a similar effort to obey any other set of imperatives." This principle has obvious implications for the laws which individuals

[2] I think myself that the theory is made stronger if "utility" is used broadly enough so that *equality* of welfare is counted as a utility.

in a community will be obligated to enact and support; they will be laws, the existence and enforcement of which will maximize long-run welfare. Similarly, it has implications for the decisions of judges and prosecutors charged with enforcing the law; they must use policies which serve long-term welfare. In general, the principle implies that criminals be treated as leniently as possible (since their suffering is itself a disutility to be avoided) compatibly with the effective operation of the law as a deterrent, reforming, and educative agency. The utilitarian principle presumably will sanction at least roughly the accepted justifications and excuses recognized as legal defenses against charges of crime: e.g., insanity, innocent mistake, compulsion, involuntary intoxication, absence of premeditation. The reason for this is that omission of punishment in these cases (or the infliction of a lighter punishment) will not reduce the effectiveness of the law as an instrument for inducing desirable behavior; for instance, a sane man will not be the less motivated to avoid committing a crime because of the thought that he would not be liable to punishment if only he were insane.

Utilitarian theories, usually understood in a simpler form than the above statement, have often been criticized. It has been said that a utilitarian would be ready to punish the insane or those who offend only because of innocent mistake, if only such punishment could be shown to serve the public good. It has been said that a utilitarian theory implies that prosecutors and judges should conspire to condemn innocent men whenever this would be useful for the public. Again, it has been said that according to the utilitarian theory there is no real difference between punishment for crime and quarantine; in both cases individuals are in effect imprisoned for the sake of the public good. A careful examination of these objections as objections to the utilitarian theory formulated above, however, will show that they have no force.

The reader may, of course, be troubled by a fundamental methodological question. "What," he may be asking himself, "are here being regarded as good grounds for accepting or rejecting an ethical principle?" This question raises large issues, which cannot be debated here.[3] It may be helpful to remark, however, that it is here assumed that an ethical principle may be accepted if and only if it is a member of a consistent and complete set of general principles, not excessively complex, which are coherent with one's *criticized* attitudes (feelings, preferences)—"criticized" attitudes being one's attitudes as they *would be* if one were completely informed about all relevant facts, and were in an impartial and normal frame of mind. The suggestion of the foregoing remarks is that a certain type of utilitarian principle is a member of such a set, whereas a retributive principle is not, or at least is a useless redundancy.

[3] The writer has discussed them in detail in *Ethical Theory: The Problems of Normative and Critical Ethics* (1959).

ᴥᴥᴥ VII ᴥᴥᴥ

RETRIBUTION IS OBSOLETE

HENRY WEIHOFEN

PROFESSOR BODENHEIMER states his thesis in such fair-minded terms that one must seem churlish to disagree with him. He admits all the objections to a retributive approach to crime and actually ends up with what I would call the utilitarian view; yet throughout his paper, he gives the over-all impression that he is criticizing that view and making defense for retribution.

The first question that suggests itself is: Why should a decent and kindly philosopher like Edgar Bodenheimer feel impelled to try so hard to find something good to say about the irrational, primitive urge for vengeance? That is what he defends, and he says so. He defines the term punishment as he uses it as "an unpleasant act which society imposes as a *requital for a wrong* committed." Requital. An eye for an eye, a tooth for a tooth. He who sins must suffer.

This vindictive concept of justice is a legacy from our primitive ancestors. Every step of progress that we have made in dealing with crime and criminals has been *away* from this concept. And every step has been over violent, emotional opposition of the advocates of vengeance. This urge to punish remains today the greatest single obstacle to the adoption of a decent, rational penal program. Whenever we fail to solve the maladjustments of our society, there is the constant impulse to turn in our impatience and anger to vindictive punishment and terror. What we very much need is greater understanding of the irrationality and self-defeating nature of

116

this atavistic urge. What we do not need are philosophical efforts to sugarcoat it with respectability.

My fundamental criticism of Professor Bodenheimer's paper, therefore, is his emphasis on a dichotomy between "punishment" and what he calls a utilitarian point of view and his apparent conclusion that there is something to be said for both. I say apparent conclusion, because, as Professor Brandt points out, his actual conclusion is not really different from the utilitarian viewpoint, and the ends he seeks could be achieved just as well if he took a stand against "requital."

The utilitarian approach, as Professor Bodenheimer says, has two ends: to protect society and to reform the criminal. That is all the criminal law can do and should do—to apprehend lawbreakers and keep them under constraint as long as public safety requires, and in the meantime try to rehabilitate them so that they may be returned to society as soon as it is safe to do so. Bodenheimer himself actually comes to exactly that conclusion, when he says that an equilibrium must be found "between the concerns of society in the repression of crime and the delinquent's interest in being readmitted into the fold of the community at the earliest possible opportunity."

Professor Brandt is right in saying that it only complicates one's theory of criminal justice to add to these objectives a demand for "requital." It does worse than complicate it; it makes utter hash of it, as G. B. Shaw said many years ago:

To propose to punish and reform people by the same operation is exactly as if you were to take a man suffering from pneumonia, and attempt to combine punitive and curative treatment. Arguing that a man with pneumonia is a danger to the community, and that he need not catch it if he takes proper care of his health, you resolve that he shall have a severe lesson, both to punish him for his negligence and pulmonary weakness and to deter others from following his example. You therefore strip him naked, and in that condition stand him all night in the snow. But as you admit the duty of restoring him to health if possible and discharging him

with sound lungs, you engage a doctor to superintend the punishment and administer cough lozenges, made as unpleasant to the
taste as possible so as not to pamper the culprit.[1]

If we are to impose punishment for its own sake, we must
decide how much to inflict. Bodenheimer says, "There must
be at least a rough proportionality between the deed and the
punishment." The Mikado said it more melodiously, but I am
not at all sure Bodenheimer would approve the Mikado's
methods of making the punishment fit the crime. Nor would
people ever agree on any formula for application. Crime and
punishment are different things, and cannot be equated. You
can take a life for a life, but beyond that there is practically
no room for the principle of equation to operate. You can't
impose a rape for a rape, forgery for forgery. An eye for an
eye is not impossible, but does Bodenheimer or anyone else
today seriously suggest putting out the eye of a man guilty of
hitting another in the eye in a felonious assault?

The nearest we could come to achieving "proportionality"
between crime and punishment would be to rank crimes in
what we decide, somehow, is their order of seriousness, and
also rank punishments in order of their unpleasantness, and
then try to correlate the two lists. Professor Brandt has discussed some of the quagmire this gets us into. Even if it could
be done, the question would remain, how far up or down the
scale of possible severity should the whole list of punishments
be pegged? Should you start with the death penalty, or with
a maximum of twenty years' imprisonment? This is a question of public policy which can only be answered intelligently
on the basis of some utilitarian objectives, the reformatory (or
demoralizing) effects of long prison terms, the *in terrorem* (or
brutalizing) effect of executions, etc. It cannot be answered
by trying to find "proportionality" between the deed and the
punishment. The seriousness of a crime is a matter of value
judgment, which will depend upon the cultural premises of

[1] Preface to Sidney and Beatrice Webb, *English Prisons under Local
Government* (1922), p. xiv.

the judge. Different cultures vary enormously in their ranking of offenses. There is certainly no universal standard. Even within our own American culture, there are surprising variations. An offense punishable by twenty years' imprisonment in one state may carry a maximum sentence of one year in another. Older statutes may reflect a view of the seriousness of a crime that is no longer current today. Such statutes will therefore prescribe punishments quite different not only from those prescribed by more recent enactments in neighboring states, but different also from the current popular standard of that state itself. Nor could this situation be met by trying to bring such statutes up to date so as to reflect current popular standards. The day is past in our society when the great majority of people accepted the same cultural norms. Ours is a heterogeneous society, and it would be impossible to achieve anything like a consensus on the relative seriousness of different crimes and the "just" punishment.[2]

For these and many other reasons, all of this abstract philosophizing about punishment as requital for crime has a musty smell about it, a smell of the professor's study. It does not breathe the air of reality, of the criminal courts, or the prisons or the institutes for psychopathic offenders. No working criminologist, or judge, or prison warden, talks this way. The people who have the responsibility for fighting crime and dealing with criminals have learned that it is pointless to talk about "how much punishment" is deserved. In the nine-

---

[2] A few years ago, a group of university students were asked to rank in seriousness 13 different crimes defined by the California statutes, including arson, bigamy, forgery, theft, assault with a deadly weapon, and attempted burglary. The students rated as deserving of most punishment the serious beating by a father of a small child. Of a group of California prisoners serving sentence for these various crimes, the actual average punishment meted out for this offense was *less* than for all but one other of the 13 crimes. The crime for which the longest average sentence was actually served was injuring electric or telephone lines, an offense which the students rated as twelfth in seriousness. Rose and Prell, "Does the Punishment Fit the Crime? A Study in Social Valuation," *American Journal of Sociology*, 61 (1955), 247.

teenth century, when sociological and economic laws were supposed to operate automatically, standardization of punishments to fit the crime had its appeal, but experience has since led to a critical re-evaluation of the entire process. The modern behavioral sciences have shown that arm-chair abstractions about the "justice" of retribution by philosophers who reject human experience [3] are sadly defective in human understanding, not to say human sympathy. The retributive approach is too subjective and too emotional to solve problems that have their roots in social conditions and the consequent impact on individual personality. Such an approach can only obstruct the job of evolving techniques for social control utilizing what we now know about the forces that control human behavior.

But, as Professor Bodenheimer says, there are those who, though they themselves may reject retribution in theory as "only vengeance in disguise," nevertheless say that we must be realistic in recognizing that the desire for vengeance is strong in men, and we must not offend this "instinctive sense of justice." But if this so-called sense of justice is unsound, then we should reject it, and not condone it. The law today is strong enough to do what is right. Furthermore, I deny that there is any evidence to support the idea that we must "come to terms with" or "yield to" this anti-social aggressiveness. There is no proof that the public is as thirsty for vengeance as this notion assumes. There is no proof of any "unbridgeable gap" between public opinion and the objectives of modern criminology. Public opinion during the past two hundred years has been rather less retributive than the law itself. It was public opinion that forced the law to become humane— to abandon capital punishment for scores of offenses, to recognize mitigating circumstances, to treat juveniles differently from adults. Juries today have almost wholly abolished capital punishment in fact, even though it remains on the books in all but nine states. As an actual operating part of our penal

---

[3] E.g., Immanuel Kant, *Philosophy of Law* (1887), p. 243, trans. Hastie.

program the death penalty has almost ceased to exist (48 executions in the whole country in 1958, as against some 7,000 murders)—and this because and not in spite of public opinion. It isn't often one meets an argument that can be called both base and baseless at the same time, but that is what we can call the sounding of a retreat before the unreal specter of an irresistible mob baying for blood.

Professor Bodenheimer discusses two criticisms of the utilitarian view. The first is that it "has a tendency to play down the claims of justice." What he means by this is that "unless it is tempered by non-utilitarian considerations it may lead to unnecessary harshness and severity in the treatment of offenders." Every utilitarian would agree that *unnecessary* harshness should be avoided; almost by definition, what is unnecessary is not utilitarian. The danger of unduly harsh treatment of offenders is a real one, but the problem is one of balancing two utilitarian concepts—respect for the interests of the individual against concern for the interests of the group. These interests are likely to be more or less opposed; releasing a prisoner now, to give him another chance, may be the most promising way to rehabilitate him, but it takes a chance with the safety of society. All we can do is to put the responsibility for making the choice into the hands of the most competent people we can find, and give them elbow room to make the wisest decisions they can. I might point out that if there is one basic difference between our political system and that of the totalitarianisms, it is that we are relatively more willing to take a chance in favor of the individual, whereas a police state is more likely to give primacy to state security. No utilitarian I know questions the soundness of that value judgment.

This problem of weighing the interests of the individual against the interests of society could not be solved in any degree by adopting Professor Bodenheimer's suggestions that we temper *both* these utilitarian objectives "by non-utilitarian considerations." On the contrary, the non-utilitarian concept of requital is much more often the *source* of unnecessarily

harsh treatment of the individual than it is a protection
against it. Those who clamor for "justice" usually mean that
they want *harsher* penalties inflicted than utilitarian considerations justify. What does a man mean when he says that a
certain crime (for example, certain Nazi atrocities) is so hei-
nous that "justice" demands severe punishment? He means
merely that the acts create such feelings of antagonism in himself that he wants to see the wrongdoer suffer, and suffer much.
This is a common human reaction—but the fact that a certain
feeling is frequently found among men does not mean that
it is commendable or justified. That a person who has suf-
fered at the hands of the Nazis should feel that no punishment is too bad for them is understandable. But this does
not make such hatred a "just" or worthy sentiment. Rather,
we should say that the creation of such hatred is among the
worst of the wrongs that can be laid against the Nazis. Our
ideal should be, and for 2,000 years our ideal has been, to
overcome such hatred, and to treat even such criminals with
decency; to do what needs to be done to protect ourselves
against them, without hate and without the deliberate infliction of unnecessary cruelty. Playfair and Sington, in a recent
book, *The Offenders,* report that the Van der Hoeven Clinic
in Holland has as a patient a man who worked for the German occupation forces as a concentration-camp guard and
committed atrocities, including probably homicide, against
his fellow Dutchmen.[4] In Holland, it has apparently come to

[4] Playfair and Sington devote a chapter to the story of Irma Grese, the
"blond beastess" of Belsen, as the newspapers called her. They trace the
childhood of this simple peasant girl, the influence of Nazi indoctrination
about the lower breeds, her romantic devotion to what she had been
taught was her duty to the German race. Her hanging, conclude the
authors, "like all the other executions for war crimes—seems to have
been useless as well as barbaric." It has not deterred other potential war
criminals, as events in Korea and even in Germany itself have shown.
On the contrary, it has done political harm. For some Germans, her story
became a legend—not a healthy legend, but one that emphasized the callous side of the British occupation. "A civilized attitude would have seen
Irma Grese as a psychological casualty of war, like many of the young

be realized that the proper approach even to so-called "crimes against humanity" is the curative one. England during the war created a center where young German prisoners of war indoctrinated with Nazism could discover liberal, tolerant ways of life. The experiment was so successful that it was continued for ten years after the war. If those whose own homelands were overrun or bombed by the Nazis and whose countrymen and perhaps family and friends were the main victims of these atrocities can find it in their hearts to offer a chance for rehabilitation to the "corrupted generation," we in America should be willing to do the same for our own criminals. And I believe we shall, if only well meaning professors will leave off giving aid and comfort to the peddlers of hatred.

There is nothing special about "war criminals" that justifies treating them differently from others. Those who try to make a case for retribution by appealing to hate and fury can also find plenty of peace-time atrocities to point to. Thus one writer invites the reader to "picture that your daughter or favorite niece was ruthlessly raped and then her belly torn open by a neurotic assailant." [5] Another asks, what of "the three monsters . . . who literally fried to death a schoolteacher who lived alone . . . ?" [6]

But as one eminent psychiatrist has said in answer to such arguments, "While the impulse to punish such persons is easy to understand, it is hardly a rational basis for determining how the criminal law shall function in order to protect society. We cannot exceed the community's willingness to be 'understanding' and 'loving' in relation to acts committed against it. However, the professionals who are to shed light

---

soldiers in all countries, who, having been trained as 'killers,' became a social problem in postwar years." G. Playfair and D. Sington, *The Offenders: The Case Against Legal Vengeance* (1957), pp. 167-211.

[5] H. A. Davidson, *Irresistible Impulse and Criminal Responsibility, in Crime and Insanity* (1958), p. 40.

[6] Mr. Justice Mackay of the Court of Appeals of Ontario, quoted in H. Weihofen, *The Urge to Punish* (1956), p. 155.

on questions of *why* these acts were committed, as well as to
find ways permanently to protect society from further depreda-
tions by such individuals, must not be hampered in their
efforts by rules which are predicated on ancient and atavistic
concepts of protection." [7]

Professor Bodenheimer's second objection to the utilitarian
approach is, strangely enough, the very opposite of the first.
Not only may it lead to undue harshness; it may also lead to
undue softness. "By focusing its attention exclusively on the
individual offender . . . it may lead to a sentimentalism which
jeopardizes society's interest in crime prevention." But the
utilitarian view does not focus its attention exclusively on
the offender; Professor Bodenheimer himself admits this. It
is concerned also for the interests of society. As already said,
individual and group interests are likely to be more or less
opposed. As also already said, in balancing those interests our
social system favors the individual more than do some others.
But that is a long way from saying that Americans generally
or utilitarians in particular are concerned exclusively with
the individual and care nothing about protection of the public.

In their concern for the rehabilitation of the offender,
modern criminologists do not take the position that punishment can never have a reformative or deterrent effect. No one
denies in toto the validity of the pleasure-pain principle of
learning. On the contrary, psychologists would say that punishment calmly devised and administered has therapeutic
value and is an important factor in personality development.
What we do say is: first, our faith in the deterrent effect of
inflicting unpleasant consequences as a response to criminality
is exaggerated; second, punishment should therefore not be
used indiscriminately (or absolutely, as a mystically, transcen-
dentally required requital for crime), but only where, upon expert diagnosis, it promises to do some good; and third, other
methods of treatment are at least as effective in many cases,

[7] Dr. Andrews S. Watson, Book Review, *University of Pennsylvania Law
Review*, 107 (1959), 898.

and punishment should therefore be considered as only one part of a well-rounded preventive-therapeutic program.

Even if we indulge our urge for "requital" in the *sentencing* of the offender, our *prison* programs must be rehabilitative in purpose. We cannot and do not want to keep all these men locked up for life. The overwhelming majority must be released eventually, and we certainly do not want to turn them out wholly unregenerated. We cannot avoid addressing ourselves to the need to do what we can to see that this steady stream of men comes out less dangerous than when they went in.

The extent to which punishment actually serves this need seems to be of no concern to those who see it only as a necessary requital for wrongdoing. But one who relies on principles to decide specific cases cannot avoid defending those principles by showing that they lead to proper consequences. Those who know tell us that punishment has some undesirable consequences that may outweigh all that can be said in its favor. It isolates the individual and is more likely to confirm his anti-social attitude than to reform him. More important, punishment can deter only by appealing to selfish fear, not to insight or moral conviction. When it succeeds, it is a victory for cowardice. At best, it can achieve only a sterile conformity, a blind obedience, not a healthy adjustment to society. We want more than merely to repress. We want to help the unsocialized child or adult to become a self-reliant, self-respecting, co-operative member of the human race.

But punishment usually stops any such constructive efforts. Having imposed punishment, we are likely to feel with smug satisfaction that we have taken care of the problem. The criminal is taken away, locked up and forgotten. We assume that he will be kept there for a long time, and that when he does come out, he will have learned his lesson.

But even if he is remorseful and resolved to reform, he needs help to carry that good intention into effect. Motivation, stimulation, suggestions, ideals, and patterns of conduct must be provided. He must be given a chance to carry his resolves and ideals into practice in social relations with other human beings. All this calls for individualized thought and effort on the part of a trained and competent staff.

The experts who deal with the problem first hand know this. The judge, the prosecuting attorney, the police officer, the probation officer, these are not usually the ones calling for harsher punishments. Any of you who have ever attended a forum or conference at which crime or juvenile delinquency is discussed have perhaps seen the pattern. These experts emphasize the need for understanding what kind of people get into trouble—the fact that 10 per cent of juvenile delinquents come from families where one or both parents have schizophrenia; that 20 per cent to 40 per cent are mentally backward, due either to heredity or to poor environment; that their parents, if not actually psychotic, are themselves delinquent, or immature, drunken, or absent. The experts emphasize the need for competent and skilled probation workers to work with these youngsters, the need for clinical and institutional facilities, if they are to be redeemed. It is always some ignorant member of the audience who then rises to say that the whole problem could be solved if you just take them out to the wood shed—give them a taste of jail—or jail their parents. Prompt to second this view is the fundamentalist hellfire and brimstone preacher. It is unfortunate when professorial musings over a supposed transcendental necessity for punishment are used to lend a cloak of decency to the performance.

Crime and criminal responsibility are not mere interesting abstractions for philosophers to amuse themselves by, dreaming up metaphysical constructs out of them. Crime is a reality, an ever-present danger which in some cases is literally a matter of life and death.

The voices of ignorance and hate are loud enough now, angrily trying to shout down almost every effort to improve criminal administration by substituting rational for irrational solutions, a rehabilitative for a punitive approach. The rationale of these programs calls for an understanding of the sociological, economic, and cultural sources of criminality, and for an understanding of the psychology of criminals and of our reactions to criminality. We need the help of all those who have the education and the insights to understand; we need them to stand up for reason and decency, and to teach and preach and fight for it. We need you.

I resent the apostles of "punishment for its own sake" arrogating to themselves words like "moral" and "justice," and implying in consequence that those who scorn their metaphysics are amoral or at least unconcerned with moral values. Surely the feeling of concern for the offender as a human being, the desire to save him from a criminal career and to help him redeem himself as a member of the human family, and the even wider concern to prevent others from falling into criminality by searching out the influences and conditions that produce those frustrating and embittering defeats, degradations, and humiliations of the human spirit that turn a man against his fellow men; the effort, therefore, to give men those advantages that will help them to keep their feet on the right path—better education, healthier dwellings, readier aid for the motherless and the widowed, and more systematic provision for the casualties of sickness, accident, and failure of employment—surely this is not a less moral ideal than that which knows only one measure of morality: an eye for an eye and a tooth for a tooth.

Half a century ago, Winston Churchill said, in essence (I do not have his exact words):

The mood and temper of the public toward crime and criminals is one unfailing test of the civilization of any country. A desire to rehabilitate those who have committed crime, tireless efforts toward the discovery of curative and regenerative processes, and an unfaltering belief that there is worth, if you can but find it, in the heart of every man—these are the symbols that mark and measure the stored-up strength of the nation.

Yes; and I would add, these are the sign and proof of its morality.

◈ VIII ◈

PUNISHMENT AND THE BREAKDOWN OF THE LEGAL ORDER: THE EXPERIENCE IN EAST PAKISTAN

K. J. NEWMAN

T HE CHOICE of this topic is partly due to the fact that the implications of partial breakdowns of the moral and legal orders that have occurred since the end of World War I have failed to have an impact on criminological thought. In 1918 Nagler [1] still did not believe that such a collapse could ever become a reality. Events were as yet to prove to what an extent legalized mass murder, the ruthless sacrifice of lives and the general unleashing of violent emotions during the war had undermined man's long established loyalties, traditions, and conventions. This in turn led to a general deterioration of ethical standards and social controls which could not fail to affect legal standards.

Whereas in the nineteenth and early twentieth centuries barbarous measures, such as the Bulgarian massacres, had caused a general revulsion in the civilized world, sensitivities now became more hardened, even in the sight of far worse occurrences. Moreover, some European governments, after World War I, abandoned the high standards of moral integrity and justice which Hegel had ascribed to the State. Being armed with all the powers of the law-enforcing machinery some states adopted methods and techniques which always had

---

[1] Johann Nagler, in his book *Die Strafe* (1918), pp. 550ff., asserted that so far every legal order had defended itself with the help of "the armor of punishment," because . . . "the absence of punishment would create a breach in the social order, the devastating magnitude of which we are unable to imagine."

been associated with criminal behavior. Before World War II, the techniques adopted by the Nazis on the occasion of the so-called "Roehm Purge" in 1934 and the assassinations by Gestapo agents of Professor Theodor Lessing and Mr. Formis in Czechoslovakia were characteristic of criminal homicide. The purges, stage-managed trials, and executions in the Soviet Union also weakened the belief in the integrity of criminal law and punishment. Finally, the extermination of millions of innocent people by the Nazi authorities during World War II profoundly shook the belief of Western man in the legal order. Our sense of justice realized that monstrous acts, crimes according to the principles of the law of nature, were escaping punishment.

The rapid emancipation of those colonial and semi-colonial countries which became independent nations after World War II has since presented a different type of threat to the legal order. This threat occurred not because a criminal group seized the government, but on the contrary, because of the weakness and inexperience of well-meaning groups of people suddenly called upon to lead their nations. Most of the trained and experienced legal and police personnel were suddenly replaced by less competent ones. What is more, the idea of national liberty was sometimes interpreted in these countries as one of solidarity, imposing a collective feeling of charity toward all members of the nation. To this sentiment was added an insufficiently developed sense of responsibility in broad strata of the newly emancipated nations.

The notion of "equality before the law" is specifically Western and had been previously unknown in areas which had for many thousands of years been under the rule of Oriental despotism.[2] On the Indo-Pakistan Sub-Continent, for example, British rule was imposed upon a society both feudal and particularistic, where ordinary men, who had no access to the seats of regional power, counted for very little. After national

[2] Carl Wittfogel, *Oriental Despotism* (1957). This work presents in many places a unique interpretation of the oriental idea of punishment. For example, consult pp. 38ff.

emancipation the new ruling classes sometimes returned to a multiple standard of legal security and law enforcement. There was one standard where they themselves, their relations and friends were concerned; another for resident members of foreign communities; a third for the middle classes. But the vast masses, living below the existential minimum and not as yet sufficiently organized through labor unions and other pressure groups, found it hard to obtain the state's legal protection.

East Pakistan, since the achievement of independence in 1947, offers an experience which is almost tantamount to a laboratory test.[3] To start with, offenses such as theft, smaller cases of burglary, larceny, smuggling, corruption, fraud, or allowing the deterioration of essential foodstuffs and medicines were not always prosecuted by the police. The cause of this apparent indifference can be found, in part, in the very great venality of the police, which is traditional to such an extent that some of the lower ranking police officers considered the taking of bribes almost as their right, as a kind of private tax,[4] and partly because a local (*Thana*) police officer who would report many crimes to his headquarters would earn a

[3] As Chairman of the Department of Political Science of the University of Dacca since 1950 I have had ample opportunity to watch the process. The deterioration was not due to a jurisdictional policy of the courts. Only in respect of the Supreme or High Courts is there a genuine separation of the judicial from the executive powers. It rather set in at a lower administrative level. Accurate statistical data are not readily available, and their collection would require an extensive survey. Nevertheless, the facts quoted above I consider reliable, because of my presence as an eye witness at a large number of court proceedings at Cacca, Chittagong, and several courts in the interior of the province, and my personal acquaintance with several judicial magistrates and high police officers, from whom I obtained personal statements; I also received statements from both citizens and resident foreigners whose property was lost due to criminal actions; the day-to-day reports of the local press over a period of eight years tell the same story.

[4] See the testimony of a former Inspector General of Police of East Pakistan in Abul Hasnat, *Justice and Peace for All* (1954), pp. 98, 99, and 105-07.

"bad name" for his locality. A good portion of crimes would thus not be reported at all. Moreover, the public, in anticipation of such slackness, would not care to report all the crimes. If the report ever reached the court, the defendant might be bailed out and the court police might conduct the case without much zeal.[5] This meant that the case would be adjourned over and over again and finally dismissed for lack of evidence or punished nominally, or, at any rate, very mildly indeed. This attitude of the police was helped by the leniency of the criminal law. According to articles 457 and 380 of the Pakistan Code of Criminal Procedure, burglary is to be punished by rigorous imprisonment up to fourteen years, yet article 561 of the same code provides for a mere admonition to first offenders, which was frequently administered.

Moreover, in a river country, such as East Bengal, where the size of the districts was far in excess of practical administrative potentialities,[6] the villagers found it exceedingly difficult to obtain police protection even against armed robberies, called "dacoities," which were sometimes combined with murder, rape, or the abduction of women. Even where criminals were apprehended and brought to book, it was not easy to produce satisfactory legal proof, and even where this was possible the courts were reluctant to impose the death penalty, and prison sentences were often preferred.[7] Adulteration of essential foodstuffs and medicines is one of the most dangerous and insidious crimes, as when milk is adulterated in a country where cholera and typhoid bacteria may be present in the water and the physical resistance of the people generally low. Adulteration of foodstuffs and medicines such as penicillin or chloro-

[5] *Ibid.*, p. 107.

[6] The largest district, Mymensingh, with 6230 square miles, has a population of 5,797,521.

[7] *Morning News*, Dacca, January 19, 1958: "Zamil Kazi, one of the 3 accused in a dacoity, was convicted to 10 years Rigorous Imprisonment by the Second Additional Sessions Judge, Dacca, agreeing with the unanimous verdict of the Jury. Two others were acquitted. The charge is loot of cash and gold ornaments costing Rupees 6.670 and the *killing of one of the inmates of the house (a woman)*."

mycetin may, therefore, frequently amount to homicide. Still criminals of this class were rather mildly treated.[8]

Before independence the officers concerned had been British, or British-guided. Their sense of what merited punishment was not diluted by a feeling of national or racial solidarity with the offenders. In this respect, independence brought about a change. There appeared a marked tendency on the part of the police to prosecute offenders only where important officials or eminent personalities showed some interest.

The process of deterioration was gradual. Whereas there was still some semblance of law and order under the Muslim League regime from 1947 to 1954 (which interfered very little with the previous bureaucratic structure), and under the following bureaucratic emergency regime from 1954-55, the situation sharply deteriorated thereafter and reached its nadir under the Awami League regime from 1956-58. Often the legal order was purposely undermined by the provincial government for political reasons. A police official who would curb an unruly demonstration would be at once suspended or transferred on the demand of a local legislator. A college principal who dared to expel violent or unruly students would be instantly removed by the Education Minister.[9] There were widespread rumors that even in cases of suspected murder, proceedings had been quashed at the behest of prominent local politicians. All this was bound to encourage criminals throughout the Province who now, without fear of punishment, committed burglaries in the compounds of high police officials and High Court Judges. While a thief was being tried by a Dacca Magistrate and was trying to get his pardon for

8 Out of a total of 324 persons tried for food offenses in East Pakistan during October, 1957, 228 received punishments, while 96 were acquitted. Of the former, 18 were imprisoned for terms varying between 2 years and 3 weeks, 187 were fined for sums amounting from Rs. 800 ($160) to 20 ($4), and 23 were both fined and imprisoned. *Morning News*, Dacca, June 15, 1958.

9 For example, Mr. Edward MacInerny, Principal of Barisal College, was suspended in 1955 because he rusticated students guilty of unruly behavior during a political demonstration.

one crime, he picked the pocket of the very Magistrate whose sympathy he was soliciting [10] and was apprehended by the clerk of the court. Loiterers entered any private compound in the cities during broad daylight to steal cooking utensils, large quantities of fruit, flowers, etc., for resale on the market. Trees were cut down in public and private gardens and thoroughfares for use as firewood, without the police even risking a glance.

Any protests to public authorities were met with the standard excuse of the extreme poverty of the populace. That this excuse was fatuous was evident from the black market and smuggling activities of wealthy men, the corruption amongst ministers and some high officials. Finally, violence was added to offenses against property; it invaded the very parliamentary buildings and put an end to democracy.[11]

In the same degree as the enforcement of the laws was neglected, the number of offenders increased. Ordinary citizens resorted to the age-old method of self-help, characteristic of a partial return to the state of nature. Suppose a cow or goat would be stolen; instead of appealing to the police for help which was of doubtful value, citizens would apprehend an offender, and before handing him over to the police give him a public and collective beating to make sure he would not escape justice. Once I found that my students had caught a bicycle thief on the campus. By the time I came on the scene the thief had been tied to a tree and thoroughly whipped and kicked by the students, who dispersed only after much persuasion, and showed thmselves highly reluctant to rely on the efficacy of legal proceedings.

How could one explain the actions of the citizens and students of Dacca? Did they inflict upon the thief, whom they had caught red-handed, a retributive punishment? Did they beat him because he had sinned, as Professor Weihofen suggests? Did they demand an eye for an eye? Requital or retri-

10 *Morning News*, Dacca, January 23, 1958.

11 See K. J. Newman's article "Pakistan's Preventive Autocracy and Its Causes," *Pacific Affairs*, 1959, p. 30.

bution is not mere vindictive vengeance. No doubt the people resorting to self-help were behaving emotionally; and yet they were certainly resorting to an act of social self-defense. From the many cows, goats, and bicycles which had recently been stolen they concluded that the more thieves went scot-free, the more cows, goats, and bicycles would disappear; it would be their property which was likely to be lost and they did not want to lose any property of which they had so little.

East Pakistan thus represents an instance where the legal and social order had partly broken down because (a) there was no certainty that punishment would be inflicted on the offender by the law and (b) even if punishment were inflicted it was likely to be so light that criminals were willing to take the risk. Even Ferri agreed that the lack of certainty in punishment leads to an increase in crime.[12] What he omitted to consider is the fact that excessive leniency in punishment in itself enters into the criminal's calculations, when he considers the possibility of evading the law. Since opponents of the retributive theory commonly base their theory on the views of the distinguished Italian criminologist Enrico Ferri, it would not be out of place to point out here two of his major shortcomings. First, his statistics were defective because he attempted to prove that the increase in crime in various European countries, in the course of the nineteenth century, took place in spite of more rigorous punishments, and yet he failed to take account of the corresponding vast increase of population. Second, in his division of population into three classes, "a morally perfect class," one of "born and habitual criminals," and a third class of "individuals not born to crime but whose honesty will not withstand a test, who oscillate between vice and virtue and from whom occasional criminals are recruited." [13] Ferri does not mention that this latter class really represents some 95 per cent of the population of a given country. It would not be too difficult to prove numerically

[12] Enrico Ferri, *Criminal Sociology* (1917), p. 221, trans. J. I. Kelly and J. Lisle.
[13] *Ibid.*, p. 228.

that the majority of offenders against the law who are tried by the courts come from this class and not from the born and habitual criminals.

One can go along with those who wish to reduce the need for punishment by establishing social conditions which make it less necessary. One may agree with those who stress the psychological abnormality of criminals, no matter whether they were acting under an irresistible impulse, or their action was due to some other mental abnormalities.[14] One can fully subscribe to the educative treatment of offenders. Still, there remains the problem of how society is to be protected against those who deliberately choose to revolt against the fundamental moral laws. The relativist approach which stresses the variance of social controls in various regions and social layers is not really of basic importance. For, as the East Pakistan example clearly indicates, John Locke's thesis that men in founding society give up their fundamental natural right of self-help only when they are satisfied that the machinery of the state will do it better on their behalf still holds and is as true as ever.[15] Though there may be variations, these natural laws are still common to mankind and easily identifiable. Let the state abdicate its functions and men will resort again to self-help.

One has to agree with Professor Bodenheimer's view that punishment should convey to the offender the expression of public disapproval, and one cannot agree with Professor Weihofen that the revulsion which world public opinion felt against the Nazi gas chambers, for example, was just an immoral hatred which civilized people ought to learn to control. To assert this is tantamount to denying the existence of a sense of justice in the human soul, and it is exactly this sense of justice which allows the average human being to remain a law-abiding citizen.

To reduce the collective feeling and demand for justice in

14 Consult in this connection, *Durham v. U.S.,* 214 F 2nd volume, 1954, p. 862ff.

15 John Locke, *Of Civil Government,* Book II, chap. VII, par. 87.

humanity to an animal impulse for vindictiveness and vengeance would be oversimplifying things. The failure of the state
to satisfy this collective feeling leads to widespread fear and
insecurity. To the community the crime appears as a docu-
mentation of uncontrolled strength or power which, at any
moment, may become directed against any one of them as the
vindication of a right which the other members have agreed
to surrender to the state. If the state fails, therefore, to repress lawless, individual action, the citizens may rightly claim
that they have been released from the social contract, and that
each is again free to do as he pleases. Hence the criminality
increases as a result of the state's failure to do proportional
justice. It is for these reasons that aversion to crime and to
the criminal who personifies it is unavoidable; unless the social group maintains its reprobation of crime it cannot remain intact.[16]

From a moral point of view, it will be argued that men are
law abiding because they are convinced that moral conduct
is right. What causes men to believe this? To assert that legal
codes can operate without the sanctions required for them
amounts to separating social codes from social controls. A
thorough analysis of the motives of human conduct will reveal that only a very small number of men, most likely limited
to moral philosophers, servants of religion, etc., practice morality and righteousness for its own sake and without the assistance of social controls. Karl Mannheim, following Hume,
has pointed to the important influence which custom has on
human conduct.[17] MacIver has explained the close inter-connection of the various codes and sanctions, consisting of a
chain starting from the religious and running to the moral
and legal codes.[18] It is undeniable that most human beings
are without any marked criminal tendencies, and hence obey
the major social codes because they have become habituated

[16] Pareto, *Mind and Society*, III (1935), p. 1248; quoted also in Herman
Mannheim, *op. cit.*, p. 160.
[17] Karl Mannheim, *Man and Society* (1954), p. 328.
[18] R. M. MacIver and Charles H. Page, *Society* (1957), p. 143.

to them. It is the sanction with its threat of an unpleasant consequence which enforces obedience, until such obedience ultimately becomes a habit with the mass of individuals. To the religious man the denial of salvation after death is an even more serious sanction than the death penalty. The habituation to right conduct in a community, which has been achieved through the prolonged existence, perhaps through many hundreds and even thousands of years, of the combined strength of religious, moral, and legal codes, all enforced by drastic sanctions, results then ultimately in the appearance of automatic code-abiding conduct. But reduce the effectiveness of sanctions for any length of time, and the codes are bound to become less effective.

If we are surprised about the lack of moral scruples which in some Asian countries are connected with petty thefts, we should remember that men used to be hanged for stealing a sheep in eighteenth-century England. Even today the legal sanctions against larceny are particularly strong there. On the other hand, in a country such as Saudi Arabia where the Shariah code of cutting off hands is still in vogue, theft is far less common, not only because of the savage sanction, but because of the close inter-connection between its legal, moral, and religious character. In India the connection of legal and religious sanctions was less intimate; for there were certain brotherhoods dedicated to crime which still used to obey minutely all the principal religious commands, as did, for instance, the devotees of the Goddess Kali. Even in Europe, law enforcement became almost impossible when, as in the case of duelling, the moral code did not uphold the legal one.

From a legal point of view the essence of crime is in its character as a rebellion against the social order. The community is not primarily interested in vengeance, but in the need of subjection to the laws on the part of the criminal. In other words, the legal order must be equipped with the means of its own self-defense. St. Augustine asserted that punishment is but the necessary and logical internal transformation of a given breach of justice. Inasmuch as the criminal is guilty of this rebellion, or is capable of being guilty, he is liable to punishment.[19]

The best explanation of the ratio of punishment was, however, given by St. Thomas Aquinas, who supplemented St. Augustine's view by asserting that every such rebellion falls under the cosmic law of reaction; for the attacked legal order has the power to hit back. Therefore *"quidquid contra ordinem aliquens insurgit, consequens est, ut ab eo ordine at principe ordinis deprimatur."* [20] What makes Aquinas' theory superior to all explanatory philosophies of punishment before and after him is the fact that be foreshadowed the sociological discovery of the close interconnection between the religious, moral, and legal codes.[21] He fully realized that just as divine retribution is the sanction of divine law, and our moral feeling is moved by conscience, so punishment corresponds to the human legal order.[22]

The reaction of the legal order is thus directly caused by illegal conduct. That such a reaction should occur at all is due to the very character of the former. Thomas, following Aristotle, thinks that crime creates a kind of inequality,[23] a disturbance of the natural social order, which demands the restoration of balance for purely utilitarian purposes, namely, in the interest of the state. But the equilibrium disturbed by the offense can only be restored by something of an equal kind; something the offender himself has to contribute, so that he may again become a member of the social order which he has attacked.[24] For this order cannot allow anybody to remain outside. What is required of the violator is called "retribution." In this sense the term "retribution" has no immediate

19 Augustine, *The City of God,* Book XII, chap. XV.

20 Aquinas, *Summa Theologica,* 12 q. 87 a1 c. Also Wagner, *Das natürliche Sittengesetz nach der Lehre des heiligen Thomas Aquinas* (1911), p. 104ff.

21 See R. M. MacIver's view quoted above which is fundamentally in keeping with that of St. Thomas, *op. cit.,* p. 10.

22 Nagler, *op. cit.,* p. 174.

23 Aquinas, *Summa contra Gentiles,* III c 140.

24 See also Nagler, *op. cit.,* pp. 176 and 177.

connection with vengeance. The literal meaning of the term is not primarily something that is inflicted, but rather something that the criminal himself contributes toward the restoration of balance. In true Aristotelian fashion, the central idea of justice simply requires that there should be a *quid pro quo*. Immanuel Kant basically agreed with this view when he understood punishment as a consequence of the moral order. In his *Critique of Practical Reason* Kant recognized that punishment should be such that it even satisfies the criminal, so that he admits that justice has been done to him. Indeed, distinguished thinkers such as Grotius or Hegel had to agree with this version of the retributive theory. This doctrine stands, because of its inherent rationality, for greater justice and thus for a more humanitarian concept.

Those who today stress the deterrent element in punishment as different from the retributive one overlook the fact that it was the theory of deterrence, and not of retribution, which led to the most inhuman punishments during the times of the worst deterioration of criminal justice from the fifteenth to the seventeenth centuries. Public executions, including mutilations (like drawing and quartering, being broken on the wheel, and so forth) served primarily the idea of deterrence. This theory admits that the degree of punishment may be greater than that required by the offense. On the other hand, if deterrence is to be coupled with very mild punishment it loses its *raison d'être* and effect.

Whether a community can afford to be mild in its sanctions depends largely on the sensitivity [25] of the legal order. Where law enforcement is rigorous, the police efficient, the community sufficiently homogeneous to be controlled by a uniform sytem of folkways and customs; where a rigorous moral order controls a closely knit community, a single crime, however serious, is unlikely to shake the foundations of the legal order. Punishment can be milder, and nobody will mistake the state's mildness for weakness. It is different in fast developing industrial societies, beset with multifarious problems of ad-

[25] *Ibid.*, p. 615ff.

justment, and plagued by constant collisions of heterogeneous groups which have no uniform set of moral standards, and where, therefore, non-legal social controls are far less effective. The social texture, and not the size of the country, is the reason why some countries have been able to do without the death penalty, and not others. But even an efficient law-enforcing system, such as exists in the United States, may be less effective in checking violent crime if such criminals are worshipped as heroes,[26] as a result of sensationalism. One can hardly watch an evening's television program on any American station without having a murder story presented in which the criminal ultimately loses, but is nevertheless presented as a vicious or mad, but interesting and brave, man who is overpowered by a large number of sleuths, and this only sometimes because of ill luck and coincidence. To those who may have some criminal potentialities such morbid publicity may well be an encouragement; even those whose lives are dull, and who may not hope for any other excellence in life and are yet ambitious, may well be driven toward a criminal career by such displays. In other words, this type of manifestation of criminal-worship sets a pattern of conduct among a certain set, particularly with the young who, with their great capacity for imitation, may be led into delinquency. It is quite in keeping with the tradition of hero-worship that the criminal is rarely caught by the law, but usually dies as a brave fighter in open combat, fighting to the last—not unlike what Adolf Hitler said he would do but did not do—thus inflicting the maximum damage on society.

Having previously stated the character of punishment as serving to subject the rebel to the social order, we clearly exclude any personal expression of vengeance. For vengeance is basically irrational; it is unjust because it strives to be ex-

26 "While it is distinctly wrong to treat every lawbreaker as an inferior human being who ought to be content with the crumbs that fall from the table of the community, on the other hand, glorification of the criminal, either by himself or the press, is the last thing to be desired." H. Mannheim, *The Dilemma of Penal Reform* (1939), p. 159.

cessive. But the legal order, in its right of self-defense, is expected to act in a rational manner to restore the equilibrium of justice; to protect the social order, its sanction, punishment, must not be excessive; on the other hand it must not be so lenient as to reduce the efficacy and surety of the sanction.

In this sense retributory punishment, as understood by St. Thomas, Grotius, Kant, and Hegel, still represents the optimal solution from the point of view of the state and society. In the face of a specific violation of a rule of the legal order society thus manifests clearly that it does not intend to commit suicide or abdicate, but means to exist and to go on existing, and to protect the moral values contained in its general forms. Important and not to be overlooked is the psychological assistance which legal punishment lends to the growth of other social controls.[27] Suppose the Nazi war criminals had been treated mildly after the war, some of them removed to psychiatric clinics, others subjected to reformatory treatment. This

[27] Interesting proof for the existence of a general sense of justice in respect to the proportionality of punishment can be found in the ancient Indian Athashastra ascribed to the sage Kautyliya: "Punishment, if too severe, alarms men; if too mild it frustrates itself. Punishment according to deserts should be encouraged." "When improperly awarded due to ignorance, under the influence of lust and anger, it enrages even hermits and mendicants. . . . Punishment unawarded would verily foster the regime of the fist—in the absence of the upholder of law the strong would swallow up the weak," quoted in P. K. Sen, *Penology Old and New*, p. 105ff. The ancient documents of the Manusamhita and Mahabharrdta represent punishment even as a highly beneficial and providential force. "Punishment alone governs all created beings, punishment alone protects them, punishment watches over them while they sleep; the wise declare punishment (to be identical with) the law." Quoted in U. N. Ghoshal, *A History of Hindu Political Theories*, G.U.P. Erich Fromm has thrown some interesting light on the evolution of what is commonly called "conscience." "In recent years conscience has lost much of its significance. Authority has made itself invisible. . . . Anonymous authority reigns . . . disguised as common sense, science, psychic health, normality, public opinion. It does not demand anything except the self-evident. It seems to use no pressure, except with persuasion. Anonymous authority is more effective than overt authority, since one never expects there is an order which one is expected to follow."

might have encouraged the growth of other Hitlers, Himmlers, and Goebbels', since there would have been all over the world men conscious of the fact that the common order of natural law could be defied with relative impunity by men able to muster governmental powers and controls. Indeed, the very fact that Stalin's similar system of governmental persecution became a negative symbol in the Soviet Union immediately after his death may not be entirely unconnected with the Nuremberg Trials.

As described in the case of East Pakistan, the possibility of a virtual breakdown of the legal order is a very grave danger today because of the vast social, political, and economic changes in underdeveloped countries. In technologically advanced communities there exists the acute peril that a relatively small group of criminals may arrogate and monopolize the means of state power. For all these reasons an energetic assertion of the legal order is more than ever necessary. If it is to assert itself it must be uncompromisingly strong against the strong; only then can it afford to be mild and merciful toward the failing, weak, poor, and psycho-pathological, provided the latter characteristics are the true causes of their failings.

✺❃ IX ❃✺

CRIMINAL RESPONSIBILITY AND PUNISHMENT

THOMAS E. DAVITT, S.J.

THE VERY RAISING of the question "Is Punishment Obsolete?" bespeaks the shift in thinking that is occurring
in some quarters regarding the grounds of criminal
guilt and responsibility. This question further implies the
change that is taking place in the interpretation of the nature
of the criminal himself as a man, as well as of public authority and law as representative of the people. For it is in
relation to this broader background that the criminal act and
its consequences take their meaning.

This paper will be concerned with the problem of criminal
responsibility and punishment in the perspective of a philosophy that considers a man to be a being with ends to be attained and who is accountable for the manner he uses the
means thereunto. Only the briefest reference to the main
features of this position, before proceeding to an examination
of punishment, seems in place here. Further substantiation
can be had elsewhere.

Prerequired for criminal guilt is responsibility for one's
actions. Such answerability derives from knowing, free decision. This presupposes that man is a unit of matter and
spirit with the unique powers of intellectual knowledge and
free decision. Men's knowledge of various objects would be
meaningless unless complemented by a choice of action regarding them.

Factors such as emotion and impulses may bear on the functioning of these powers and thereby lessen or even extinguish

143

freedom and resulting responsibility. But a lessening in itself
is not extinction. The amount of light by which we see may
be diminished until it is completely absent. As long as there is
some light, seeing is possible—albeit in varying stages of perfection. Likewise the amount of freedom with which we make
our decisions may be lessened even to the point of being non-
existent. But insofar as there is some degree of freedom, to
this extent there is free decision and responsibility.

Knowledge and soundness of mind, in this view, are pre-
requisite conditions for responsible conduct. They are no
guarantee that a man will act rightly. The power of free discretion can be knowingly used for self-interests in opposition
to the public interests of law, as is the case in the criminal act.
Such free opposition to law is the core of culpability. Ignorance and insanity preclude the possibility of such knowingly
decided action. Their indicated remedy is education and
therapy. Hence, the criminal act taken formally is an indica-
tion neither of ignorance nor of insanity. It is a sign of the
deliberate misuse of the power of decision.

Law, in this philosophy, is a directive judgment on the part
of lawmakers as to means necessary for the common good. It
is an instrument of public authority, which itself is but an expression of the delegated authority of the people. Hence, the
criminal violation of a law represents the personal opposition
of the criminal's judgment and desire to those of the persons
in public authority and of the people themselves.

In essence, punishment is the deprivation of a good, consequent upon the violation of a law, and against the will of the
violator. Deprivations imposed by law are of property by fine,
of liberty by imprisonment, of physical well-being by flogging,
or of life itself by capital punishment.

Punishment must be related to a criminal act. Otherwise it
is not punishment in any meaningful sense. A judge might
arbitrarily impose a deprivation on those who, in his estimation, would profit by it whether they were guilty of a crime or
not. But if he did, the deprivation—unrelated as it would be

to any particular lawbreaking act—would not be just nor would it be a punishment. It would have no reference to a deliberate decision to violate the law and could not serve as a deterrent from future lawbreaking acts. Hence, before any benefit can be drawn from punishment, either for the criminal himself or others, the criminal must first have been guilty of a crime and be punishable for it.

What precisely are the grounds for which deprivations are imposed on the criminal? The grounds are a two-fold injustice. First, the criminal's act is an invasion of the rights of those who sustain immediate damage from it. Such are the victims of murder, arson, robbery, rape, and the like. Even if there were no man-made law prohibiting these acts, they would nevertheless be an infringement of the claim of these individuals. The criminal's act is a breach of the commutative justice that private individuals owe to each other.

Second, the criminal act is an invasion of the rights of the people themselves and their representatives to whom they have delegated public, lawmaking authority. The criminal has breached the people's wall of protection—the law—and has thereby endangered their common good. He has violated their claim to peace and security. By the exercise of his free decision to break the law, the criminal has put his own interests before the interests of the community. He has set his own desires against the desires of public authority representing the people. Hence, his criminal act is also an infringement of the contributive justice that individuals owe to the community.

It is in regard to this contributive injustice that the rationale of legal punishment is to be found. For, of greater significance than the damage inflicted by the criminal's act on individual victims, important though it be, is the harm done to the community by the deliberate flouting of its law and public authority.

Regarding this double invasion of rights, justice demands an accounting. A rectification must be brought out. Otherwise the rights of individuals and the community could be invaded with impunity and the whole purpose and force of law immediately nullified. Men would find themselves in a "state of nature" as bad as that hypothesized by certain political philosophers.

Reparation as far as possible, then, is due to the individual victims of the criminal's act. This would be demanded by natural justice whether or not there was a statute providing for it. But such a restoration could be handled as a matter of civil law.

A redressing of the criminal's refusal to be directed by the law, however, is more significantly due to public authority and the people it represents. In putting himself above the law, he has subjected the law to himself. If this condition is to be corrected, it must be done by some action on the part of the public authority that constrains the criminal to follow its directives. This occurs when the criminal is made to undergo deprivations imposed by law. In this manner the pre-eminence of public authority is ultimately reasserted over the criminal. He allowed his own desire to outbalance the desire of public authority. The enduring of deprivations against his desire now counterweighs the rebelliousness of his desire. The imbalance of justice caused by his criminal decision is, to this extent, corrected. The people and their public authority are ultimately vindicated.

This vindication should be distinguished from vindictiveness or revenge. The distinguishing mark of vindictiveness is pleasure at seeing the offender deprived of something against his will, however unjust the reason. The vindication of public authority is characterized by the desire of protecting the rights of the people, which is a matter of justice and not of emotion.

The reaction of public authority to criminal opposition by repressing it through deprivation finds a parallel in nature. Opposition to the ordered structure of a being, say an organism, elicits from this being a reaction that represses the opposition. This is necessary if the identity and functioning of the being which is being attacked is to be preserved. So also in law, the criminal's opposition of his will to that of public authority is repressed by his having to submit to deprivations imposed by this same authority and against his will. Only in this manner can the uniqueness and effectiveness of public authority be maintained. For it is in the prospect of such repression that the possibility of deterrence lies.

There is also another way in which the vindication of public authority takes place. It exemplifies still more clearly the connection between the violation of a law and the deprivations that follow as a consequence.

Laws that are not arbitrary have justifying reasons. The grounds for a law restricting the speed of automobiles is the factual relation between excessive speed and the preservation of limb and life. There is a limit of speed beyond which a car cannot successfully negotiate a curve, the center of gravity of cars being what it is and the angle and bank of curves being what they are. This relation of speed and safety can sometimes by scientifically ascertained. A series of fatal car accidents on a highway may cause lawmakers to enact legislation restricting speed on this particular road. Corps of traffic engineers can discover what this limit of safe speed is. According to this factual situation, even if there were no statute restricting speed based on the finding of traffic engineers, the driver who exceeded the safe limit would be certain to run off a curve with resulting injuries and possible death.

This complexus of facts does not change when it is embodied into law and made the content of the directive judgment of public authority. Hence, when a driver violates what natural prudence should have dictated and what legal prudence demands, he incurs willy-nilly the deprivation exacted by the physical laws expressed in the nature of things which now has been incorporated into the content of positive law. The violator is deprived of the good condition of his car, of his own physical well-being, and perhaps of his very life. And the directive judgment of public authority, which decreed that a certain limit of speed was necessary if these consequences were to be avoided, is now vindicated.

These deprivations which follow immediately from the

content of a law are more closely related to the violation of a law than are the deprivations, such as fines and imprisonment, which are extrinsically added by the law. Although the intrinsic sanction of law is more obvious and immediate in such cases as the one just discussed, it nevertheless occurs in all violations of a well-founded law, that is, a law based on a factual means-end relationship.

Deprivation, then, in being a rectification of opposition through repression is also capable of causing deterrence. The deprivation which the driver of the speeding car unwillingly endures as he lies injured alongside the road as a result of violating the law, may have a pedagogical result. He himself may effectively learn that it is to his advantage to follow the directive judgment of public authority and he may be actually deterred from future violations. His desire and decision in the future may be aligned with those of the lawmakers. Others, passing by and observing his plight, may also be moved to reach the same conclusion and be likewise deterred from future infractions. For, "tragedy is the great teacher."

There is no assurance, however, that such a learning will take place. Experience shows that some "never learn." Deprivation alone does not inevitably effect a change of desire and decision. In the process of undergoing the deprivations which public authority exacts in vindication of itself, some respect for law may be acquired. Fear also of this authority may be engendered by the prospect of having to submit to similar punishment again. But respect and fear do not necessarily denote a complete rehabilitation of the mind and will of the criminal. Such an interior reconditioning may have to be brought about by entirely different motives.

The kind and amount of deprivation should be related to the criminal act. But the criminal act, as noted, is not simple but complex. It is an injustice against individuals and society and demands a rectification that has both retrospective and prospective implications. Hence, deprivations to be effective must be related to all these aspects of the criminal act.

The most obvious mode and degree of deprivation is that of strict equality. Such is the *lex talionis* which demands "an eye for an eye and a tooth for a tooth," or cutting off the hand that stole the bread or the tongue that did the calumniating. Here the measure is material correspondence between the crime and the deprivation. It has been claimed that such a norm is the only one giving assurance of complete satisfaction for a crime. But the time when the formula of talion can be held up as the ideal of just punishment is past, as is the day when it could be maintained that the rendering of justice demands torture as an indispensible means for obtaining conviction by confession, or burning at the stake as the only sufficient penalty for certain crimes. We have come no small distance since then.

The notion of complete satisfaction is, to a great extent, illusory. Although there is something reparable in every crime (the state of mind and will of the criminal) there may also be something irreparable (the damage inflicted on the victim). Besides, the measure of strict equality is inapplicable in many crimes, such as when a person's good name has been destroyed, when sexual integrity has been violated, when government secrets have been treasonably betrayed, and so on. Moreover, the history of the *lex talionis* affords evidence enough that its use was frequently motivated by revenge. Other forms of deprivations, then, must be considered.

The alternative to strict equality of punishment is proportional equivalence. A deprivation that has a measure of correspondence to the criminal act may be as effective as one of strict equality. Men sentenced to life imprisonment for murder ofttimes attempt to commit suicide. They prefer death to life in prison, especially if there is no prospect of easy parole. A proportionally equivalent deprivation can take account of other ends to be accomplished besides rectification and deterrence. Life imprisonment can offer the possibility of rehabilitating the mind and will of the prisoner if means conducive to education and motivation are at hand. For it is one thing for a man to observe the law because of his fear of incurring the evil of punishment, if he opposes it; but it is another thing for him to keep the law because of his desire to do what is good for himself and others, by following it. An equivalent deprivation can also represent a recognition of the fact that the punishment meted out can seriously affect innocent and needy persons. Because of the closeness of the family bond, the situation where the criminal is the father of a large and poor family is a common instance of this.

In determining what such an equivalent punishment should be, however, the injustice done by the criminal to both the individual victim as well as to society must be borne in mind. It is true, as already noted, that in one sense the vindication of the rights of society is of greater importance than the reparation of the damage done to the immediate victim. But this does not mean that the injustice to the victim can be allowed to slip from view. As criminal law now stands, attempts to make the punishment fit the crime consist for the most part in scaling the quantity of the deprivation and not in varying its quality. Most punishments take the form of a certain amount of fine or imprisonment which is adjusted to fit the list of misdemeanors and felonies. And although such deprivations may somewhat satisfy the rebalancing of the injustice done to society by the lawbreaking act, they have no relation to the damage done to the victim. Their proportion to this part of the injustice they caused is mostly imaginary.

What is needed is greater use of initiative and imagination on the part of legislators and judges in conceiving of deprivations which take both aspects of criminal injustice into account and also contribute to the emendation of the mind and will of the criminal. Instances of such punishments are not wholly lacking. In some places vandals are made to work and pay the cost of their vandalism in whole or in part, drivers have their licenses revoked to prevent more accidents, those guilty of bastardy must support their progeny, to mention only a few examples. But the imposition of such deprivations is not widespread and constant enough. The obvious difficulties involved in determining and administering punishments of this nature do not absolve us from the duty of attempting to do so. It behooves legislators and judges to see to it that the deprivations imposed on criminals have some proportional relation to the injustice done to the individual victim as well as to society.

The problem of criminal responsibility and punishment, then, points up perhaps as sharply as any the relation between philosophy and law. Any displacement in the philosophical strata is bound to cause reverberations on the legal level of the criminal act.

If a philosophy of man is adopted which maintains that his actions are but the consequence of an unbroken chain of biological causes and that any idea of free, undetermined decision is but an illusion, the logical consequence is either a new notion of punishment or a relinquishing of the concept all together. Only such background thinking could account for the artless confusing of all punishment with talionic revenge and the suggestion that the whole notion of punishment is obsolete and should be abandoned.

The intimate relation between philosophy and law is inevitable. After all, the key question in law is the same as that in life: What is a man, his origin, his destiny? Political and legal philosophers would only be acting economically if they first ascertained the direction in which the answer to this question lies, before embarking on an attempt to find the solution to the problem of criminal responsibility and punishment.

❧ X ❧

ON JUSTIFYING LEGAL PUNISHMENT

JOEL FEINBERG

BEFORE WE CAN ANSWER the urgent practical question of whether legal punishment is obsolete, we must first provide answers to the two anterior questions presupposed by it. These are: (1) What is legal punishment? i.e., what does the word "punishment" mean as used typically by legislators, judges, lawyers, and others concerned with the workings of the criminal law? (2) What are the appropriate principles to be used in justifying punishment as a general legal practice? The inquiry into the nature of punishment, of course, has a certain priority over the question of whether punishment is in fact justified, for one cannot decide whether legal punishment is obsolete until he knows what legal punishment is, and what it does. But once we know what sort of practice is designated by the phrase "legal punishment," and what are the formal criteria which must be satisfied by this practice if it is to be justified, then, apart from the relevant empirical facts, we have all the data we need in order to reach a verdict.

The importance of a definition of "punishment" is often underestimated by writers eager to attack or defend our legal or penal systems. If our inquiry into the meaning of the word "punishment" is undertaken hastily, as a mere preliminary to our efforts to answer the important practical question raised by Professor Bodenheimer, then we are in grave danger of begging that practical question in our very definition of "punishment." For example, suppose that a philosopher brings with him to a discussion of the justification of punishment a ready-made ethical or political theory according to which any political or legal institution is justified and proper if and only if it does such and such. Now suppose he defines "punishment" hastily and incautiously, as simply the doing of such and such. Then, of course, it follows that on his justificatory principles the practice of punishing criminals *is* justified. From the abstract logical point of view there is nothing wrong with this sort of procedure; but if our philosopher has unwittingly allowed his theory of the principles to be used in justifying punishment to creep into and so determine his definition of "punishment," without carefully checking that definition against the actual use of the word in legal contexts, then he will have contributed nothing but darkness and confusion to the whole discussion. It is important then that we endeavor honestly and independently to answer the question about definition on its own grounds without being influenced one way or another by the standards we bring with us for evaluating institutions.

I wish now to propose a definition of "legal punishment" which, though generally similar to Professor Bodenheimer's, differs rather sharply from his in one important respect. My definition is derived from an examination of a few clearly recognized standard examples of legal punishment, that is, cases which are such that all of us would agree in identifying them as instances of legal punishment regardless of the theoretical commitments which may divide us on the further question of justification. Consider then the following examples:

1. Jones is arrested for driving his automobile 80 miles an hour on a section of highway where the posted speed limit is 25 miles per hour. He is tried in an authorized court according to due process of law, pronounced guilty by a judge, and sentenced to thirty days in a House of Correction and deprived of his driver's license for a period of one year.

2. Smith is a citizen of South Africa of the Caucasian race. He is arrested for violating a law which prohibits the entertaining of Negroes in the homes of white men, tried in an

authorized court according to due process of law, pronounced guilty by a jury, and sentenced by a judge to six months penal servitude, the maximum penalty allowed by the statute he violated.

3. Green is charged with the murder of his wife. He is tried in an authorized criminal court according to due process of law. It is officially decided by the court that Green did fire the shot which killed his wife, that he did it intentionally and not by accident, and that he is, and was at the time of the crime, legally sane. He is pronounced guilty, sentenced by the judge to die in the electric chair, and six months later, after all remedies have been exhausted, he is electrocuted under conditions specified by law.

All I wish to claim for these three examples is that all of them are perfectly clear examples of legal punishment, however they may differ in other respects. The word "punishment" is of course vague; there are many other possible examples of punishment which are not so clearly recognizable as the ones I have cited. As certain important features of the standard examples drop off, we get a continuous shading into the uncertain region of borderline cases, metaphorical uses, and analogical extensions of meaning. The cases I have cited, however, are clear and noncontroversial models of legal punishment, and insofar as some other case differs from these models, to that extent we would be reluctant to call it a case of legal punishment at all.

My definition of "legal punishment" then will simply consist of an enumeration of the more conspicuous features of the standard examples I have cited. I take these to be the following:

1. In each case some intended loss, deprivation, or suffering has been inflicted on the man punished. Of course, Jones may be an odd fellow who enjoys the House of Correction and did not really like driving anyway; Smith may actively have desired his own imprisonment as a means of publicizing the fight

against his government's racial policies; and Green may have wished nothing so much as to die: in which case none of the three men in the examples may have considered his punishment to be any kind of loss or deprivation. Nevertheless, each of these men was treated in a way which would normally be regarded, in the vast majority of cases, as the infliction of loss, deprivation, or suffering, and certainly each was deprived of some of the normal legal rights of a citizen of his country.

2. The presumed suffering or deprivation was inflicted by some recognized legal authorities after a trial according to due process of law.

3. It was inflicted because the victim was presumed to have violated a law.

Any legal system which incorporates practices having these three features can be said to be, or to contain, a system of punishments. On the other hand, any legal system which lacks one or more of these features might more appropriately be called by another name.

Professor Bodenheimer's definition requires more of a system if it is to warrant the name "punishment." He requires that the presumed infliction of loss or suffering be a "requital for a wrong," and although he does not say so explicitly, he means, presumably, a *moral* wrong. I am not sure I wish to quarrel with his use of the word "requital." In its most generic sense, as in the expression "requital of love" it means simply "a returning of"; and since one can requite love with hate, or hate with love, a requital in this most generic sense need not even be a returning in kind. If Professor Bodenheimer's intent in using the word "requital" is simply to indicate that any judicial infliction of loss, in order to count as an instance of punishment, must be infliction *for* something done, or *in response to* or *because of* something done, then I surely agree with him that punishment is requital. A judge who tells a defendant that although he has done nothing illegal, he is to be punished for it nevertheless, commits more than an outrage to justice; he has so flagrantly misused the word "punish" that his statement is little more than nonsense. Punishment, to be punishment, and properly so called, must be punishment for something or other; that is, it must be some sort of "returning," or requital.

Professor Bodenheimer makes this point clearly, but I am less satisfied with his account of what it is that legal punishment is requital for. Legal punishment, he tells us, is requital —not simply for a violation of law—but for a "wrong," and thus he suggests that presumed moral guilt, and not mere guilt in law, is a necessary condition to be satisfied by any judicial transaction which can be given the name "punishment." Notice that Professor Bodenheimer is not here claiming, as some of the classical retributive theorists claimed, that punishment *ought* to be inflicted only as a response to moral guilt; rather he is telling us that judicial infliction of pain counts as punishment only when it *is* a response to, or requital for, moral guilt. Now I think that this part of his definition has several disadvantages. In the first place, on this definition many of the cases generally called punishment are not really instances of punishment at all, and this is true even of some of the standard examples of legal punishment. Mr. Smith, the South African in my earlier example, deliberately and from the highest moral purposes, violated a law of his country. His soul surely was not stained with sin as a result; but though he incurred no moral guilt thereby, there is no question that he was punished for his act, and that his punishment was legal punishment. In general, whenever a man violates an unjust law, partly because he believes it unjust, he incurs no moral guilt, yet he can be punished for it, and his punishment in one sense might even be *just,* if we mean by that simply that the courts, in his case, fairly and impartially administered the wicked and unjust law. Moreover, a man might deliberately violate a perfectly just law of his country while honestly but mistakenly believing it to be unjust, and if he acts conscientiously and with high moral purpose in so doing, he can hardly be regarded as wicked or sinful; yet his punishment remains punishment and is properly described as punishment for all that.

Similar is the case of a man who violates some law (for example a business regulation) of whose existence he was wholly unaware. Such a man is usually called imprudent but not (necessarily) immoral, and there is no doubt that people do get punished for their imprudence.[1] Moreover, there are other, usually minor offences, whose punishment carries no more import morally than the penalties in a football game. While these penalties may be only borderline cases of punishment, there is no doubt that they are not intended to be retribution for sinfulness. But the greatest drawback of a definition of "legal punishment" in moral terms is that it tends to obscure the discussion of the justification of punishment, it invites equivocation, and makes possible the begging of some of those practical questions which have traditionally divided utilitarians and retributivists. I would recommend then that all reference to moral wrong-doing be excluded from a *definition* of legal punishment.

We come now to the second of the two questions presupposed by the practical question whether punishment is in fact justified, namely, to what criteria must we appeal in deciding the case for or against punishment? What considerations about punishment as defined above are relevant as *reasons* either for preserving or for discarding punishment as a general system of legal practices? This question does not call for case-making one way or the other; it asks instead for a statement of the rules to be followed in case-making, not when we are dealing with an issue within a legal structure, but rather when we are passing judgment on the legal structure as a whole— so to speak, from the outside.

Now it seems to me that we must justify a general system

[1] This point is well made by S. I. Benn. See his "An Approach to the Problems of Punishment," *Philosophy*, XXXIII (October, 1958), 325-41.

of legal practices in much the same way that we try to justify any general social practice, or any political, legal, or economic institution. We must ask ourselves what are the benefits and advantages yielded by the institution in question, and then we must compare its advantages and drawbacks with those of the proposed alternatives to it. Justification is always justification of something to someone against something else. To justify, for example, the economic system of so-called "free business enterprise," one must list the benefits yielded by the system and then compare them very carefully with the alleged benefits of the various proposed alternatives to it, with the aim of discovering where the balance of advantages lies. This is, in fact, how the argument between socialists and defenders of capitalism generally proceeds. The defender of capitalism claims greater productivity and greater security from governmental infringements of individual rights as unique benefits of his system; and the socialist claims that an elimination of the defects of character which lead to crime and a reduction of social tensions between classes would be beneficial consequences of his proposed alternative. The issue between them, of course, cannot be conclusively settled in the absence of the necessary empirical data; but the important point is that so long as such things as economic abundance, security from fear and anxiety, peace and order, are recognized by both parties as advantages, and such things as hunger, anxiety, tension, and conflict are recognized by both parties as disadvantages, then reasoned case-making on both sides, and rational give and take of argument, are possible.

One justifies an institution, then, by demonstrating that it yields greater benefits and has fewer disadvantages than any of the proposed alternatives to it. Thus far my answer to the question of how institutions are to be justified, insofar as it refers only to benefits and advantages, seems to be the traditional utilitarian answer. But I am not entirely satisfied with that answer. Our list of criteria is not yet complete, for one might appropriately ask at this point, "Benefits for *whom?*,"

"*Whose* advantages?" This is where justice comes in. Some institutions, for example slavery in ancient Greece, might very well yield more benefits on the whole, and in the long run, than any alternative system, and yet be flagrantly unjust.[2] I would like to propose, then, as a second criterion, that the benefits of an institution should be as equally distributed among those whose interests are involved as is possible. Ideally a general social system—particularly a political or legal system —should yield advantages, directly or indirectly, for all citizens alike; but if this is impossible in principle, then we can at least specify that the more widespread and equally distributed the benefits of the system, the better, and especially that the benefits of the system should not be made possible only at the expense of some substantial subsection of citizenry.

Human interests being as diverse and variable as they are, it may be impossible to name anything whatever that would be equally advantageous for everyone. On the other hand, there are some values which approach rather closely to this ideal. War might be a benefit to a handful of reckless adventurers or profit-mad munitions makers, but to almost everyone else it would be a calamity. Bread manufacturers, I am told, get rich during times of depression, but it is clearly in the interests of almost all of the rest of us, directly or indirectly, that we preserve the general prosperity.[3] Unemployment compensation directly benefits the unemployed, but it

---

[2] For a thorough and cogent statement of the difficulties involved in reconciling purely utilitarian principles with our ordinary notions of (distributive) justice, see H. M. McCloskey, "An Examination of Restricted Utilitarianism," *Philosophical Review*, LXVI (October, 1957), 466-85.

[3] Even though a bread manufacturer would profit *directly* from a depression, one might argue plausibly that nevertheless the preservation of the prosperity is *indirectly* in *his* interests too; for the widespread bitterness, angry mobs, riots, and other ugly social phenomena which generally follow in the wake of a depression can badly weaken public order and pose a very real threat even to the rich man's personal liberties.

also benefits indirectly almost all of the rest of us insofar as it contributes to economic stability. It is in the interests of everyone [4] virtually without qualification that the science of medicine continue to make advances, that public sanitation be kept at a high level, that there be no rampaging epidemics, black plagues, or other natural disasters; that peace and order not be replaced by chaos and disorder, that social intercourse be smooth and not violent; that there not be (in Hobbes's unsurpassable words) "continual fear and danger of violent death, and the life of man solitary, poor, nasty, brutish, and short." These, then, are typical of the kinds of benefits and advantages widespread and equally shared, to which one must appeal in justifying a social or political institution.

We come at last to the justification of punishment. I should make it plain at once that the question Professor Bodenheimer asks us is *not* "How is any particular instance of legal punishment to be justified?," but rather the more general question, "How, if at all, is punishment as a system, or general practice, or 'social institution' to be justified?" Every lawyer knows, simply in virtue of his training as a lawyer, how particular instances of punishment must be justified. In particular cases, jurists attack or defend, uphold or overrule sentences of punishment by appealing to the wording of statutes, to the relevant legal precedents, to evidence, and so on. Professor Bodenheimer's more general question is a far more difficult one. He asks us why we should ever punish anyone, why we should have the kind of criminal law and penal system we now have instead of some alternative system in which there is no such thing as punishment. This more difficult question

---

[4] I am using the expression "X is in Y's interest" in such a way that it does not entail "Y desires (wants, actively seeks, appreciates, etc.) X"; nor does it entail "Y knows (or believes) that X is good for him." I believe there is such a sense of the locution, and that it is a common and familiar sense. I am aware however that such a sense is badly in need of further clarification, but unfortunately that is too big a task to undertake here.

is not addressed to jurists and lawyers as such, but to legislators, political reformers, and political and legal philosophers.[5]

I am not going to make a detailed case for punishment. I have neither the empirical information nor the time for that. I will simply indicate in brief outline what kind of a case could be made by anyone who applied the justificatory principles stated above to punishment as I have defined it. Such a case would begin with an enumeration of all of the widespread and equally distributed benefits of the system of punishments. The case-maker would then ask his opponent to perform a series of experiments in his imagination, asking himself just what life would be like under each of the systems alternative to punishment, including no system at all. The case would then conclude with a comparison of the advantages and disadvantages of each alternative and a demonstration that the balance of advantages is with the system of punishments.

It seems to me that there are certain obvious advantages of a legal system which provides punishments. Under such a system, I know what the law forbids and what penalties it provides for disobedience, and thus I can plan my affairs accordingly. I can also anticipate or predict, with far greater accuracy than is possible under any other system, how others will behave toward me. Furthermore, the law informs me of the "price" I must pay for anti-social behavior, but in a sense leaves me free to decide in each case whether it is worth pay-

[5] The distinction between justifying a legal practice specified by a set of rules and justifying a particular action, which falls under the rules, obvious as it may seem, has not always been clearly recognized by writers concerned with the problem of justifying legal punishment; and failure to understand this distinction has caused much avoidable confusion. For a discussion of the logical basis of this distinction and its use in resolving the traditional controversies between utilitarians and retributivists, see John Rawl's very important article "Two Concepts of Rules" in *Philosophical Review*, LXIV (January, 1955), 3-32, and Anthony M. Quinton's equally important article, "Punishment," in *Analysis*, 14 (June, 1954), 133-42. The latter is reprinted in *Philosophy, Politics and Society* (1956), edited by Peter Laslett.

ing the price.⁶ Because the criminal law recognizes certain
excusing conditions, I can make my plans in perfect confidence that I will not, by accident, blunder my way into prison
and have my plans ruined. In short, the law maximizes the
effectiveness of my choices and decisions, helps me anticipate
the future and plan accordingly, diminishes anxiety and insecurity, and deters by threat private individuals who might
otherwise cause me great damage. Furthermore, I think a case
could easily be made that the law could not yield these benefits for me nearly so effectively without the system of punishment. Finally, and most importantly, the advantages I have
cited are advantages shared alike, or nearly alike, by all.

So far I have simply presented the outline of a *prima facie*
case for punishment. A conclusive argument would go further
and examine each of the possible alternatives to it. One alternative, of course, would be no system at all, no criminal
statutes, no courts, no prisons, nothing perhaps but governmental recommendations, admonitions, and exhortations urg-
ing people to be nice to one another. Such *ad hoc* pronouncements would be about as effective in controlling human
behavior as are presidential exhortations in controlling in-
flation. It would take very little argument, I am sure, to convince anyone (even a hardened criminal under the present
system) that life under such a "system" would indeed be "solitary, mean, nasty, brutish and short."

We can derive other alternatives to punishment simply by
dropping off, one at a time, each of the defining characteristics
of legal punishment mentioned above, that is, each of the
three salient features of my standard examples of punishment,
and we could then proceed to examine the institution which
would result from each exclusion. Suppose, for example, we
consider institutions which bear some superficial resemblance

⁶ For an ingenious interpretation of the criminal law as a kind of
"pricing system" designed to maximize the effectiveness of each individual's informed choice, see H. L. A. Hart's "Legal Responsibility and
Excuses," in *Determinism and Freedom in the Age of Modern Science*
(1958), pp. 81-103, edited by Sidney Hook.

to punishment, but differ radically from it in that they do not require that judicial inflictions of loss always be *for* something, i.e., that they be *requitals.* Under such systems, violation of the law would not be a necessary condition for the deprivation by governmental tribunal of some of the normal rights of citizenship. Professor Bodenheimer discusses two such alternatives to punishment, those which he calls "measures of social defense" and "treatment of offenders" (where "offenders" presumably is given a broader interpretation than "proven violators of the law"), and curiously, these are the only alternatives to punishment he mentions.

Neither the system of social defense nor the system of therapeutic treatment, as Professor Bodenheimer describes them, require that the infringement of a legal statute be a necessary condition for the operation of the system's machinery. That is to say that, unlike punishment, neither involves the notion of a requital for overt infraction of rules; and in this omission lies the chief failing of each. Under the system called "measures of social defense," I could not possibly be as confident as I am now that I will never end up in prison; I would suffer from considerable anxiety; and I would be unable to predict with confidence the consequences of my choices and decisions. Under the system of "therapeutic treatment," I would be subject to unpredictable restrictions of my freedom at the whim of some board of "experts" on moral health. Under both of these alternative systems, citizens would be subject to certain losses and deprivations, not as predictable consequences of their own deliberate behavior—that is, not as requitals—but simply because, in the opinion of certain governmental authorities, they have dangerous attitudes or character defects. It seems clear then that the system of punishments has certain obvious advantages over any alternative system of social control which does not require guilt in law as a necessary condition of its operation.

Most critics of the practice of punishment, however, have not proposed that a system be substituted for it in which restrictions and inconveniences can be inflicted on persons who have violated no law. Most liberal and humanitarian critics of punishment have proposed a much less drastic alternative to it, namely a system of requitals for law-breaking which lacks another of the essential features of punishment, the requirement that the requitals be unpleasant to the law-breaker. They have proposed that when (and only when) a person has violated a law, been tried according to due process and found guilty, he should be sent to some frankly therapeutic institution where, in the highest humanitarian spirit, the most advanced techniques of psychotherapy be utilized to rehabilitate him. The motives behind this proposal are laudably humane, but it takes very little consideration to discover that what is proposed is quite unworkable. Insofar as this proposed system is a genuine alternative to punishment, it suffers from one glaring disadvantage, and if it is patched up to avoid this disadvantage then it ceases to be a genuine alternative to the system of punishment. To see why this is so, we need only ask what would happen under this system to the offender who refuses to submit to therapy, runs away from the rehabilitation center, and continues his career of crime. Two answers are possible. Either the rehabilitation centers are made so very pleasant and attractive that no one would ever wish to escape them, or else legal force is used—the whole apparatus of armed guards, bars on the windows, and so on. In the former case, the system would have the fatal disadvantage of not only failing to deter crime, but of actually encouraging it; and in the latter case, it would differ in no essential respect from punishment.

I think that most of the humanitarian reformers who claim that punishment is obsolete do not really mean what they say. They really mean that many of the usual accompaniments of punishment—spite, cruelty, pointless moralizing, and so on —are obsolete, and in this I think they are right. Restriction on an offender's liberty is, generally speaking, an injury to him. Most modern penal reformers do not wish to eliminate this injury; they wish instead simply not to add insult to it. They recommend taking advantage of a prisoner's confinement by making every possible effort to rehabilitate him; but this would be a supplement to legal punishment, not a substitute for it.

It seems likely to me, then, that when punishment as a general practice is compared with the most plausible of its proposed alternatives, the balance of advantages is clearly on its side; but there is nothing in my remarks, I hope, which can be construed as a blanket apology for the status quo. While punishment as such is not obsolete, I am sure that many particular criminal statutes and judicial procedures are, and that many aspects of our penal system are badly in need of reform. All of these piecemeal reforms can be made, however, without doing away with any of the features which are essential to the system of legal punishment.

It remains to consider what kind of case can be made against legal punishment. The case for punishment can be made simply by citing its rather conspicuous advantages. Apparently the strongest argument against punishment—at least the only argument which Professor Bodenheimer seriously considers—is that punishment is somehow incompatible with a metaphysical theory called "determinism." I, for one, fail to understand how determinism can affect the issue one way or another. Determinism is the theory that all events, including the deliberations, choices, decisions, and actions of human beings, are the effects of previous determining causes, and thus are in principle, though not in fact, predictable. I do not know whether determinism is true or false. Indeed I do not even know what would count as evidence against it. But it seems clear to me that the benefits and advantages which I have cited as justification of the system of punishment are truly benefits and advantages whether or not determinism is true; and the disadvantages of alternative systems are truly disadvantages whether or not human behavior is in principle predictable. I conclude then that determinism has not the slightest tendency to impugn either the justice or the utility of legal punishment as a system of social control.

But why have so many writers thought otherwise? I think

the explanation, put very briefly, is as follows. In order for a person to be properly held responsible for some past action, it must be true of him that he was, in Professor Bodenheimer's words, the "true author" of that action. According to some writers, if determinism is true then this condition never holds, and consequently no one is ever really responsible or answerable for what he does. It follows then that in every single case of legal punishment, pain or loss is inflicted on a person who was not really responsible for what he did, and hence that all punishment is an abominable injustice.

I do not think that this argument against punishment will stand careful scrutiny. It does not follow from determinism that men are never the "true authors" of their deeds. It is a solid and unquestioned fact that sometimes men do things not because they have been tortured, coerced, hypnotized, blackmailed, or threatened, but simply because they wish to do those things. If determinism is true, there is a causal explanation for this fact, but it does not cease to be a fact simply because it can be explained. To say that a man is the "true author of his action" is not to deny that there were antecedent conditions sufficient to produce that action; rather it is to deny that there were antecedent sufficient conditions of a *certain sort* (conditions which included threats, coercion, irresistible impulses, neurotic compulsions, etc.[7]), or to deny that there were, at the time of his action, sufficient conditions for his action *which did not include his own intentions or wishes in the matter*,[8] or both.

I conclude then that the justification of legal punishment as a general practice is to be found in the benefits it yields directly or indirectly, not just for a specially privileged group, but by and large, for all of us equally; and that the theory

[7] The point of denying that such conditions as these were among the causes of his action is to show that his action was "voluntary" in the sense of *avoidable*.

[8] The point of denying that the causes of his action did *not* include his own intentions or wishes in the matter, is to show that his action was "voluntary" in the sense of *intentional* or *non-accidental*.

of determinism is no real threat to it. Determinism is not incompatible with punishment as such, but it is incompatible with self-righteous anger,[9] hatred, and cruelty toward the criminal. But then, self-righteousness, hatred, and cruelty are equally incompatible with indeterminism or any other theory. In a state of civilized society, I think it is safe to say, these attitudes and emotions *are* obsolete.

[9] This is to be distinguished from so-called "moral indignation." The distinction is not at all easy to make, but I would think that in order for an attitude toward a criminal to qualify as "moral indignation" at least the following conditions must hold: (1) It must be free of all elements of personal prejudice, spite, and malice; (2) it must be directed at the criminal not simply because of the harmful effects of his crime but because of the defects of character manifested in the doing of the crime; (3) it must be "universalizable" in the sense that the "indignant" person would be prepared to hold exactly the same attitude toward any person, including himself, who manifested the same character defects in any action criminal or not; (4) it should not be an expression of the primitive urge to hurt in retaliation for hurt nor of any wish that its object suffer pain for its own sake.

It is an open question (and indeed, a psychological question beyond my competence to investigate) whether an attitude satisfying these conditions could properly be described as *anger* at all. My suspicion is that such an attitude would be more "sorrowful" than "angry."

PART THREE

RESPONSIBILITY IN MODERN GOVERNMENT

POLITICAL RESPONSIBILITY IN A DEMOCRACY

F. H. KNIGHT

MY TOPIC I take to be the responsibility of political officials to "the people," in a democratic state. Responsibility is a field too vast for an attempt at mapping in any detail on this occasion; but an audience of political and legal philosophers should tolerate a brief consideration of verbal usage and some much needed definition of terms. We regularly say that a cause is "responsible" for its effects. I mention this usage only to stress the wide coverage of the word and to begin narrowing it down. The responsibility which concerns us here is of course human responsibility in a free society. It is exercised in a two-fold framework of positive causality. One kind is called "scientific," the other "historical." Both relate to human phenomena, chiefly social and cultural and in some sense mental, and hence the methodology differs notably from that dealing with non-human nature. Insofar as the social sciences, including history, deal with mind, their data are not secured through direct sense-observation; hence they are not literally empirical, and, in particular, experimentation has little place. As the use of responsibility for positive causality illustrates, we lack the terms needed to distinguish between radically different concepts, beginning with "observation," and "fact." A first point needing emphasis is the limitations of the knowledge that would be required for intelligent social action —the basic practical problem to be explored. It is notoriously difficult to learn from history, and while the limitations of the social sciences in the stricter sense, for prediction or the guidance of action, invite discussion, it cannot be undertaken here.

In its primary meaning, responsibility is a moral concept. The personnel of government are, logically speaking, the agents of a society as a whole, and the major premise for discussing social action is that an agent ought to be responsible to his principal as, indeed, the word "agent" implies in this case. He ought to act exclusively in the interest of the latter; and another two-fold axiom of a free society is that the individual is in general the best judge of his own values, hence his judgment ought to be final, unless there is an obviously conclusive reason to the contrary. He must be "responsible" for himself, his own conduct; but more fundamentally, responsibility is roughly equivalent to moral obligation, and every member of any human society bears the general responsibility, or obligation, to obey its laws. Since for free men moral responsibility does not suffice, society has organs or agents for "enforcing" the laws, and its first practical task is that of "holding" these agents responsible to itself as a collective principal. Accordingly, our discussion must give some attention to the meaning of law—its several meanings. The laws in question define "standards," specifically of conduct, what is "right" or what men "ought" to do. Thus they present a categorical contrast with descriptive laws, of science or history.

Law is first of all the product of history, and a glance at primitive or "early" law seems in order. As the words placed within quotes above indicate, law itself, which defines responsibilities, is a moral concept. Primitively, it was essentially moral; its content was given by the *mores,* those usages which men felt as imperative. The laws of human society are distinguished by this characteristic. There had "always" been laws in the descriptive sense, before there were men, or life; law is pervasive in nature. But they were "obeyed" (as we say, lacking a passive verb for conformity) without compulsion, automatically; the first men doubtless obeyed laws somewhat as M. Jourdain had been talking prose since childhood, without knowing that he had. Compulsion became necessary because man as we know him, as he evolved in and out of some form of animal society, is naturally a law-breaking animal. He is a social animal—both by necessity and by choice—but as having to be "made" to obey law, he is more distinctively "the" antisocial social animal. This trait seems to go with awareness of the laws, which must have developed along with various urges to non-conformity. Somehow he became both selfish and romantic as he became more "rational."

We know little indeed—and doubtless never can know much —about human beginnings. But we can be sure that somewhere along the course of prehuman evolution an "emergence" occurred, in which the instinctive basis of previous behavior was largely replaced by "culture," in the anthropological meaning. The patterns ceased to be fixed and transmitted by biological inheritance through the "gene" mechanism, which gave place, in the main, to social inheritance through imitation of their elders by the oncoming generation. "Somehow," the instincts of the evolving hominid were attenuated into vague "drives," without specific content, which was learned, as indicated. The laws may have still been as purely descriptive as before, their functioning as automatic and unconscious, but now they were a matter of "conditioning." In any case, we must recognize another emergence (whatever was the order in time) when men, or proto-men, became aware of the laws, and began to feel them as compulsive. The whole two-fold transition, we may guess, was connected with the acquisition of speech, and language is now the main example of nearly pure cultural phenomena. However, the mental life mediated by speech is more conspicuously emotional than cognitive or intellectual, and what is instrumentally rational has had progressively less and less relation to the biological ends of survival and increase. In the familiar phrase of David Hume, reason is the slave of the passions, and these are not in the main biologically oriented. The conditions of life set limits to their vagaries, but the direct objectives are often squarely opposed. Civilized men often use their intelligence to trick their fellows and to circumvent nature, and not only in such matters as diet and sex, but in the whole "higher life." Their thinking is centered on *quality* of *experience,* more or less in conflict with physical "quantity of life." The body and its processes are treated as instrumental to the "goodness" of life, an inversion of what must have been the original relation of mind to body. And their ideas of the good, as manifested in conduct, including speech, are diverse and strange, beyond the possibility of any simple analysis.

As we view it in our own society, law, in the narrow meaning, "jural" law, is an area within a much broader category of imperatives for conduct. It is that part of "moral" law which is formally enforced by prescribed penalties for infraction, administered by designated social organs or agents. The moral law in turn is a vague intermediate realm between the jural law and a heterogeneous collection of proprieties, usages, or customs. It is intermediate as to compulsiveness and the social sanctions enforcing it. At the opposite extreme from the jural laws are those which are almost purely cultural, hardly present to consciousness; for illustration, again, the laws of the language of a community. Above these, but still below moral laws, is the area of "manners," laws which need no explicit enforcement because people are anxious to conform. They are said to be "enforced" by such psychological traits as liking the approval of one's fellows and disliking or fearing the opposite. An especially important sanction is ridicule. Somewhere back in pre-history (long before speech?) men acquired laughter and weeping and the former largely displaced the anger reaction as a social compulsion. (Humor is commonly cruel or obscene or both; these traits are not found in animals; and both are interesting as norms overlapping aesthetics and morals.)

A conspicuous feature of culture history is change through "drift," which tends to diversity, as illustrated by the multiplication of languages. Human nature evolved through the ages in small-scale "tribal" society, in a constant state of actual or potential hostility; and the problems of our society are largely due to the vast size of the units. A modern state is far too large for primary acquaintance and hence for primitive morality to function effectively. Thus it tends to sub-divide along spatial or more artificial lines into more or less antagonistic sub-groups. Man is naturally a partisan and a gangster, expressing at once the social and anti-social interest. Human society differs from that of animals in its conflicts of interest between individuals and component groups, and between both and the needs of the larger unit. The conflicts that create serious problems occur mostly between groups, from the family up to the national state, the locus of the rivalries that are now most menacing to freedom, to civilization, and to life.

Certain features of early law will help to define by contrast the situation and problems of modern democracy. First of all, the laws were simply "there"; there was no thought of changing them, they were "sacred." They had originated in commands of supernatural powers, and these would punish infractions, inflicting penalties on the society which tolerated disobedience as well as the guilty individual. Yet human agents were concerned with law enforcement; we should think of these as agents of society, but primitive men viewed them as agents of the "supernaturals." For obscure reasons, the agents were commonly of two kinds, religious and secular. Both were thought to derive their position from the same divine source, but the secular power has been less strictly custombound; this doubtless because its primary function was leadership in war, or the hunt, activities not reducible to a set routine. Ostensibly, the authorities would not make law at all, but merely declared and executed the sacred law. However, application of law to cases inevitably involves some change. We may think of the "medieval" social order, which was highly primitive in essentials, notably the rigid formalism of the law; pleading was by rote, and a verbal slip would forfeit a case. Primitive law was not primarily a law of personal relations so much as relations between the tribe and the spiritual powers it recognized. Insofar as it had to do with the former, it was a law of tort rather than of crime. The latter was "sin," its main content religious—sacrilege, or blasphemy, or heresy. A puzzling but vital feature of a religiously sanctioned social order is that it prescribes elaborate dogmas to be "believed," including myths purporting to explain the origin of things and the course of history. Myths took the place of science and authentic history in liberal thought.

The laws, being "static," would naturally be known to all —at least they specified an authority to answer any possible questions; hence the responsibility of men was purely moral. The alternatives of choice were simply to conform and obey, or to defy admitted right and duty. There were no problems of conduct, in the proper "intellectual" meaning, even for the enforcing authorities; the law fixed the procedure for dealing with cases, the punishment for crimes and compensation for torts.

All this was practically inverted by the vast culture revolution which replaced medievalism with modern liberalism. Responsibility for conformity and obedience gave place to those of Freedom, sacred and hence static norms to the idea and ideal of Progress, not automatic, but to be achieved and directed by intelligence. Freedom and Progress are aspects of the same thing, since freedom is "for" improvement and progress is to result from freedom. The substance of freedom is that each person is by right the final judge of his own values, which does *not* mean self-interest implying "selfishness," or any opprobrious connotation, but only that freedom is in general "better" than dictation by authority. This basic assumption is antithetical to "original sin." Freedom to satisfy personal desires is axiomatically limited by the equal freedom of all; i.e., the ethics of free association based on mutual agreement upon its terms. In fact, practically no individualist has failed to recognize various needs for legal compulsion. The classical economists in particular had much to say about taxation and functions of government in addition to policing market freedom to prevent force and fraud.

The Liberal Revolution took place in two stages. First, the Renaissance and Reformation displaced the Church by "the state" as the supreme authority over thinking and conduct. But as this meant the new states, absolute monarchies under dynasties ruling by divine-right, the change hardly altered essentials. It was important indirectly, because military competition forced the new governments to accept and encourage the development of trade and science, already under way, as sources of new wealth, the sinews of war, science functioning as the basis of rational and progressive technology. But western culture also gave birth to a new interest in knowledge for its own sake, hence in freedom to seek and publish new knowledge. This was the substantive achievement of the "Copernican Revolution," whose final and basic result was the liberation of the mind from traditionalism and dictation by state or church. Thus "truth," to be judged by weighing evidence, came to be the primary human obligation or responsibility, replacing eternal and immutable truth revealed once for all, and "interpreted" by an absolute authority. Truth of course includes "right," (truth about right) particularly as embodied in laws. (Truth originally meant loyalty—the German *Treue*.)

The second and directly more important stage of the revolution took place in the age of the Enlightenment and after, only a few generations ago. Its primary social achievement was the democratization of monarchic government. But this was inseparably connected with economic liberation ("laissez faire"), the freeing from state control of the "economic order" operating through free exchange of goods and services at prices fixed in free "competitive" markets—with freedom of enterprise. From this time forth, the regulation of this mechanism, or its eventual replacement in particular functions by political agencies, has been the major responsibility and task of society, acting through law and government. Notable is the restriction to a defined area of "right" conduct, renouncing the effort to define intellectual truth or to dictate belief, in any field of judgment.

Liberal democracy introduced for the first time in history genuinely "social" problems (responsibilities), problems to be dealt with by society as a whole, with formally equal participation by all normal adults as citizens. In a theoretically ideal democracy, there would be no literally compulsory law or government, no relation of ruled to rulers; rule would be purely advisory. The laws would be simply rules fixing the terms of association, agreed upon through free discussion by those who are to live under them, and they would be obeyed without punitive enforcement. Political organization would at most register and publish such rules. This, be it noted, applies to the citizens, i.e., outside the family. For "infants," freedom and responsibility have no meaning; these and the "helpless," regardless of age, are dependents and some authority must be responsible for them. Family organization can only be mentioned, as vitally important in creating responsibilities for society as a whole, through failure to meet those that might ideally belong to it. The family is the minimum real social unit; "familism" is a more correctly descriptive name than "individualism" for the principle of liberal society.

Government exercising compulsion is necessary, first, because men will not freely agree on what the laws are, what conduct they require, and, secondly, will not always conform to laws recognized as right, or the best possible under the circumstances; hence "moral" laws are not enough. Thirdly and more important, they will still less agree on what the laws "ought" to be, and the fact and ideal of progress require agreement in that field also. Actually, the fact of changing laws makes conformity to law much harder, since no one can know at all accurately what is the law in problematic situations that constantly arise. The law must always be what somebody in particular says it is, which is a task for some "authority," to be designated by the law itself. This is far more the case under changing conditions, apart from the necessity of an authority to decide the details of what the law ought to be, and to "legislate." Much solemn nonsense has been published about government of laws "and not" by men, and also about government by "the people." It must always be both; if all agreed about the laws, government would not be necessary; at best rule is "by" a majority, "of" minorities, and even this ideal cannot be very closely approximated in reality. There must be a presumption in favor of law against authority, within limits, and when there is no sufficient reason to the contrary—as there is a presumption in favor of maximizing liberty against law, beyond what is necessary, and with the same qualification.

The general fact which underlies the problem of governmental responsibility is that a human group—at least one of appreciable size—can act as a group only through some individual as its agent. Occasionally the agent may be a very small group agreeing directly, but normally within any ruling group the same situation arises as in the society itself. In "political" politics, the agents are called "representatives"; in any case they exercise a *delegated* authority. The task of the politico-legal organization is to define the scope of the responsibility delegated and "hold" its agencies to action within that area— as far that is, as purely moral obligation and their own judgment will not suffice, and the machinery itself will work only about as far as it is backed up by "moral" pressure. The problem can only be sketched here in general terms, ignoring more concrete matters such as criminal law, family law, and business law. The law directly in question is constitutional and public law, which is chiefly procedural, in contrast with substantive law, civil or criminal. In legal terminology it is not a law of agency, which deals with the responsibility of a principal for the acts of this agent, but the logical converse, the relation of a fiduciary or trustee. Technically it is not that either, though it is immediately defined by courts, as a matter of constitutionality. As elsewhere, there can be no clear line between questions as to what the law is and what it ought to be; whoever decides cases must make constitutional law also, within limits that cannot be defined by a formula. (This is true even under the "fixed" law of primitive conditions.) I pass over constitutional legislation by the people, under whatever amending procedure is provided, or ultimately through mass disobedience or insurrection and civil war. In British legal history, under the system of case or court-made law and no written constitution, laws have often been changed by being ignored, until a crucial case has forced formal legislative action. In such cases the fiction is likely to prevail that the action states the real law at the time, the change having been effected by historical, i.e., "moral" forces.

The prior and really primary task of democratic political machinery is to organize discussion and so to establish the requisite agreement as to what the law ought to be—what changes ought to be made. It then publicly registers the result, usually in terms of general and rather vague objectives, leaving details to the discretion of the sequence of social agents who make and apply the stated laws. Such responsible discretion involves partly a factual judgment of what public opinion demands (or will "stand for"), partly an ethical judgment on what is really better or worse for the society. The citizens themselves vote on a vague mixed judgment of the better policy with appraisal of personalities to be trusted for discretion as to competence and moral dependability. In our own politics, the main provision for holding the agents or representatives responsible is a limited term of office, with eventual but rarely used impeachment or prosecution for criminal malfeasance or breach of trust. The wish of an office-holder to continue in office may be absent, and anyhow may be supplemented by appeal to his (moral) loyalty to his party or other former supporters. In any case, the principle of agency law applies: the principal is responsible for the acts of the agent, whom he appoints to act on his behalf under delegated authority.

The primary responsibility of the people—the principal in this situation—is to reach through discussion a reasonable agreement on the commission given to their agents, their powers and duties—i.e., to establish a fairly definite public opinion. (An *opinion* on the "better" social policy; decision by a majority in terms of special or factional interests is the chief menace to democracy, but that form of irresponsibility cannot be elaborated here.) If an effective public opinion exists, there is relatively little likelihood of a governing personnel acting very far contrary to it, regardless of constitutional form and legal powers. A dictator cannot rule by force—except as, unhappily, force can be used to "create" a public "will" adverse to the real interests of his subjects. Such coercion is primarily deception, and rests on the willingness of human nature to be deceived along certain lines, by appeal to well-known emotions. It is stupid to condemn freely chosen agents for carrying out their commission, or doing what they must do to be elected, even for making promises they know are deceptive—short of legal fraud. But this is what "the people" typically do, exhibiting the attitude which in large measure underlies their being misled. The same phenomena appear in business relations as in politics, with similar consequences.

To be stressed is unity of *opinion* about what is *desirable*. Social problems arise out of conflicts of "interests," which may be either subjective desires—the "mere tastes" about which there is no argument—or value judgments. In either case, they must be discussed in terms of judgments treated as objective. Desires can only be asserted, which will only intensify the conflict and never tend towards agreement. Judgments as to what is socially better or worse, as grounds for legal change, look to the future, taking account not only of living dependents incapable of responsibility, but also of the yet unborn— ideally to the future of civilization. The public interest is not limited to reconciling, by compromise or otherwise, interests of either sort advanced by living responsible citizens. The responsibility laid on the citizens of a democracy—historically quite recently and suddenly—is indeed an onerous one. It begins logically with delimiting the area of conduct to be subject to enforced law, as distinct from that in which more literal freedom is to prevail, subject only to "moral" compulsion with its informal sanctions. This is hardly discussed explicitly, being decided by positive legislation in the former sphere. All must be done by selecting and "commissioning" agents, as indicated; it involves electing primary agents part of whose commission is to appoint others in more detailed roles.

A look at actual "politics" suggests that it is contrary to human nature seriously to try to use analytical and critical intelligence in any major part of the task. Apart from man's inherent romanticism and intellectual laziness, this may be explained in part by the historical novelty of the situation, and in part it is perhaps due to sub-conscious recognition of the forbidding magnitude of the responsibility itself, which a little analysis will bring out. The knowledge required for intelligent social action, on which agreement must be reached, is to a very limited extent available, or even possible to achieve. It covers most of the recognized fields of intellectual inquiry, beginning—or ending—with the "theory of knowledge" itself, since truth, as a problem, means new truth, and is a matter of valid methods for the pursuit and establishment of truth. In this field, men need to know what can be done— politics is the art of the possible—and then what ought to be done. The "how" of action is less important at this time, since existing democratic machinery is fairly adequate, if wisely used for solving the other two problems. Most immediately in point for the first task are the various "social sciences" (so-called) dealing with the nature of man and of society, rather especially psychology and history, and particularly the history of culture. Their role is to *predict* the course of events, as it would be in the absence of action, and the consequences of any proposed action. Their *limitations* cannot be considered in any detail here, but need emphasis since one of the worst evils is that people expect too much. That is chiefly because of romantic and conceited notions of what can reasonably be expected—due less to "honest" ignorance or error than to "prejudice." Wishful-thinking, especially "moralizing," is preferred to a serious effort to be critically intelligent. In the natural sciences, all this does relatively little damage, because there manipulative and visual tests "force" agreement, about as far and as fast as this is socially necessary.

These last remarks apply even more to the second major field of knowledge: what ought to be done, the knowledge of objective values or ideals. Here the methodology contrasts even more sharply with that of the natural sciences. What is required is agreement on nothing less than the meaning of social progress, finally the progress of civilization as such. That serious intellectual discussion of the problems is not natural to man is attested on the one hand by the manifest absurdity of most of what passes for "argument" in politics—both "political politics" and the essentially similar politics of organizations other than the state, notably "business" and the relations of government to business, and social relations at large. On the other hand, one who is rather an outsider may dare to mention the "mess" made of the discussion of values— specifically moral values—when it is explicitly undertaken by the specialists who should furnish intellectual leadership: the ethical philosophers. Yet one thing we do know about the nature of the world and of man: they are such that it is certainly better not to act unless it can be done in a fairly intelligent way; the chances are overwhelming that the results of acting at random or on impulse will on balance be bad—and acting on false knowledge or "prejudice" is still worse. But one or the other is typical of the common man, while the moral philosophers multiply controversy over "theories," which also are largely absurd. They rather typically rule out all discussion, either by an appeal to mystical intuition, or by propounding a scientistic-mechanistic view of man, or, more commonly, by contending that value judgments are "nothing but" subjective individual desires, emotions with no cognitive basis or content. Those who attempt to discuss values as values typically follow ancient tradition, formed in pre-liberal society; they hardly come to grips with the problems of modern democracy.

In particular, they talk nonsense about the major internal problem (I pass over international relations) which is the right role of legal compulsion in economic relations. This obviously calls for *comparing* the functioning of the business order with that of democratic politics, and both with what is ideally desirable and possible. The value theorists shirk the responsibility of understanding the economic order, in theory or as it works in reality, and rarely indeed seriously try to understand both systems of organization. Politico-legal action may be needed in order either to establish and maintain market freedom or to replace this with political agencies where such action can be counted upon to yield socially better results. It should not cause surprise that lucubration about values in the abstract, building on ancient tradition, sheds little light on current problems arising out of freedom, or even that it tends more to promote controversy than to establish agreement among the disputants themselves.

The basic "fault" of human nature is reluctance to assume *intellectual* responsibility—specifically in the newest problem field, factual knowledge about men and society, and critical judgment of social values and institutions. The root of it is confusion of personal or small-group interests with critically formed opinions about objective rights and right. At long last, quite recently in history, men have learned—been forced to admit—that truth about nature is not given once for all, sacred, and hence eternal and immutable, but is to be responsibly pursued and progressively achieved. This has come hard, as the names of Galileo and Darwin suggest—and that of Freud could be added, pointing to error in the opposite direction, and to the enormously greater difficulty of being objective where knowledge of man is in question. Having learned, at long last, that natural events are different from human choices, many "best minds" have concluded that these must be like natural events, their problems to be solved by the "scientific method." What men most need still to learn about themselves is their propensity to make any strong wish a conviction of right, and conversely that any opinion naturally becomes an interest, to be promoted rather than critically examined or impartially discussed. The obvious need for agreement commonly takes the form that others ought to agree with "me," and their failure to do so is imputed to some unworthy motive. Man is still animistic and moralistic— as shown by the permeation of our language of discussion by these meanings, underlying superposed descriptive connotations, as mentioned earlier.

Thus what should be discussion turns into name-calling.

An outstanding weakness of free society is that liberals, as idealists, tend romantically to over-stress Freedom, neglecting the inevitable role of tradition and authority as the basis of any social order. But uncritical idealism tends toward dogmatism and authoritarianism as the alternative to anarchy and chaos. So, Freedom finds expression less in discussion than in a free-for-all contest in persuasion, which, contrary to common usage, is a subtle and insidious form of force. The first step, naturally, is competitive "screaming" to get attention. Conspicuous among the passions which intelligence is used to serve is rivalry, the predilection for a contest, with victory as the *summum bonum*. Both politics and business, and in large part other social relations, are organized in terms of "competition," which has no (instrumentally) rational place, since every victory is cancelled by a defeat. This motive, however, is not in itself evil. It is the spirit of play, and it is a good thing, within limits, to convert work into play, which is itself good, under certain conditions. It should be a "good game," regulated by "sportsmanship" which, along with workmanship, is a supreme ethical value for a free society. And where substantive values are at stake, as in the serious affairs of politics and business (and science and culture) they must be "valid" values, and must be given precedence over victory as the end. Paradoxically, a serious objective destroys the play spirit, and the combination is difficult; but a certain "right" kind and amount of the latter may be a spur to the pursuit of human excellence.

Ubiquity of the agency relation is a fundamental feature of free society, along with Freedom-and-Progress. The progressive view of knowledge as ever subject to increase and corrective revision results in the specialization of its pursuit. One consequence of this, in turn, is that specialists or "experts" are everywhere and constantly making decisions for others or giving them advice. (Another consequence is that "education" becomes a problem, which it hardly is in primitive society—

but that must be passed over here.) Counselling involves an agency relation, with vast responsibilities, and creates extensive responsibility for society, i.e., for law and government. A simple illustration is the relation between doctor and patient. The doctor is an agent of the patient, but has *power* over him—in this case power of life-and-death. The power is limited by various social devices, but finally and chiefly by moral responsibility. In over-simple terms, but essentially, the freedom possible to the patient is that of choosing his doctor, and of terminating the relation at will—if he can! We cannot here go into details; the point is that under modern conditions freedom is largely that of choosing agents, of deputizing actual decision-making. This fact makes the control of one's conduct in so far indirect, and severely limited. The content of delegated power can be defined with various degrees of precision, but even a simple errand involves some amount of discretion. Usually, the agent has more or less "authority" over the end as well as the means. For the patient, the end is "health" but his first need for the doctor is to tell him whether or not he is sick and therapy is needed, or can do any good. The main regulative force in free society is competition between principals seeking agents and especially between would-be agents seeking principals to advise; more conspicuously the latter, for reasons too complex to recount here.

The situation is vastly complicated when an agent represents a group, as its members will normally have different interests and opinions about the group interest. In the free economy, the "entrepreneur," as final decision-maker, is the agent at once of consumers and of those who furnish the labor and property-services employed. He must have considerable power, but this he gets and keeps by satisfying all parties "better" in their judgment, than competitors for the role. Their freedom is that of dealing with one or another of the latter. In a special sense the entrepreneur is "responsible" to his consumers, whose wants he must not only satisfy but anticipate in advance, at great cost and with great risk of loss. As things naturally work out, he partly "makes" the wants as to details—but all in open competition, a fact usually ignored by those who cry out against the "power" of advertising and salesmanship. Even the patient's selection of a doctor is largely ruled by market competition, more or less formally free. Politics is a similar competition for the agency role, so set-up as largely to suppress the price factor—which the medical profession also does, and business managers attempt, as conditions permit.

The last important point to be stressed is that the choice of an agent can rarely be very "rational." This is axiomatic insofar as real power is delegated. To choose a doctor intelligently, the patient would need to know extant medical science—hence would not need a doctor—and in addition know both the technical and moral qualifications of the available candidates (not to mention the matter of price, and considering only knowledge, apart from manual skill).

The "moral" of our tale is two-fold. First, discontent is largely due to expecting too much, in particular from the economic order, and then from the political order as an agency for remedying its defects, real or supposed. This is connected, secondly, with shirking individual responsibility to understand the possibilities and choose intelligently among alternatives. Instead, people blame their agents for the dissatisfaction they experience. In politics, in particular, they virtually ask for disappointment, by compelling those who compete for positions of leadership to promise more than can be performed, in order to be chosen. Citizenship in a free society involves new and heavy *intellectual* responsibility; or, more accurately, moral responsibility has largely taken the new form of an obligation to act as intelligently as one can, to increase intelligence in the world, and then to be satisfied with the progress reasonably to be expected in view of the limitations of knowledge and insight, and of other conditions set by nature and human nature of the time and place. This responsibility contrasts greatly with that imposed on men by earlier forms of society, in which choices are "purely" moral. With the emergence of a free society, mankind has undergone a second and greater "fall" from innocence into responsibility. This new status has vastly increased the difficulty of conforming to existing standards by agreement, and added the vastly greater one of constantly raising the standards and embodying them in new laws. The former task was theoretically possible, the new one is not; there can be no final solution of social problems, for each step forward always creates new openings for advance. The notion of "perfection," meaningful under "static" conditions and ideals, is now absurd and must be given up in favor of achievable progress. To reach reasonable agreement on the meaning of the good as the better, not of perfection, and to co-operate in promoting the advance of civilization is the responsibility of man in our age.

XII

THE DILEMMA OF ADMINISTRATIVE
RESPONSIBILITY

CARL J. FRIEDRICH

A MONG THE SPHERES within which the problem of responsibility is of primary importance, administration ranks high. No large-scale administration, no rationalized bureaucracy, whether governmental or non-governmental, is possible, without making the staff members responsible *for* their work, and *to* their superiors. Eventually that means under democratic constitutional conditions the general public or one of its numerous subdivisions, such as shareholders, members of churches, trade unions, and the host of other organizations which employ a staff. If "to be responsible" means to be in the habit of acting in such a way that one can *answer* (*respondere*) for one's acts and omissions, then every official or employee has to be responsible *for* his work *to* someone who has engaged him. Responsibility seems to be a condition *sine qua non* of workable administration, an ineluctable quality of all administrative personnel. These bare and elementary statements, self-evident as they seem, raise some very difficult questions, however, for which the answer is not easy to give; an attempt will be made here to adumbrate several lines of approach.

The key difficulty arises in conjunction with the ground upon which possible answers might be based, if the administrator is challenged to explain his actions. This answer is needed, even if no challenge occurs, because the relationship between A and B involving responsibility of B toward A presumably contains the potentiality of such challenges. Hence responsible conduct is rational conduct in the sense that it is

189

capable of reasoned elaboration. Consequently, responsible
conduct is closely linked to the problems of authority.[1] Whenever B is responsible to A, the presumption is that A has conferred upon B discretion to act upon certain issues, to decide
them on A's behalf, i.e., to choose between several available
alternatives or to discover a new one, not arbitrarily, but in
accordance with what the situation requires.

"What the situation requires," is the decisive stipulation
which raises the key difficulties. For an understanding of the
requirements of the situation may call for expertise, for technical knowledge which may be possessed only by a professional. Responsibility thus has two facets, two aspects which
may be called the *personal* and the *functional,* respectively.
The personal aspect is related to what the person or persons
to whom the respondent is responsible desire or prefer. Such
preferences may be explicitly stated in commands, orders, or
suggestions. They may also be anticipated by the respondent,
as he is influenced by the persons to whom he is responsible.
In this personal perspective, a responsible official is one who
responds to what is required of him. If his superior asks that
he accomplish a given task, he will do all that is needed to
fulfill it. In many situations of administrative activity this
simple carrying out is all that matters; both the principal and
the agent, the superior and his subordinate, are aware of what
are the technical requirements, and so there can be no problem.

It is, however, a common occurrence in all situations calling
for communication between persons, that misunderstandings
arise. The superior may have wanted something else than the
subordinate understood him to demand. Or he may have
failed to communicate what he wanted for various reasons.
In such situations, the responsible person will use his judgment. When he recognizes that the request or purpose makes
no sense, he will act differently from what the instruction
seems to demand. But his action will be responsible only if

[1] Cf. the author's paper on "Authority, Reason and Discretion" in
Nomos I (1958), pp. 28ff.

the respondent can justify what he has done, that is, when he can answer any query that his superior may address to him in the circumstances. Even if it then develops that what he has done is not what the superior wanted, the reasonable superior will accept such an answer. He will not say (or think) that his subordinate is an irresponsible person. In all these and related siutations, the responsibility is therefore a personal one.

This personal responsibility is transcended, however, in those situations wherein the respondent has a technical knowledge which is not at the disposal of the principal. Some years ago, I wrote of this aspect in the following way:

Administrative officials seeking to apply scientific "standards" have to account for their actions in terms of a somewhat rationalized and previously established set of hypotheses. Any deviation from these hypotheses will be subjected to thorough scrutiny by their colleagues in what is known as the "fellowship of science." [2]

In situations of this type the responsible official is guided by the function which he fulfills. As the scope of functions of modern governmental administration has widened, the difficulty of securing that kind of responsibility has become increasingly urgent. A vast number of technicians of every variety, engineers, economists, agronomists, medical and natural scientists are continually confronted with situations which require the highest degree of technical skill and knowledge. Often, the lives and welfare of thousands of people depend upon the effective employment of such skills and knowledge. Unless a sense of responsibility to these higher standards is assiduously cultivated in an administrative staff, breakdowns in operation are unavoidable.

This sense of responsibility is, properly speaking, a sense of workmanship or craftsmanship. According to Veblen, who gave considerable prominence to this "instinct of workmanship" in his poignant analysis of industrial life and technical civilization, it is a "sense of merit and demerit with respect

[2] "Public Policy and the Nature of Administrative Responsibility" in *Public Policy,* I (1940), 31ff.

to the material furtherance or hindrance of life." He added
that "the proximate aim of all industrial improvement has
been the better performance of some workmanlike task." [3]
To be sure, Veblen thought mostly of the worker in an industrial plant, or on a farm, but the notion is relevant to any
situation in which special technical knowledge is required for
the effective carrying out of a given function. In industrial
organizations it becomes increasingly important as persons
rise in the hierarchy of organization. At the top, although
there exists a general responsibility to the shareholders, this
responsibility cannot be made effective by following their
wishes, except for the maximization of profits and the growth
of the enterprise. Only a marked sense of workmanship, and
an appreciation of the standards of first-rate performance can
render the executives of such organizations responsible. Chester I. Barnard, in a well-known study, wrote some years ago:

Executive responsibility, then, is that capacity of leaders by which,
reflecting attitudes, ideals, hopes, derived largely from without
themselves, they are compelled to bind the wills of men to the
accomplishment of purposes beyond their immediate ends.[4]

This statement focuses upon very general notions of goals
rather than the technical knowledge of a particular field of
activity, such as the manufacture and sale of a particular commodity, but it implies the capacity to lead an organization—
a particular kind of technical knowledge which relatively few
men acquire. For a general theory what is important is the
exclusiveness of the knowledge and workmanship of the respondent as it transcends the competence of the principal in
numerous relationships of power, rule, and influence.

For this gulf of technical knowledge which separates the
professional from the layman causes the most serious conflicts

[3] Thorstein Veblen, *The Instinct of Workmanship and the State of the
Industrial Arts* (1914). Cf. also chap. VI, "Responsibility and the Sense of
Workmanship" in *The New Image of the Common Man* (1942, 1951) by
the author.

[4] Chester I. Bernard, *The Functions of the Executive* (1938), p. 283.

arising in the field of administrative responsibility. They are most serious in the government service, because the prevailing tendency to stress the *will* of the principal, be it the people or its representatives, creates an irresolvable conflict. Only an approach which will bridge the gap between the personal and the functional aspect of responsibility can show a way out of these difficulties. But before we take up this line of reasoning, it may be well to deal with a related point. There is a fairly general belief still widely held that the public and parliamentary bodies could, on a basis of personal responsibility, secure the required conduct on the part of officials. Now there can be no question that a good deal more could be done than is actually done. Congressional committees continue to play a considerable role in bringing about a measure of administrative responsibility.[5] But the delegation of broad discretionary powers is spreading all the while. More than twenty years ago, the Committee on Ministerial Powers in Britain issued a report which gave a good deal of attention to the increased use of a clause, known as the "Henry VIII clause" which empowers the appropriate minister "to modify the provisions of an Act he is called upon to administer so far as may appear to him necessary for the purpose of bringing the Act into operation."[6] Both in Britain and in the United States, the cry has gone up about irresponsible bureaucracy, and eventually a law dean rather over-dramatized the situation by proclaiming "the passing of parliament" and the impending arrival of dictatorship.[7] The trend is universal, and

[5] Note particularly the work of the special Committee on Government Operations which has looked into many situations where irresponsible conduct was spreading; its *Reports* are a veritable mine of specific detailed information for the student of administration, and of the problem of how to make the government service more responsible.

[6] Committee on Ministers Powers, *Report* (1936) Cmd. 4060, p. 61. There they said: "We consider that the Henry VIII clause is a political instrument which must occasionally be used."

[7] G. W. Keeton, *The Passing of Parliament* (1952), esp. chap. VI, Cf. also Lord Hewart's *The New Despotism* and W. A. Robson's well-reasoned answer in *Justice and Administrative Law* (1928; 3d ed., 1951).

the only remedy is in terms of reinforcing the technical standards. John Gaus once wrote:

The responsibility of the civil servant to the standards of his profession, in so far as those standards make for the public interest, may be given official recognition. . . . Certainly in the system of government which is now emerging, one important kind of responsibility will be that which the individual civil servant recognizes as due to the standards and ideals of his profession. This is his "inner check." [8]

More than twenty years have passed since then, and the evolution of governmental and other bureaucracies has certainly taken place along these lines. Everywhere the professionalization of administrative work has gone forward, until today a "science of public administration," complete with research institutes, international congresses, and programs in all major universities clinches the argument about the "inner check" which must reinforce the crumbling institution of parliamentary responsibility.

These standards are, of course, by no means just "administrative" standards. They are frequently derived from fields of advanced technical knowledge, such as medicine, engineering, and the related natural and social sciences, as mentioned above. Typically, there exists a *communis opinio doctorum,* as the scholastics called it, a fairly generally agreed view as to what is sound. This broad common agreement is at times obscured by the sharp disagreements which arise among persons "in the know" about advanced positions in these several technical fields. But most of the time, it is not too difficult for the "insiders" to tell the professional from the charlatan.[9] Responsible conduct (c) is conduct in accordance with such technical

[8] John M. Gaus, "The Responsibility of Public Administration," in *The Frontiers of Public Administration* (1936), pp. 39-40.

[9] A very vivid portrait of the range of issues involved may be gained from a "case" involving the science of statistics as reported in Harold Stein, "Attack on the Cost of Living Index," *Public Administration and Policy Development* (1952), p. 775ff.

standards (s): c(rf) c(s). It is one of the most familiar instances of conflict in government that the B's possessing a certain technical competence are convinced that a particular line of conduct is required of them, when judged by technical standards, while a different conduct is asked of them by those A's to whom they are personally responsible. The A's may be the public or they may be the people's representatives, or even the official superiors of such responsible persons, comprised in a bureaucratic hierarchy. According to the old and generally sound rule that "the experts shall be on tap, but not on top," [10] it is held that technical (functional) responsibility in such instances must give way to personal responsibility. This may be stated by modifying the above formula to read $c(rf) + c(rp) = c(s)$, so that the formula as first given holds only when $c(rp) = c(rf)$, that is to say, when the A's to whom the B's are responsible desire that the standards of the particular functional field shall be the basis of action. One field in which these issues are particularly bothersome is the military. Issues such as the abolition of the horse cavalry or the balancing of the several services, the development of particular weapons and the like have continually given rise to bitter fights, usually carried forward by men of conviction, "idealists" who felt deeply the responsibility cast upon them by their technical knowledge. Famous instances, such as Billy Mitchell's struggle for an adequate airforce, and de Gaulle's determined, if unsuccessful, efforts at modernizing the French army merely highlight a continuous problem.[11]

The solution which our simple formula suggests is politically speaking the democratic one. It is, however, often objected to, both in general and in particular instances, on the

[10] For further thought on the democratic implications, and the problem of "workmanship" see my *The New Image of the Common Man* as cited above, footnote 3.

[11] For several interesting analyses see the contributions to *Public Policy,* VIII (1958), especially the papers by E. L. Katzenbach, pp. 120ff. and P. N. Wrinch, pp. 151ff.

ground that the damage resulting from a technically erroneous
conduct may be so great—although unknown to the A's who
are in control of the responsible officials—that the official who
is technically competent is really responsible only if he takes
a stand, uncompromising in terms of his standards, for the
"right" action or policy. The over-ruling consideration is said
to be the "public interest." Such arguments become particularly sharp and perplexing in such fields as the military, where
the very existence, the survival of the A's may be at stake and
depend upon the responsible conduct of the B's. Now the
public interest is a broad and many-faceted category [12] which
cannot be broken up into technical fields. Not only is there
the problem of coordinating the several technical fields with
each other, but there is also the more general interest in the
maintenance of a particular kind of political order. Typically,
medical science may suggest interference in highly private
matters, police and tax collectors, and even Congressmen, may
correctly or incorrectly consider that a certain way of carrying
on their work will give superior results vital to the well-being
or even the survival of the political order they serve and feel
responsible for. Yet, such several lines of conduct may be rejected by the public and its representatives, because they violate values which are basic and constitutive of that particular
order itself. There is no ultimate way of determining what
the public interest is, except by consulting the public. But the
manifest danger of miscarriage of responsible conduct suggests that safeguards need to be maximized to make sure that
the public has had an opportunity to learn of all the different
implications of a given line of conduct of action or policy.
Here the issue of the extent to which responsible officials
should be permitted to address the public at large, to expound their views in press and public lecture, arises. It can
manifestly not simply be answered by prohibiting such activities, as the old authoritarian tradition of government service

[12] E. P. Herring, *Public Administration and the Public Interest* (1936),
chaps. I-III.

is inclined to do (and still does in many governments and in practically all business concerns), but that some limits must be placed on such appeals seems clear.[13] These limits can only be worked out, however, with careful regard for the problem of responsibility, that is, how to render the bureaucracy as responsible as possible.

When looking at the issue from this viewpoint, it would appear that generally responsible conduct becomes possible only within the context of a widely discussed public policy. It is in such public policy that personal and functional responsibility are united and in a sense transcended. But even under highly effective arrangements for determining public policy by a balancing and merging of the community's values, beliefs, and interests with the technical requirements of a given field of endeavor, there will be a range of conduct on the part of public representatives which is at least controversial in terms of responsibility. Policies, like laws, cannot be made sufficiently detailed to fit all situations, and therefore must leave much to the discretion of those who operate and execute policies. The extent of such discretion varies and is extended or contracted to some extent at least as a result of technical considerations, but as we said at the outset, it always involves three notions, namely (1) that a choice between several existing alternatives can be and indeed must be made, or that (2) a novel solution is found, an innovation or invention made, and (3) that such a choice or innovation is not

[13] For further elaboration of these problems see the author's paper, cited above, footnote 2, pp. 22f. Cf. also James C. McCamy's *Government Publicity* (1939). Senator McCarthy's activities brought out still another angle for which see R. G. McCloskey "The McCarran Act and the Doctrine of Arbitrary Power," *Public Policy,* IV (1953), 228ff. The British situation, still dominated by the *Official Secrets' Act,* is rendered reasonably sound by the traditions of questions in parliament and the "letters to the editor," especially of *The Times;* for this syndrome see Herbert Morrison's remarkable *Government and Parliament—A Survey from Inside* (1954), pp. 256ff. (questions) and p. 268ff. (public relations) and Bernard Crick, *Reform of The Commons* (1959).

made arbitrarily, wantonly, or carelessly, but in accordance
with the requirements of the situation.[14] This means that
ordinarily discretion operates within a framework of rules,
implementing them and elaborating them, as suggested in
the comment of the Committee on Ministers' Powers quoted
above. If we ask what is to exclude arbitrary, wanton, or careless choices, the answer will be in terms of responsible conduct. A person of discretion, i.e., a person exercising discretion
as it is intended to be exercised, is a person who will conduct
himself in accordance with the instructions or the anticipated
reactions of a superior or ruler and in line with the technical
requirements of the function he is exercising. Such discretion
can be conferred, because the A's holding power in its various
forms, and/or possessing authority, are able to find persons
who will be ready to act in such a way as to be able to answer
for their conduct.

A modern administrator, especially in the so-called underdeveloped countries now being modernized, is in many situations dealing with problems so novel and complex that they
call for the highest creative ability.[15] This need for creative
solutions effectively focuses attention upon the need for positive action. The popular "will" has little content, except the
desire to see the maladjustments removed. A solution which
fails to do so, or which causes new and perhaps greater maladjustments is wrong, and may properly be called irresponsible, if it can be shown to have been adopted without proper
regard to the existing sum of human knowledge concerning
the technical issues involved, and just as much so, as if it was
adopted without proper regard for the existing preferences in

[14] The vital second point, possible innovation, was not included in my
earlier treatment of discretion, as cited above, footnote 1; it is a vital
dimension of freedom, for which see my *Puerto Rico—Middle Road to
Freedom* (1959), chap. I. Cf. also Morris Cohen, "Rule versus Discretion,"
Law and the Social Order (1933), pp. 257ff.

[15] Cf. Donald Wilhelm, Jr., "The Place of Public Administration in the
Overseas Technical Assistance Programs," *Public Policy*, VI (1955), 182ff.,
and P. Abelin, ed., *La Fonction Publique International et l'action inter-
nationale d'assistance technique* (no date—c. 1958), several papers.

the community, and more particularly its prevailing major-ity.[16] This is very generally and increasingly appreciated. The bestseller success of a recent novel high-lighting precisely this issue is eloquent testimony to such public acknowledgment of the issue of responsibility which stands at the heart of the drama there depicted.[17] The responsible administrator is re-sponsive to these two dominant factors, technical knowledge as well as popular sentiment. This proposition applies equally to policy formation and execution. The administrator can no longer be considered responsible if he relaxes with the comforting excuse that he merely is called upon to execute existing policies. This is particularly true in the field of foreign and defense policy, but applies equally to other fields as well. "To govern is to invent," Governor Munoz-Marin likes to say. It is the ultimate meaning of administrative re-sponsibility.

One final aspect of administrative responsibility calls for brief comment and that is its "enforcement." If government and other officials are to be responsible, how can they be in-duced to respond? The notion of "enforcement" is, in its most antiquated form, based on dismissal. To this day the general practice of private organization, and the smaller and hence more primitive, the more so, is to rely upon the power to fire a person as the basic method for maintaining responsible con-duct. But the spread of tenure provisions which protect offi-cials and employees against such dismissal, except where defi-nite malfeasance is involved, have restricted its availability. This is well, because many of the subtler forms of responsi-bility can not be elicited by this crude and brutal device. Organization machinery, like physical machinery, is evolving more refined tools for accomplishing its more difficult tasks. Dismissal resembles an axe or butcher knife—tools which are not useful for raising trees, flowers, or beef cattle, though ade-quate for cutting them.

[16] Very interesting cases in Arthur Maass, *Muddy Rivers—The Army Engineers and the Nation's Rivers* (1951).

[17] William J. Lederer and Eugene Burdick, *The Ugly American* (1958).

Whenever the need for action is the primary problem in responsible conduct, the technique of dismissal is decidedly crude as a method for securing conduct responsible and responsive to the preferences of the principal. Hence modern governments have had to rely to an increasing extent upon other methods to induce their officials to act in "the public interest." Five major kinds of measures appear to contribute to the bringing about of administrative responsibility.[18] First, there are the disciplinary measures short of dismissal, such as fine, reprimand, temporary suspension, reduction in salary, and transfer to another post. Since these are punishments, they raise the problems discussed in another section of this volume. They exhibit the limitations of all penalties. Based on the psychology of fear and discouragement, they are more likely to prevent misconduct than to elicit good conduct. Second, there are the promotional measures—promotions, salary increases, titles, orders, decorations, and rewards and prizes for novel ideas. Based upon the psychology of encouragement, these are much more likely to induce officials to maximize effort "beyond the call of duty," as the American military like to put it. Third, there are financial measures of control and audit of expenditure. Based on the rule of anticipated reactions, they serve to bring about financial responsibility, but if narrowly administered, they often hamstring initiative, prevent necessary action, and therefore should themselves be subject to careful review. Such institutions as the Bureau of the Budget in the United States have raised as many issues as they have solved, as far as securing responsible administration is concerned.[19] The fourth way of bringing about administrative responsibility is the time-honored method of judicial

[18] For a more detailed discussion of what follows see my *Constitutional Government and Democracy* (1950), pp. 398ff. and the literature cited there, as well as the leading texts in continental administrative law, such as Hauriou, Vedel, Jellinek, Forsthoff, as well as the modern American treatises on Administration, like Simon, Smithburg & Thompson, L. D. White, F. Morstein-Marx, Chester I. Barnard, and Albert Lepawsky.

[19] See the imaginative critique by Arthur Maass "In Accord with the Program of the President?" *Public Policy,* IV (1953), 77ff.

measures, based upon the civil and criminal law. Such judicial measures are inherent in any constitutional government, based as it is upon the rule of law, but, like dismissal, they are more apt to prevent wrong-doing than to induce responsibility for action and initiative. Finally, fifth, there exist today, as previously suggested, the modes of approval and disapproval which have for so long been a decisive factor in the *esprit de corps* of the learned professions. There is plenty of evidence to suggest that officials working in all the more esoteric fields of government service, the ever more numerous scientific activities, both national and international, are more sensitive to and more concerned with the criticism made of their activities by their professional peers than by any superiors in the organization they serve. Such professional standards and criticism have for a long time been crucial in maintaining the responsibility of the judiciary, possessing life tenure and no determinate superior. Whether the standards related to the principles of the science of administration itself will become sufficiently firm to reinforce such professional standards in other more established fields it is too early to say. There are some favorable signs, especially in the English speaking countries which are paralleled by the increasingly realistic approach of Continental administrative law, the principles of which have been developed over the years by special courts, notably the Conseil d'Etat in France. When such institutionalization occurs, the professional standards become assimilated to judicial measures as a means of maintaining administrative responsibility.

In conclusion, it may be said that the ways by which administrative responsibility can be secured are many, and that only a combination of all of them offers the prospect of securing the desired result. But such measures must not be allowed to obscure the fact that only within well developed policy can responsible conduct on the part of administrative officials be expected. As we have seen, well developed policy means a policy developed with the active and responsible participation of the officials who are to execute it. As the sphere of public administration is further and further extended, and the size of organizations correspondingly enlarged, the understanding of the nature and conditions of administrative responsibility become decisive for the survival and well-being of all communities, including the world community. The dilemma posed, on all levels of government, by the potential conflicts of personal and functional responsibility is a permanent one. It can only be resolved, in each instance, by the constant evolution of public policy, adequately discussed and rationally adapted to changing situations and their requirements.[20]

[20] This dilemma is only a special instance of the more general problem of "reason of state" in a constitutional order; see for this my *Constitutional Reason of State* (1957).

◈ XIII ◈

REFLECTIONS ON POLITICAL INTEGRITY

WARREN ROBERTS

HOWEVER THE CONCEPTS be defined, political responsibility implies political integrity. The concept of integrity in politics has always posed special problems, some of which have been pressed by recent emphasis on existential truth as contrasted with political decision. A legislator, however, sees personal convictions merge into agreement on action and give that action its only source of sustained power. He thereby gains an impression that truth emerges from the political process. Integrity, personal or political, may be viewed as but a time-dimensioned aspect of processes of integration, integration being defined positively or ideologically as the co-ordination of capacities and negatively as the reduction of inner conflict. A study of integrative processes affords insight into the meaning of rational political adaptation and the functional evolution of law.

The approach is practical for it introduces political behavior by consideration of political norms. Experienced politicians come to feel the need to define the kind of honesty that does visibly triumph.

The concepts of responsibility and political integrity may be oriented in at least three possible directions. Both concepts have normative overtones. In addition they raise questions concerning the political capacity of men for self government [1] and of expectations and obligations within organization. The concepts also suggest certain prime movers in political action. This is particularly true of the term "integrity" for it touches on the need for self-consistency, and so helps clarify the nature of political competition.

[1] Carl Friedrich, *The New Belief in the Common Man* (1942), chap. III.

As the "lie-detector" indicates, man experiences internal tension when reporting other than the truth as he sees it. And just as dispute over personal honor is *per se* an altercation, so any serious difference over the logic and consistency of political action will itself mark a change in political allegiance. Man must visualize a world with order enough to allow him meaningful activity, and his actions do themselves constitute an important part of his world. Though he cannot hope for complete order and predictability a voice within him pleads always against those words and actions that are contradictory and self-defeating, so that his world shall not seem a tale told by an idiot.

The need to define the nature of man's constant reintegration in face of changing environment challenges all of the skill and learning of the social scientist. To describe the processes whereby men adjust to new economic environment is less difficult than to describe man's rational response to the more radical changes in the political world. To describe constitutions whereby men may alter laws is less difficult than to describe the processes whereby men in search of ways to personal integrity may change constitutions. Yet survival demands increased effort to provide concepts adequate to these subtleties.

The social scientist, thinking back over the immeasurable tragedies of the last generation, perceives that the loss of the European marchlands accompanied a degree of nihilism understandable in the light of Western political-economic collapse. His conscience whispers that more honesty and care might have saved the center of the world that fatal, momentary, fragmentation. His present task would seem to be to define, establish, and preserve market places of agreement. The problem lies within the bounds of logic. The proximate imperatives of the political challenge, to the theorist as well as to the practitioner, are in fact set by political competitors, each of whom bows to native and competitive obligations to follow consistent lines of action not unrelated to the events and occasions of the world about them. Above all else the

Yeats nightmare symbolized discontinuous engagement.[2] Order is not static but flows from continuing processes of relationship among all varieties of people.

The problem is to define more explicitly the truth-in-process that emerges from specific campaigns and draw from known details of political integration an increasing number of generally applicable principles. The apparent lack of integrity in politics does reflect peculiar difficulties in attaining it and most political competition is directed at the conquest of these difficulties.

The model of political competition begins with known steps in personal adjustment to changes in environment. Assume a man disturbed by a new need, remediable by known governmental techniques, or by the appearance of new techniques remedial of old needs, or by the two types of change proceeding simultaneously. At first, say students of psychology, the form and meaning of the new situation is vague; next, the several parts become differentiated, and then people learn processes of integration and articulation.[3]

At first glance the alleged order of the last two steps appears open to question. Ability to differentiate might seem to accompany rather than precede experience in articulation. Yet students of government recognize here a most important point. Phenomena of tension, uncertainty, and speculation accompanying political change weigh most heavily while a new association is analyzed in advance of full participation. The tension of uncertainty might be expected to rise from the moment of *prima facie* differentiation through the tactual abandonment of the old and the integration of the new.

2 Things fall apart; the centre cannot hold;
  Mere anarchy is loosed upon the world,

  . . . .
  That twenty centuries of stony sleep
  Were vexed to nightmare by a rocking cradle,
  And what rough beast, its hour come round at last,
  Slouches towards Bethlehem to be born?
                    (W. B. Yeats, *The Second Coming*).
3 Gardner Murphy, *Personality* (1947), pp. 66, 333, 345, 619, *passim*.

As William James observed, men choose because they must redirect energy, so that the search for integrity has a dynamic, active dimension. Each part of the on-going adaptive movement has its own verification, and together they form sequential models of action. The weight to be accorded any part will vary from moment to moment as well as from individual to individual and scientifically supported conclusions in this area accumulate slowly. Yet simplified models appear in many kinds of writing, and these are enough to suggest working classifications of norms.

Two standards of action are underlined by Cervantes' reiterated conclusion that the road is better than the inn. The view was shared in part by Veblen, who emphasized the force of the sense of workmanship as distinct from the claims of the pecuniary goal.[4] To a degree both may receive support from Bergson's stress on the supreme values found in *the becoming*. With another emphasis novelists like Anatole France and H. L. Humes [5] have insisted that the idealized image, though never reached, kept men on the road. Bergson was more inclined to give credit to the *vis-a-tergo,* the kick from behind, a phrase enthusiastically embraced by Henry Adams as consonant with his astringent conclusion that politics is organized hate.

It seems unlikely that any single model fits all situations, yet some tentative generalization is necessary for the purpose of discussion. Despite the specific and persuasive arguments of Carl Jung, whose definition of the creative libido would appear to support the road-inn aspect of the model, the present writer is inclined to side with Bergson and Henry Adams on

4 Thorstein Veblen, *The Instinct of Workmanship and the State of the Industrial Arts* (1914), I, 27, *passim.* Carl Friedrich, *op. cit.*

5 H. L. Humes, *The Underground City* (1958), p. 524. Explaining the common refusal to believe Lenin's open and frequent identification of the enemy not as the Czar but as the liberal, Humes muses on the power of illusion. "A world without illusions is a world without order, and a world without order is terrifying. It leaves the soul in chaos. To be so deprived is the one torture beyond human capacity to survive."

political motivation. Except for those who are particularly inclined to "dream collectively," politics requires more unreasoning personal surrender than most other relationships. The existentialists are not wholly wrong. Uniformity is the bane as well as the blessing of law. To an important degree, also, the romantic vision of the idealized inn may be but the inverse image of discontents, hates, or fears, or some unconscious memory of the remedy of these discontents. Does not the certainty of law stem less from hope than from fear or fear of fear? Tentatively we shall here symbolize the standards by which men judge consistency by the term "need-remedy" convictions, the word "need" including dissatisfaction or antipathy, the hyphen serving to recognize moving relationships and tension, and the term "remedy" recognizing the road or the inn or both.

Political conviction in this sense means a time-space dimensioned feeling of the relatively grave importance of a need and the relatively encouraging promise of a remedy, the need and its inferred remedy being two sides of the same coin, separated by degrees of venture and speculation. Because the campaign moves toward legal decision and government action, need must be defined as that which is to be remedied, as the remedy takes its meaning from the need. One has political integrity to the degree that his words and actions relate to needs as they appear to him in their relative importance and remedies in their relative effectiveness.

Without denying the satisfactions of the road we must observe that change of direction does not come from the road itself, but, rather, the contrary. The enjoyment of the road, and the institutionalization of the road, act against change, even in the face of new need-remedy possibilities. Dialectic excess is made possible in part by the fact that men will delay new political action until their personal integrity is seriously imperilled. Therefore, revolutionists like Trotsky try to disguise the extravagance of their purpose, the phrase "not peace, not war" taking on a specific Hegelian meaning.

We are trying here to go behind the equilibrium theory
of law [6] to help define the gestation of law in a functional
manner. Men learn to work together for new law out of a
sense of wrong growing from visible or tactual experience and
from a related hope in the practicality of remedial action.
However complex and volatile their motivations, they are
caught for the moment in a tension of contrasts, sharing their
new convictions by use of new abstract symbols developed by
sympathetic intellectuals. We do not here intentionally differ
with Cervantes. Even war may exhilarate.

Parties represent and clarify alternatives. Men turn to the
party whose proposals most conform to their personal convictions, and party effectiveness, therefore, depends on speed
of perception of the nature of new, commonly felt, wants and
new remedial opportunities. Lubell's conclusion that the
dominant party is that which is the more sensitive to the immediate issues seems at first glance, therefore, to be a truism
but it does lead us to seek the cause of minority deviation.
Some of the minority may be insensitive to the world about
them. Some may be perverse, truculent, or arrogant. But the
inability of the members of the minority to give the same
priority to need-remedy issues as do the majority stems also
from differences in personal experience. If the minority were
to embrace alien need-remedy convictions they would violate
that bent for self-consistency controlling all other behavior.
The rock-ribbed members of the party, pressed to accept
planks compromising their "principles," ask "What are we
fighting for?" and lose interest. Even under threat of armed
invasion a defensive alliance "with the devil himself" brings
twinges of conscience and concern for the future.

A party's will to dominate appears to come from its radicals, for partisan competition is "expensive" and the party depends for its life on members willing to "sacrifice" on behalf

[6] On which the present writer once offered parastastical evidence; cf.
his "State Taxation of Metallic Deposits," *Harvard Economic Series,* 77
(1944), chap. 4.

of the cause. Those to whom this "sacrifice" is no sacrifice are found in the extreme rather than in the moderate element of the party, for to this more radical group the opposition represents an irrational, demonic, threat to a whole way of life. The New Deal demand for social security legislation offered an answer to something the conservative core of the Republican Party failed to see even as a practical question.[7] Whole ways of life here conflicted.

On immediate issues the integrity of the party is rooted in the integrity of this radical core and on loss of membership the party first shrinks to this core.[8] In a world of change and continuous new challenge, the preservation of the party requires deference to fighting faiths. Over time, however, procedural integrity (mores of integration) must include more receptiveness than comes naturally to the militant.

This requirement of procedural integrity is normative and it is also pragmatic. The very antipathy of each core toward the other demands victory and victory requires enrollment of moderates in large numbers. Furthermore, whenever populous tradition has tended to sanctify majority decision, defeat shakes core morale. If issues change so sharply that the party seems unable to retain consistency of action the core will disintegrate, perhaps taking the name of the party with it. Age and personal debility may combine with economic mobility to smooth the transition, and cortical reflection while out of office will help the party gather its dialectic capacity to leap-frog the opposition. Still we must not dodge the central truth that the more distant this core may be from the national (or global) norm the graver the danger of decline of the party.

[7] Among the rural German-English populace of Decatur County, Indiana, those on land not blessed by the latest glacier had traditionally voted Democratic against their richer neighbors, but moved toward the Republican fold on the advent of the New Deal. (Unpublished study by John Mitchell, Greensburg, Indiana.)

[8] Following this line of reasoning, the Democratic Party should ordinarily not be the first to suggest a sales tax.

Especially in a shrinking world some conflict between the
norms of integrity and the norms of integration is unavoidable. Yet the conflict is reduced by some tendency of these
two standards of transaction to alternate in importance. The
imperatives of integrity are most compelling at moments of
decision, whether by election, revolution, or war. To enjoy
the trust of its constituents each party must show its self-
consistency on substantive matters. In the bitter legislative
session of Indiana in 1959, the Republican party officially
fought to retain the "right to work" law, while the Democratic party as openly fought to repeal it, despite every likelihood that if the law remained on the books it would serve as
an issue with which the Democrats would gleefully torment
the Republicans in the critical election of the following year.
Faithful to its expressed convictions the Republican minority
ruthlessly used its control of the Senate committee on labor
to keep the issue from the floor.

The unity that follows the vote is preceded by unity and
decision within the contending parties, but between these
"moments of truth" the party must harken to the needs of the
members of the middle group it would attract. It will sharpen
its perception of general ills and exert maximum ingenuity in
evolving remedies. It will organize and exercise its capacity
for conviction even while concealing its less popular, more
esoteric, desires. At the same time it will try to paint the
whole of the opposition the color of some radical element
therein.

The term "conviction" carries a different meaning to the
Westerner than to the follower of Lenin. The Western connotation stresses the responsibility of the voter to himself and
accords less weight to leadership. In the frontier tradition,
especially, conviction is personal, derived from experience,
and relatively more sacred. For the guidance of political edu-
cators everywhere, however, we must continue to point out
that this respect for existential impression has acquired feasibility by reason of personal humility, sympathy, patience, self-

possession, and related convictions of a procedural nature, including belief in natural law, faith in modes of representation, or antipathy to disturbances endangering productive activity.

Yet again we cannot avoid the hard fact that the force of personal procedural conviction tends to vary inversely with one's distance from the moral line of substantive conviction. A radical, seeing no reason in the arguments of the opposition and madness in the threat of its success, is more concerned to defeat it than to abide by the rules. For this very reason the radical will tend to challenge the procedural convictions of the moderates. For unless he has tested the constitutional limits set by the community he may doubt his own strength of character. Sometimes the result is an upheaval that destroys the old center, but in a strong democracy many campaigns are lost because of apparent violation of the accepted norms of representation.

The act that set the stage for the final victory of Mr. Eisenhower over Mr. Taft, in the Republican convention of 1952, was an unscheduled broadcast by Mr. Dewey, describing to the American public the allegedly unorthodox methods by which Taft delegates had been named in Georgia. The inpouring telegrams responding to this broadcast marked the turn of the tide. But parties may also lose from lack of the vitality needed to take soundings, and in an inchoate society constant exploration of constitutional limits is as important as constant effort to improve and stabilize them.

Conviction may also mean the active process of convincing or an *agit-prop* act of causing people to feel the importance of some need-remedy proposition. Though more evident in Communist usage this sense of the term is also found in Western dictionaries. Here the responsibility of leadership is more evident. Leaders should be sensitive to social menace, clear-sighted in espousal of remedies, personally effective in communication of their better convictions, and aware of the virtues and values of continuous activity.

Once the validity of a conviction is established, as Marx and Lenin established in their followers a belief in the evils of capitalism and built hope in the dictatorship of the proletariat, then in the coin of this established value, party members may persuasively offer and receive assistance and build elaborate co-operative organizations.[9] The stronger a common conviction, the smaller the coin required for persuasion. The party will seek the most productive balance of the two processes, bargaining when further salesmanship seems profitless. Ease of persuasion marks a society whose inherent conflicts of conviction are resolved for the time, even though the value denominators of smooth persuasive exchange have been implanted by threat, as between master and slave.

Like active conviction on substantive issues, active processes of procedural conviction are many-faceted and appear in all the norms men follow when they represent themselves or attend to the representation of others, in or out of formal politics.

Tolstoy, in *Anna Karenina,* observed that recently freed serfs, long guided by custom, could not be induced to change their ways even for the sake of higher income. They had come to identify self-consistency with tradition. Tolstoy suggested "education" as the path to broader values. Half a century later the Communists, trying to supply their growing industrial centers with food, found the Kulak unresponsive either to the money they could offer or to persuasion of a more ideologic nature. They then liquidated the Kulaks and promoted in their place farmers whose convictions made them

---

[9] In a sense, of course, processes of conviction are persuasive in that new convictions are analogically related to the old. But for those who have practical responsibility for uniting heterogeneous groups, the *agit-prop* or suggestive processes for creating the common denominators of exchange need special emphasis. The concept of implanting values appears much clearer, for instance, in the ordinary connotation of *ubezdhat* than in *peithein*. Alex. Inkeles, *Public Opinion in Soviet Russia* (1950), chap. I. F. S. C. Northrop, *The Taming of the Nations* (1952), in his references to Monlin. Salvador de Madariaga, *Spain* (1930), chaps. II, VIII.

more susceptible to available means of persuasion. And conviction of the validity of authoritarian decisions must include, as Koestler said, the thought that "No. I" might, after all, be right.

To summarize this concept of integrity, the focus on needs and the inference of remedies appear as related parts of any single occasion of the exercise of political responsibility, by leaders and by ordinary citizens. The norms of responsibility demand search for and definition of short run and long run truths emanating from experience. Part of this truth concerns the substantive issue but part concerns modes of representation and agreement. Political integration issues in the reduction of conflict so that change comes by consent rather than by destructive violence. Basically, men are able to persuade each other in view of the coercions they severally experience, and discontents are focused by emphasis, by suggestion of the practicality of relief, and by idealism. Values are activated by suggestion and defined by analogy. The need and the remedy attain their meaning together. Yet the somewhat greater speculative element of the remedy lessens its practicality as a political concept, and the wise politician, therefore, maintains stress on commonly felt fears or discontents rather than on remedies, thereby retaining a valid foundation for his program, however he might be compelled to revise it.

To the moderates the learning problems of the right wing and the left wing on any given issue appear to differ. The left is composed of those already aware of the needs to be served by, e.g., a proposed road and these must learn from the right the costs argument against the undertaking. The right wing, seeing the costs and not being convinced of the value of this particular road, must learn the factors producing the crusade. The left then suffers frustration, the right, anxiety. The left sees a cause arbitrarily checked, the right sees threat of arbitrary change. Both may become enraged.

The right wing and the left wing on any issue appear then to differ markedly in the nature of their political strength and their vulnerability. The left wing sounds more merciful, the right wing more ideologic. During the process of change the left wing stresses immediate needs, the right wing tends to cite mores and customs, emphasises constitutional principles that might, if followed, deprive the left of power, and tries to place the new proposals in ludicrous relation to old values.

Therefore, the left wing must actively redefine principles and ideology in terms of its new convictions, and the right wing must seek to be practical. If both succeed they will move toward agreement, the left having covered its vulnerability to the charge of being unprincipled and the right its sin of blindness to need. If neither so corrects itself and if new needs are widely felt, the left wing in a fluid society, being more practical, is likely to take over and remain indefinitely in power, while the conservatives vent righteous indignation and unrighteous malice, caught in the misplaced concreteness of abstract ideas.

Let us now turn to a slightly more explicit identification of campaign tactics and their integrative effect. Defying the danger of academic reprimand we shall here term the component parts of politics "integration" and "the needle." No common usage adequately denotes the complex positive requirement that a political leader identify general evils, arouse enthusiasm over vaguely perceived and largely untried remedies, and lay a necessary positive foundation for sustained attack. Negative, divisive politics comes more naturally. Men joyously taunt the enemy for his inconsistencies, trying to isolate the extreme opposition by shaming or producing uncertainty among the moderates. Yet for this negative purpose parties often rely too much on words, assuming agreement on the meaning of those words. Inconsistencies are best exposed by better positive programs. The numerous "anti-Communist" groups on various continents serve an important purpose but they cannot easily symbolize practical positive aspects of the Western liberal revolution. Politicians must concentrate on the convictions of people in the middle group; and the integration of a successful party must therefore include a redirection of energy satisfactory to marginal adherents as well as to the core.

Consider the inner conflicts of those addressed by William Jennings Bryan. Here, for instance, is a jobless man in a great city, burdened with a sense of family obligations voluntarily assumed and knowing himself to lack virtue as virtue is measured by the traditional economic standards of a self-reliant people. His sense of personal guilt is deep and abiding. Now comes the voice of the Great Commoner, accenting the element of social tragedy and denouncing a deflation to which creditors had assented and from which they draw profit. To the unfortunate and destitute, listening to his words, the weight of personal responsibility grows a little lighter. Under the symbol of the crown of thorns, personal suffering seems at one with the sufferings of mankind.

Now the whole of the Leviathan reconsiders its convictions. The left needles the right for selfishness, the right needles the left for irresponsibility. The middle class acquires new doubts. Given the existing level of discontent, decision turns on the relative merits or demerits of proposed techniques of remedy. In the Leviathan as a whole political integrity develops in the form of agreement on the evil of monetary instability, and issues in decision to adopt the gold standard and improve the banking system. But intellectual integrity has room for doubt and unanswered questions.

In the light of history the rise of production of gold and silver, under way during Bryan's campaigns, would have rendered bimetallism unnecessary and, probably, disastrous. Yet prediction at that time was difficult, and against the charge of irresponsibility we must record the tragedies consequent on a generation-long deflation. Some element of speculation being unavoidable, the responsibility of Bryan's leadership must be judged in part by his presentation of a choice of a lesser evil among available alternatives. He helped reduce the distance between the extremes if only by asking a politically practicable question. Across the Leviathan, somewhat left of center, he helped form a fault line of disturbed and uncertain voters,

216 WARREN ROBERTS

symbolized by no less sophisticated an observer than Henry Adams.[10]

Adams' conception of the elements in the case resemble our own. Studying this issue in the light of the technological display of the Chicago Fair, he concluded that the American people did seem to be driving or drifting unconsciously to some point in space, not impossible to fix. Though "the banks alone, and the dealers in exchange, insisted upon it," the people with no great enthusiasm moved toward the gold standard. The choice had not been impulsive:

> For a hundred years, between 1793 and 1893, the American people had hesitated, vacillated, swayed forward and back, between two forces, one simply industrial, the other capitalistic, centralized, and mechanical. In 1893, the issues came on the single gold standard, and the majority at last declared itself, once for all, in favor of the capitalistic system with all its necessary machinery. All one's friends, all one's best citizens, reformers, churches, colleges, educated classes, had joined the banks to force submission to capitalism; a submission long foreseen by the mere law of mass. Of all forms of society or government, this was the one he liked least, but his likes or dislikes were as antiquated as the rebel doctrine of State rights. A capitalistic system had been adopted, and if it were to be run at all, it must be run by capital and by capitalistic methods; for nothing could surpass the nonsensity of trying to run so complex and so concentrated a machine by Southern and Western farmers in grotesque alliance with city day-laborers, as had been tried in 1800 and 1828, and had failed even under simple conditions.[11]

Here, briefly sketched, was the majority, with its capitalistic extreme and its grudging allies, the dissident minority, the author as prototype of the troubled fault line, and a glimpse of the process of adunation. The majority repressed its fear of monetary deflation out of a greater fear of monetary chaos, and rejected silver for gold.

The term "forgotten man" has all the elements of an effective needle, posing personal suffering in the form of social

[10] *The Education of Henry Adams* (1918), chap. XXII.
[11] Henry Adams, *op. cit.*, p. 345.

obligation and inferring a callous indifference on the part of those in power. Its employment in the United States covers a succession of historically related evils and reforms. William Graham Sumner, in 1883, used it against welfare spenders, arguing that in order to succor the weak and improvident the benevolent had leagued with politicians to burden the diligent and far-sighted.[12] But his crude equation of poverty with personal weakness also revealed that inconsistencies are relative and that to shame men for inconsistency requires the offer of better alternatives. Here lies the handicap of the detached elite, working in a qualitative dimension without the quantitative or movement evaluations registered, albeit imperfectly, in any viable political process.

Walter Page, in 1897, in a speech in Greensboro, North Carolina, argued that the real forgotten men were the poor and uneducated classes of the South, duped by a "little aristocracy" into a proud acceptance of an illiteracy that ran to 26% even among white Anglo-Saxons.[13] Charging a ruling class of "professional Southerners" with exploitation of material, religious, and intellectual poverty, and encouragement of class and sectional prejudice, he set them at war with themselves. The obvious practicality of his proposals for educational reform exposed a contradiction between the responsibilities and the performance of members of the Southern elite. They, defending their integrity, "excoriated" him as a renegade Southern Yankee, and during the melee the phrase "forgotten man" found a place in the indelible imagery of the South. The great majority agreed with his diagnosis and therewith began the "educational awakening" of the South.

Other things being equal, the effectiveness of a new charge is forecast by the outcry it causes, for the exposure of inconsistent behavior causes or exacerbates internal conflict and produces pain. Yet the nature of the response will depend

[12] William Graham Sumner, *The Forgotten Man and Other Essays* (1918), pp. 466ff., A. G. Keller, ed.

[13] B. J. Hendrick, *The Life and Letters of Walter H. Page* (1922-1925), 72ff.

too on the self-consciousness, the sense of public obligation, or the political sophistication of the subject of attack. Here we approach problems of tactics too complex to be covered by this paper.

Roosevelt, using the same term in his call for a "New Deal" did no more than vaguely hint at remedies and culprits. Yet in the existing state of world tragedy the poignancy of the terms and its suggestion of negligence angered leadership in both parties.[14] In the ensuing realignment he did, as charged, set class against class. Later the phrase "economic royalty" served to inflame an already tender suspicion of the unjustifiable inequity and to suggest an arrogant indifference to the plight of the unemployed. But these hard words unaccompanied by acceptable action would have been ineffective.

Some most effective slogans require time for maximum impact. In this respect the politician effectively if unwittingly applies in reverse some of Pavlov's experiments. Whereas Pavlov achieved emotional disturbance by slow reduction of signal differentiation,[15] the politician begins by making distinctions at first invisible to many, using words that only after active illustration carry to the listener the meaning the politician wishes to convey. Playing for competitive advantage in the long pull the politician tries to present a new approach to which a new majority will eventually adhere. Many, perceiving no new meaning in the differentiation, become enraged. All cool off as the distinction becomes clearer, but by then opposition leaders have fatally committed themselves.

Time, a change of issues, insight, victory, or a sense of resignation, combine to reduce the linear dimensions of the

[14] Arthur Schlesinger, *The Age of Roosevelt, The Crisis of the Old Order* (1957), pp. 136, 292.

[15] In Pavlov's laboratory the dog was shown a circle of light and then fed; when an oval was presented no food was given. The oval was then made more and more circular until the ratio between the semi-axis was $8:9$ or less, at which ratio the animal could no longer make discriminative responses, and bit, barked, jerked, and squealed with excitement in a neurosis usually lasting for several months. (Prescott Lecky, *Self-Consistency* (1951), pp. 119-120).

Leviathan on old issues. Of the radical American party-groups existent at the turn of the century, all but the Communists had become ineffective by the end of the thirties, and not only because of the menace of Fascist, Nazi, and Soviet types of socialism. The depression, accenting their grievances, had also brought remedial action.

Can we say, exactly, how domestic and global aspects of politics suddenly became inseparable? During the pain and anger of world economic collapse men had largely reserved their sympathies for their own kind. Foreigners were viewed through narrowed, provincial, half-perceptive, eyes. Men grew apart when understanding was most crucial, and the world lost its center. The collapse of the militant will of the Axis then cost the aggressors a considerable ideologic disintegration, and even the righteous indignation of the victors retreated before a sense of guilt and a deepening anxiety. The pain of conflict and the tensions left thereafter increased the eagerness of men to meet the needs of those they had as yet small means to understand.

Search for criteria of personal responsibility in a troubled, shrinking, world became the *force majeure* of the twentieth century. Global alarums drew to foreign areas that sensitive, docile, resourceful, attention which is precedent to any knowing-known relationship.[16] New transactions marked the emergence of a global ecumene in which men tried to bring into some logical balance the costs and gains of distant actions. Arguments of conviction and persuasion produced increasingly ubiquitous values. The contention of A and C for the loyalty of B produces a common language. But values change with issues and changing issues clarify themselves through competing organization. Unfortunately, organization appears to the unorganized to be no more than a weapon, when in fact it offers the only means by which the integration of values through common experience might be made continuous.

The period remains revolutionary in that modes of organ-

16 Arthur F. Bentley, *Kennetic Inquiry. Science* 112 (Dec. 29, 1950), pp. 775-783, esp. fn. 5 on Royce.

ized representation are underdeveloped, so that leaders in each community must try to translate exogenous events into endogenous guide lines.

In the campaigns of 1952 and 1956, each party out of power gained some votes from the war-weary.[17] On issues over which few can trust their existential impressions a much greater burden of responsibility falls on political leaders. Political response to public fatigue with the cold war shows lack of integrity to the degree that a decision to lessen the cost of the contest lies clearly outside American hands.

But the problem also places responsibility on the intellectual to help improve political mechanisms so that the voter may have a clearer and more continuing view of the battle-front and may then appraise Western efforts more in terms of effectiveness and less in terms of cost. The same machinery must afford means whereby people move toward agreement on need-remedy values in substantive and procedural matters. The imperatives are obvious but in fact the existential barriers are formidable and the complexity and expense of effective effort promises to exceed any Western experience.

Russia by her newly acquired subtlety pays tribute to the effectiveness of Western criticism of her more ruthless procedures. But whether in truth as in appearance she no longer represents the reactionary extreme against the world liberal revolution is not a matter for idle speculation. Political survival requires constant testing of permissible and effective modes of representation. In many cases these procedural norms can best be tested by presentation of new substantive issues. Laotian development under Western leadership is thought by some to have driven the Chinese to raw aggression.[18] In other areas, Western lethargy over land reform has allowed Communists to masquerade as liberals. Substantive issues, pressed

[17] On the 1956 campaign, cf., *U.S. News and World Report*, 141 (Nov. 15, 1956), p. 84.

[18] General C. P. Cabell, Deputy Director CIA, UPI dispatch, *Boston Daily Record*, October 7, 1959.

vigorously, may drive the opposition to extravagant defensive action. Here is justification for the economist's claim to first responsibility for definition of issues. But the intensity of the conflict may exceed economic reason, and if no substantive issue appears, the restless retinues may hurry to the dueling ground without one.

PART FOUR

RESPONSIBILITY OF CITIZENSHIP

✸ XIV ✸

INSTITUTIONAL FRAMEWORK FOR THE DEVELOPMENT OF RESPONSIBLE CITIZENSHIP

NORTON E. LONG

CIVIS AMERICANUS SUM may have the same pompous and hollow ring as its imperial predecessor. Of the three sources of Western democratic citizenship that infuse it with its complex and precarious values, scarcely more remains than did of the Republic in the Empire. The traditions that Roelofs analyzes so well in *The Tension of Citizenship* [1] have worn thin and can only with the greatest difficulty be given renewed operative meaning in the mass metropolitan society of the modern nation state. Certainly it is difficult to make the Periclean ideal seem relevant in the trivia of the garden city suburb or the crowded inhumanity of the urban ghetto, and the individual's statistical significance in the Gallup world of the national election is a scarcely more heartening exercise in realizing a significant concept of the good life.

Far easier of realization would seem our Hebraic heritage of citizenship as loyalty and service to the national mission. Such loyalty, hopefully in caricature, is bruited much abroad by Congressional committees and true believing patriots. But for this type of loyalty, unbalanced by other limiting commitments, the status of subject serves as well as citizen; in fact the modern world would seem to tend that way.

The third strand of our precarious civic heritage that Roelofs points to is the limiting Christian view of man's private occupation. While rendering to Caesar what is

[1] H. Mark Roelofs, *The Tension of Citizenship. Private Man and Public Duty* (New York, 1957).

225

Caesar's, he preserves for God what is God's, and in doing so demands a privacy in which to pursue his individual salvation.

The complex of these values does indeed involve the prideful participation of the free citizen in a community whose life is fashioned to achieve the ethical self-realization of its citizens. Side by side with this we are bound to a loyalty to the nation and its service. Critically viewing each of these pursuits and goals is the private self seeking wisdom and salvation, involved yet aloof, and in that aloofness free to make a vital contribution to the multiple values of the western democratic ideal. In a real sense, responsible citizenship in our political culture must be built on each of the disparate elements of our history and each element requires institutional support for its embodiment.

The Periclean ideal is embalmed in the turgid rhetoric of our civics texts and is reduced to the mechanized absurdity of an advertising council "Get Out The Vote" campaign. The ritual of civic participation verges on the mass demonstration of totalitarian loyalty. All conception of citizenship as an active individual ethical role is lost. The older ideal persists in the nostalgia for the New England town given classic statement in the writings of Jefferson and deToqueville. The watered-down content of this ideal lingers in the apologias for suburbia, where democratic participation becomes a kind of conspicuous civic consumption of high honorific value and low content. For the most part, Greek citizenship is a residue in the culture, provocative of sentimental attitudinizing and little more. Yet this value as a motive for accepting the responsibility of participation in public life is, along with the Stoic values of Plutarch and Cicero, a major piece of building material out of our past for any significant new construction. Can the Greek conception of citizenship in our mass national state be given more than the homage of copy book rhetoric?

Certainly the nation can scarcely be a society of friends sharing a common conception of the good life to whose support and realization the state is dedicated. The problem of size caused even so ardent a Graecophile as Rousseau to despair of anything beyond his Geneva, though he appears to have had some hopes of federalism. The only major theorist of federalism, Althusius, seems to have had little influence on modern conceptions of citizenship. American theorists such as Madison and Calhoun show more concern for federalism as a device for the deconcentration of power, the balancing of interests and the prevention of majority tyranny than as a hopeful vehicle for providing some modicum of active citizenship for the too numerous members of the nation state. Burke clearly felt a nexus of institutions leading through family, hamlet, and shire to the nation itself, institutions which for him at least provided graded significant roles. The thrust of Rousseau's influence was certainly toward abolishing the lesser corporations whose particular wills might distort or destroy the general will. For him perhaps Burke's mediated loyalties were entangled in the unprofitable edifice of mud. The autarchy of the Greek city state can hardly be permitted to city, county, or state without these entities becoming, in Hobbes' sense, worms in the body politic. Fitzhugh's Greek Democracy of the South rears its head and Governor Almond hauls down the Federal Flag. The ancient question, whether the good man and the good citizen are the same, poses itself with respect to incompatible citizenships in city, state, and nation. The good citizen of Norfolk may be a bad citizen of Virginia and once again a good citizen of the United States.

The possibility of contradictory ethics being involved in the differing levels of government raises real problems for the apologist for a Greek view of citizenship. For the natural rights philosopher, for whom the institutions of government are not so much instruments for the perfection of man as mechanisms for protecting a naturally perfect endowment, this problem does not arise except as a flaw in the mechanics. But while natural rights individualism solves some problems by treating governmental institutions as mere machinery, its failure to infuse them with value in Selznik's sense creates problems of another order.

A jealous concern for government as an instrument for the protection of individual rights might motivate the active citizenship of the eighteenth century rationalist realists of the Constitutional Convention. It can scarcely succeed in motivating the necessary manpower in the quality and quantity needed to man the civic table of organization of today. In addition, its implicit faith in an almost Smithian production of the public good from the governmentally balanced contrarieties of private interest progressively loses its appeal. Besides, the eighteenth and early nineteenth century grammar of civic motives had a large mixture of *Tully on Offices,* to say nothing of a Pauline concern for the temporal order.

The appeal of the Greek view of citizenship lies in its recognition that political institutions are not mere instruments for the achieving of results but are institutions infused with value. The process of politics in this view is valued for its own sake as providing significant roles for the realization of man's ethical potential. While the efficiency of the governmental process in coping with problems common to all political orders is an inevitable and major consideration, the Greek view of citizenship regards the capacity of a political order to provide significant roles for the realization of the citizens' moral potential as a major criterion of its value. In this sense the political order is valued not just for what it produces but for the keen sense of citizen participation in the enterprise. As socialists like DeMann have argued for the workers' sense of dignity and meaning in the productive process as a value independent and even above his pay, so one may argue that the citizen needs the opportunity of meaningful civic action beyond the mere enjoyment of good government.

This line of argument would lead to an evaluation of local, state, and national governments in terms of their capacity to provide ethically significant roles for citizens. Local and state governments would have worth, not simply as devices to prevent centralization, but as valuable means to widen the pos-

sibility of active civic life. A major purpose of these governments would be to attract and hold the active participation of
citizens who might well be lost in the undifferentiated apathetic mass of a centralized nation state.

A principal obstacle to applying the Greek concept of
citizenship to the modern state has been sheer size at the
national level and sheer lack of significance at the local level.
Can the affairs of a city or a state be given sufficient meaning
to provide anything like the challenge to human potentiality
the Periclean ideal demands? Some pride of citizenship remained in the cities of the Hellenistic monarchies, and even
in those of the Empire, but the older vitality was gone. Possibly any such vibrant vitality as Thucydides depicts would
be incompatible with superior national allegiance. When war
and foreign policy are no longer part of the stakes of power,
some of its tragic significance is lost to politics.

Yet the Greek ideal of functioning at the top of one's bent
along some line of excellence in a significant field of action is
surely applicable to our thinking about all levels of government. It is especially applicable if we are to call successfully
into play the resources of generous ambition that are squan-
dered in commercialism and escape. The stakes here are much
more than the education of the lower orders in the responsibilities of municipal housekeeping that Mill saw as a chief
value of local self-government.

As the United States becomes more and more a nation living in a few tens of metropolitan areas, the quality of its local
citizenships may well become of critical importance. Will the
inhabitants of these faceless and formless aggregates be
citizens or resident or even transient aliens with no commitment to the local area beyond the friendships of commerce
and pleasure it affords? One wonders whether resident aliens
of New York are likely to prove active citizens of state or
nation. Local citizenship is enervated by a sense of political
inefficacy in vitally influencing its neighborhood affairs. Remote municipal bureaucracies are unresponsive and where, as

in Kansas City, an enlightened city manager has attempted to give vitality to neighborhood citizenship, it has required tender care of an anaemic growth, and in its critics' view has been little more than the manager's machine. The patent need for restoration of neighborhood vitality in cities like New York and Chicago is matched by the need of a more readily workable political system for local problem solving at the metropolitan level. In one sense our cities are so big, with populations so lacking in locality roots, that they provide no meaningful activity where the citizens live. In another, our metropolitan areas are divided among so many jurisdictions that they present well nigh insuperable difficulties to the active citizens concerned with the responsible government of the metropolitan area.

While it is doubtful if the average man thirsts to be a Greek—he has been taught to be a consumer of politics, a client rather than a self-directed principal—there are still some who find a merely private and Epicurean free ride on the body politic a painful frustration of their personal potential and ethical need. For these the escape to the garden suburb seems to split the personality and confess defeat, even when, conscience driven, they return to the cave to man the board of directors of the community chest, the hospital, or the settlement house. Absentee political landlordism is productive not only of a bad conscience but, even more, of a sense of the failure to develop to the full the potentiality of one's personality in the ethical medium of politics. Dean Acheson, who should certainly know both the pains of public life and the cultivated pleasures of private society, has given eloquent testimony to the compelling attraction of large affairs to at least a remnant of Americans. This remnant is a vitally important leaven to the civic lump. Democracy, as Irving Babbitt pointed out, even more than other regimes depends on the quality of its leadership. It depends on the self devotion of a natural aristocracy to the precarious leadership roles of a mass society. In fact the eliciting of the efforts of this natural aristocracy, its education for the responsible conduct of affairs and the provision of a significant and accessible *cursus honorum* are major requisites for institutionalizing responsible citizenship.

The great city and the emerging metropolitan area threaten us with the example of Babylon, which Aristotle scornfully noted was so little a true city that half of it was captured before the other half knew or cared. The formless mass of megalopolis offers the temptation to resign oneself to the abandonment of the risks and arduous efforts of self government to an imperially efficient administration such as the Port of New York Authority or the T.V.A. A hard pressed and thin blooded elite may prefer its chances in a bureaucratically administered polity to the irksome and mudstained competition of a populist democracy where Cleons are in their element. The Yankee retreat from Boston to the suburbs, the courts and the gerrymandered state legislature has not stopped short of the brush fields of Vermont. Even there the respite has been short.

But while the frustrations of the mixed up mess of metropolis and the anonymous mass of the great city present a kind of formless futility, they have another and encouraging side. Whatever else they may be, they are not trivial. The issues of metropolitan life are momentous. The resources of the emerging metropolis are such as to challenge the imagination. The possibility, even the necessity, of a great age of cities confronts us. These cities will either be the theaters of a cultural and political renaissance or their promise will be lost in a shapeless, mindless mass of metics whose best hope is to be well administered and only moderately plucked for the pains.

Commentators from Kenneth Galbraith to Walter Lippmann agree that to the individual consumption of the past will be added an enormously increased public consumption. As our society moves toward a four day work week, the civilized use of leisure is a problem whose public import goes far beyond parks, beaches, and expressways. The Center of the

Performing Arts and Lincoln Square may be a grandiose, isolated real estate venture or a harbinger of a growing civility.

Throughout our metropolitan areas there is a stirring on the part of business and civic leaders no longer content to let the future of the communities take its unplanned course. As yet these leaders fumble in the ritual do-gooding of the civic committee, the ceremonial luncheon and the press release. The roles of a local regime responsibly governing its territory are barely beginning to take form and capture the imagination of men dedicated to the proposition that government is, or ought to be, irrelevant. It is still but a short while since Coolidge said the business of the United States is business. When the President says this, who could be blamed for minding his own? In fact, of course, Coolidge was not advocating a selfish materialism. For him, as for Carnegie, business was a private occupation, a Calvinist dedication. Curiously, business is a calling but politics is not. This is not surprising in Protestantism and especially, given its anti-urban bias, not surprising as an attitude towards urban politics. But it is at first sight odd that Catholicism, with its urbane tradition and emphasis on the doctrine of the common good, should have failed to give spiritual support to the political vocation. Catholicism's main emphasis has been on a largely private morality with scarcely a critical glance or sign of encouragement toward the public sphere. Where either faith has manifested itself it has, with exceptions, in the main been concerned to demonstrate the complete compatibility of its communicants' faith with an almost blind allegiance to the nation state. The similarity of Protestant and Catholic outlooks on politics is less surprising when it is remembered how deeply American Catholicism is imbued by Jansenism. We owe a heavy debt to the seminary of Maynooth. Few would see the state as merely a remedial institution occasioned by human sin whose proper symbol is the hangman, but many would see it as rightfully little more than the policeman of Locke if not of Herbert Spencer.

Little Rock is a symbol of the critical importance of the

local regime. While Governor Faubus' intervention upset local plans for token integration, the collapse or acquiescence of moderate leadership in the city was a portent of the political anaemia of the organization man. Little Rock represents but one, though a major one, of the tensions that will test the quality of citizenship in communities north as well as south of the Mason-Dixon. It is characteristic of Little Rock that local action has world-wide consequences. Here the issue of race in a nonwhite world in the grip of the cold war posed the problem of responsibility as starkly as possible. A whole complex of urban questions of only slightly lesser magnitude will make governing our urban centers a task of the highest seriousness.

If this estimate of the situation is correct, one favorable answer can be given to the question as to whether the Greek view of citizenship can be given operational reality in the context of American affairs. The emerging metropolitan areas in which the bulk of our people will live can be structured to create governments whose resources and problems would be such as to provide the kind of scope needed for the type of citizenship envisioned in classical theory. The possibilities of a richly pluralist culture which a galaxy of great American cities might sustain could capture the imagination of the spiritually underemployed now lacking a significant medium for creative action. As we move into an era of greater and greater public consumption, the sustenance of the arts and the refinement of life, as well as the presently burning questions of housing and the conditions of mere existence, will be more and more major functions of urban government. The new city in the terms of Burke may well become a partnership in all art, all science, all culture with a significant concept of the good life as a vital common aspiration. The apostles of metropolitanism are coming to realize that the vision they are seeking is something more than a better means of moving traffic, an improvement in the plumbing, or even an increase in the competitive position of the local economy. It is the possibility of attaining a shared common goal of a better life. The recreated city of the metropolitan area offers the hope of a significant manageable field of civic action in which a warmer sense of fraternity can be realized than in state or nation. That this is not a utopian dream is given some evidence by the New Haven renaissance that has given Mayor Lee fame and political fortune, while energizing and uniting an apathetic and mutually antagonistic citizenry. Given the heavy expenditure of federal funds, New Haven's experience may have less general applicability than its publicists claim. What is significant in the experience is the evidence it gives of the potential of an old and moribund city to develop a feeling of community, a kind of local *moi commun* and a pride in citizenship. Lee seems to have tapped a general longing for a visible fraternity and the deep desire in the ordinary man to see cathedrals built. Much of New Haven's urban renewal is of no direct economic benefit to its inhabitants, but the ferment of civic excitement is apparent in all social classes. Whether this sense of a revived shared civic life can be maintained without the charisma of Lee and the perhaps more important hypodermic of federal funds is problematic. The reality of the pent up psychological demand for local citizenship is a hopeful fact for those interested in institutionalizing responsible citizenship.

Perhaps the first task of securing responsible citizenship is the development of the sense of a *moi commun*. There have to be citizens who feel responsible and they have to have something to feel responsible for. There must be quite literally a public thing with which they identify and which they are concerned to support. The mere inhabitant of the big city such as New York may feel little more identity with the city than the shopper in Macy's basement. Like a Goth in the Roman Empire with his vote for a weapon, he may conceive himself as plundering an alien edifice. His very insignificance and lack of sense of power contribute to a feeling of political amorality. Why indeed should he care and what difference would it make if he did? The Irish of Boston who fought their way up from the docks have never accepted their responsibility for self government. Plundering the Yankees, even when in practice it means impoverishing their own people, became a political way of life. A demagogic squandering of civic capital by leaders lacking in permanent identification with the community and followers who are even less aware that their own substance is at stake is the nightmare of big city democracy and on the national scale the great beast of the Hamiltonian imagination.

The kind of individualistic imperialism, as Seilliere called it, that has no institutional loyalty but maximizes a personal profit at whatever cost, is not unknown in corporations and even in churches. In a sense the ethic of the robber barons was one of personal rather than corporate aggrandizement. Today the organization man of the large corporation, and the management too, are wedded to their corporation as an alumnus to his college, almost as the peasant to his farm, seeking its maintenance and increase with the highest goal to hand it over to the coming generation. Carl Kaysen in his article on monopoly depicts a priest-like hierarchy devoted to tending the corporate "national interest" with every consideration of reason of state. The plant sociologists, as Lloyd Fisher and Clark Kerr have called them, hope to unite management and workers alike in the soul-adjusting environment of the new corporate polity. Whatever their deficiencies, corporations, churches, and universities are capable of enlisting loyalties and devotions on the part of members who can identify themselves with them and regard them as a patrimony to be tended for its own sake and for coming generations. The corporation's capacity to enlist this kind of allegiance transforms the footloose, profit-seeking, salary-seeking economic man into the good corporate citizen.

This attitude of corporate management and organization man suggests that at least for some institutions we can develop both loyalty and a sense of responsibility for the future. However, corporations, churches, and universities provide enduring roles for their members in a way that governments only do for their bureaucracies. Were our party structures sufficiently institutionalized to be stably related to the govern-

ment levels, they might sustain roles whose occupants could
regard government with the same attachment and responsibility as management views the big corporation.

Quite clearly in the class of citizen we have a wide range of
roles and attitudes. There are those who are in active contention to man the public offices, and of these there are those who
are merely birds of passage as well as those who in a sense
make a profession of public life. The differing levels of government provide different theaters of action with better or
worse critics and media of criticism, wider or narrower, informed or uninformed audiences, and the like. The lack of
party institutions tends to an individualism of action that at
the very least will be devoid of corporate responsibility, and
the amorphousness of the political class limits its capacity to
develop sustained roles and norms of action. The old pros of
the legislative clubs of Washington do, however, develop rules
of the game and court diarists such as William White give
them institutionalizing support in the press.

The polity of Athens was built on a substructure of slaves,
resident aliens, and other noncitizens. In the American city
there are no slaves and the number of resident aliens, even if
one counts among them citizens of other states, is not so large
as to endanger the preponderance of the legal holders of local
citizenship. Yet the political psychology of slaves and metics
may be present in a majority of the legal holders of local
citizenship. Legal citizenship and ethical citizenship have no
necessary coincidence. Civic rights and the vote may be merely
political weapons in the hands of aliens who regard existing
institutions as potential spoil and their political power not
as an office of self-imposed trust but as a battering ram. The
Aristotelian view of citizenship as membership in a shared
ethical community is an essential addition to legal citizenship
if that category is to imply an accepted commitment and
office. While the ritual of naturalization is mawkish and over-
much a tawdry American Legion ceremony, it at least reflects
an awareness that physical residence by itself does not produce the desired quality of citizenship as an automatic by-

product. With the native born, apart from a compulsory course in American history and a monotonous pledging of allegiance to the flag in the schools, the office of citizenship is attained with the same ease as growing up. It is a free and unearned gift and, given a natural rights philosophy, perhaps it ought to be.

Actually, to speak of citizenship coming as an unearned gift for the mere passage of birthdays overstates the case. The historically developed processes through which the culture is socialized in the United States includes the socialization of the political culture. This culture includes, along with the abstract legal definition of citizenship, sets of social habits and expectations that give it practical meaning. The bum in the park has the same vote as the banker in the bank. Dr. Gallup's sample survey will count them each as one. But aside from Dr. Gallup and the voting machine, no one else will count them as politically equal units. The legal class of citizen masks a wide variety of roles that are socially sustained. Despite a devotion to democracy that went as far as the use of the lot, Athens too had leading citizens. Our multimember state legislature districts approach a lottery though they rest on no such consciously democratic principle as the lot.

The active citizens who form a relatively open governing class overlie a largely passive majority who consume government and exert their influence through the political market place. In a sense, the slaves and the resident aliens of Athens have been given the vote. The gloomy pages of Thucydides furnished the conservatives of many a state constitutional convention with arguments against an expanded suffrage. Indeed how could irresponsible demagoguery be contained if the politically active were to compete for the suffrages of slaves and metics? The experience of American cities, for all the failure that Bryce deplored, has not borne out the fears of those who saw in universal suffrage the threat of stasis. In part this may have been due to the devices taken to damp the force of faction, but there have been few rural and scarcely any urban Daniel Shays. The primary fear of civic irresponsibility, the fear of class war producing a city of the rich and a city of the poor, has not materialized. The nearest to this has been the physical secession, not of the plebs, but of the optimates to the suburbs.

Expansion of the ranks of the citizenry has necessarily meant a dilution of significant participation, especially as the town meeting of agrarian democracy has faded into the past. The successive accessions of new classes to the suffrage in Anglo-American constitutional history were impelled as a means to defend the subjects against the exactions of their rulers. The winning of the initiative was a long process. The first job was not to govern but to win the right to assent to taxes. The suffrage for many citizens is a means not so much of self-government as of self-defense from those who rule and a way of ensuring active competition for their favor. This legal right of protest is a kind of minimal form of citizenship. Even when not exercised, it is the political shotgun on the wall. It helps to insure one kind of responsibility on the part of the regime, an enforced sensitivity to any substantial element of the population armed with the effective right of the suffrage. Of course this does not mean that demands will be responsibly made or responsibly met. It does mean that one condition of responsible government is that no appreciable element of the community should be politically powerless. Universal suffrage also provided the legitimatizing myth of consent for the regime. One might consider the power to protest as the most general and elementary citizen role. This is the voice calling attention, in Lord Lindsay's sense, to the fact that the shoe pinches.

While it is necessary as a means of enforcing responsibility on the active citizens who conduct the government that all should have the right of voicing their grievances in a compelling manner, this inevitably involves the fact that the power to voice one's grievance is also the power to sustain or defeat a policy and a government. The ignorant, the apathetic, the irresponsible can powerfully determine the course of a government with which they feel little identification and to whose measures they have given little thought. Whether it be fluoridation or foreign policy, their intervention is a real price that must be paid.

Related to the general role of protest is the role of pressure group member. Here the citizen may not only be voicing his demands as a consumer of government policy, but, in addition, showing responsible concern for the government in terms of some notion of a common good. Farm Bureau Federation, Chamber of Commerce, C.I.O.-A.F.L., even the American Legion, must at least pay lip service to the compatibility of the proposals with a more general public interest. In fact, the leaders of the major pressure groups may acquire a degree of identification with government affairs that makes them an effective part of the governing class. The organized pressure groups provide offices and staff that support an important part of the personnel of American public life. As institutions they provide their members more effective linkage with government and public policy than the political parties. The member of the C.I.O.-A.F.L. receives a wide variety of political education, as does his counterpart in the Chamber of Commerce and the Farm Bureau Federation. While this education is partial and biased, it makes a plea that is far from one of naked self-interest. Civil rights and foreign policy are combined with bread and butter unionism. Lenin paid high tribute to trade union consciousness as a device for anchoring the proletariat in the constitutional order and his bitterness toward trade union leaders is a testimonial to their role in the public life of democracy.

A highly important role of responsible citizenship, but one without much institutional support, is that of supporting the rules of the game. The good citizens of Clinton, Tennessee, who disapproved of the Supreme Court's decision but thought it should be obeyed nonetheless are a case in point. Responsible citizenship involves support of the rules. The existence of such a body of opinion means that hotly contended issues can be kept within the bounds of accepted procedures. These procedures are valued for themselves despite their outcome in the particular case. Press, Bar Association, Civil Liberties Union, churches, and other associations provide some institutional support for a citizen role in which people stand up and are counted in support of observance of the rules. The current struggle over the Fifth Amendment is one that shows the very limited understanding possessed by citizens who have a general ideological commitment to supporting the constitution.

While the support of the rules of the game involves a very general interest, it is probably expecting too much to hope for a comparably general public support. However, as in so many cases, if anything like an appropriate elite takes a stand, its representative position in the society will insure a broad support based on its leadership role.

Lippmann in his *Public Opinion* expressed the view that Jefferson had been oversanguine in his expectation that a free press would automatically fulfill the informational needs of a democracy. In this particular work Lippmann was himself sanguine that the problem of the requisite knowledge for informed public decisions in our democracy could be met. His later work, *The Phantom Public,* was far less sanguine.

Informed, responsible citizenship, like so many other activities of our civilization, requires a division of labor. The citizen must in effect delegate the task of developing information and policy alternatives in particular areas to specialized publics. What is true of the arts is true of politices as well. The general public at best can be a critical audience of the civic drama. Specialized production, development of new ideas, will depend on off Broadway. The Walter Lippmans are the Brooks Atkinsons, and their publics, though influential, are but a fraction of the mass. Responsible citizenship is carried on in a Foreign Policy Association, a Civil Liberties Union, a Citizen's Housing Council, a Welfare Federation, and similar associations that assume the task of developing policies in particular fields. The associational life of the community provides the main framework for the development of expertise and the assumption of responsibility in particular policy areas. Specialized media of communication such as the maga-

zine *Foreign Affairs,* columnists like Lippmann, newscasters
like Murrow, become institutions for the crystallizing of special publics along with the universities and the churches. They
provide the interested citizen with something to do if it be no
more than listen to a Murrow broadcast and discuss it within
his circle.

Clearly these activities in no way compare with the ecclesia
or the law courts of Athens. The problem of mass democracy
is its almost inevitable deficiency of institutions for vital participation in the community's public life. Responsibility for
something one takes no active part in is difficult to arouse
and maintain. We are becoming a nation addicted to spectator
sports, and politics bids fair to be just another one of them.
Lack of personal participation does not prevent the fans from
being rabid partisans, a fact that has been known since the
Greens and the Blues of Byzantium. It is also interesting and
perhaps of some encouragement that the average baseball fan
is more rational in his judgment of the sport than is the average citizen in his judgment of politics. The baseball fan in
defending his judgment can refer to objective standards, statistical data such as earned run averages, hits, errors, fielding
chances, and the like. His judgment, while not unemotional,
has the grounds for intellectual responsibility not possessed by
the ordinary citizen in politics. This quality of responsibility
in the audience is supportive of responsibility to accepted
standards in the players. In the theater, if the audience demands vaudeville, it is difficult to perform tragedy.

In the structuring of a responsible audience, reporting by
the media and the special role of the accepted critics play an
important part. The sports writers are to the ball players what
the dramatic critics are to the Broadway stars. In this respect
the political stars are somewhat alike. While the mayor and
his staff in New York affect to shrug off a critical *Times* edi-
torial with the scornful comment that the paper couldn't elect
a dog catcher, they hurry out to buy the paper as if it provided the opening night's reviews. The mechanism of re-

sponsibility operates through an elite public who develop standards and methods of evaluation that are accepted by officials and more general publics alike.

The hopeful character of the developing new metropolitan areas is the opportunity to structure a significant theater for civic action. If this theater can be made sufficiently brilliant, it can attract to local public life an array of talent now uninvolved, in elections. The grounds of responsibility are its acceptance and a medium for sustained action. The great city provides the possibility for massing the thin and separated elites that concern themselves with the whole gamut of affairs from foreign policy to public housing. Hopefully, such a massing of elites will produce local regimes with a broad and programmatic sense of responsibility because their interaction will relate culture, art, and politics as facets of the great city and media of action for its leading citizens. The politicos will have a theater.

The danger that intense local life will have the effects that Rousseau feared seems far less in a period when local regimes can only survive within a strong nation. The Burkean view of a mediated loyalty in which valued local institutions support and strengthen the nation seems more likely. By providing truly significant fields of action for the minorities that leaven the civic lump, vital local politics can attract the energies and the identifications of talents now lost, indifferent, or frustrated.

A final word on Roelof's third strand of citizenship, the private occupation. As the strength of practicing Christianity and Judaism ebbs in a period of merely outward acceptance, the traditional bulwarks of western man's private life and right to it are weakened. The perfervid demands for an all-embracing loyalty and the mounting attack on the Bill of Rights show the extent to which we have lost appreciation of the importance of the private conscience to the public good. The responsibility of the citizen to labor at his own salvation and at some point weigh the acts of the state in a conscience for which he alone bears the responsibility is no longer accepted with the same assurance that a more religious epoch accorded. However accepted, as academic freedom or scientific vocation, the need for free citizens with free consciences is critical to a free society. With the churches uncertain how to render the limitation on Caesar, we are forced to find a secular and ethical expression for a religious truth. The fellowship of science has found how hard the yoke of secrecy and loyalty is to bear, given their commitment. Here the tension of citizenship between national loyalty and service and the private occupation are intense and unsolved. Faith requires us to believe that we can have our cake and eat it too: serve our nation and save our souls.

METROPOLITAN CITIZENSHIP: PROMISES AND LIMITATIONS

JOHN W. CHAPMAN

T HE MAIN PURPOSE of the following remarks is to lend support to Norton Long's enthusiasm for the revival of a spirit of metropolitan citizenship. This I seek to do in perspectives, both theoretical and historical, somewhat different from those which he has chosen to elaborate. It is apparent, I think, that the rebuilding and the institutional retooling of our metropolitan areas have distinctive contributions to make to the development of responsible citizenship. These contributions should not be underestimated, nor should they be exaggerated. Hence I wish to draw attention to their limitations in a cautionary way and to point to other and more comprehensive encouragements to responsibility.

By responsible citizenship I mean lively concern about the consequences of one's actions, especially their impact upon others, combined with adequate understanding of social and economic relationships. Here adequacy implies not perfect knowledge or foresight, but rather knowledge of the kind that a reasonable person could be expected to rely on in important decisions. Responsible behavior is rational behavior essentially. The standard of rationality is not ability to do higher mathematics or symbolic logic. It is, as C. I. Lewis points out, the disposition and the ability to take account of the future, not to do today what one will regret tomorrow. In this sense, responsibility and rationality are as much the functions of attitudes as they are of more distinctively intellectual operations.

To develop and to sustain responsible attitudes requires a

grasp of the connections between human dynamics, the ways in which psychological processes are related to one another, and institutional structures. Probably we should need to know rather more than we do at present about how attitudes are formed and how they are sustained in order to predict with any high degree of confidence whether an evolving institutional pattern will weaken or strengthen responsibility. Moreover, in respect to any given society the difficulties inherent in systematic analysis will be enhanced by the need to take account of historical considerations. Even initially esoteric metaphysical doctrines such as existentialism may be expected eventually to influence political orientations. Or rapid urbanization may hinder the development of responsible attitudes, but when this is combined with an inheritance of unresolved social conflicts, the problem of responsible citizenship may become acute. Economic organization must also be taken into account. Where economic relationships spread their web beyond the area embraced by men's sense of solidarity, the late Lord Lindsay often argued, irrational responses to events and disappointments are bound to be encouraged. This proposition, which for Lindsay was essentially a diagnosis of the plight of western civilization, applies as well, or better, to the situation that exists in many metropolitan areas, fragmented as they are by inherited and increasingly inappropriate political boundaries. In such a situation perhaps one may hope, possibly expect, that new ethical ideas will emerge to ease the tensions and to create a new sense of unity, more in keeping with economic and social realities.

One such idea appears to be that of metropolitan citizenship. My present aim is to assess this idea in an historical perspective, and so to make available the results of political thought about responsibility to those directly engaged in the work of reconstructing the institutions of the metropolis.

The idea of metropolitan citizenship offers an alternative to Hobbesian conceptions of political responsibility. It promises also to be a corrective for the Rousseauistic emphasis on the smaller, more intimate groupings of neighborhood and community. But metropolitan citizenship is an idea essentially Aristotelian, both in its origins and expectations. Those to whom it appeals picture an age of city-states in which urban loyalties, evoked by common problems and sustained by architectural symbolism, stimulate moral and cultural vitalities. In practice, there is another Aristotelian facet to the metropolitan revival, in that privately accumulated wealth may be expended for public purposes, as appears to be the case in the Pittsburgh Renaissance. Remarkable as the changes wrought may be, the question posed is whether any refurbished Aristotelian view of citizenship can be entirely adequate to the demands of modern societies, large, mobile, and technologically oriented as they are. For us a somewhat more Hegelian, more comprehensive perspective—perhaps best elaborated in terms of John Stuart Mill's concept of the "spirit of political institutions"—seems more appropriate.

Responsible action in a national, and an increasingly international, context requires not so much the further development of geographical attachments as it does the formation of common objectives, and common standards, to which active minorities and leaderships may be responsive, and by which their performances may be evaluated. Human rationality depends for its cultivation and its support upon no single set of institutions, and it manifests itself through diverse channels of influence. Governments do not only respond to men's attitudes and expectations, but help as well to shape these, perhaps in ways that are decisive. It is noteworthy that in the recent past we have witnessed a vast improvement in the standards of urban politics, of the federal bureaucracy, of the exercise of corporate power. Debilitating insecurities have been brought under control, the level of education and political sophistication of the electorate has risen, and with it all the tone of public life has improved. These results have no single cause, nor does their momentum depend upon any single institutional focus. They are the cumulative product of pressures and standards generated by an interlocking pattern of institutions, political, social, and economic.

To be sure, it is difficult to envisage a world in which emotional commitment to a locale is not an essential ingredient of a good life. But the sorts of satisfaction which promote survival of liberal democratic ways of life are likely to be in the future less geographical and more ethical in origin. And men have shown themselves to be capable of forming both kinds of attachment, one to the place, the locality, and the other to the ethic, the standard. Both kinds of attachment can unify, both have the power to make men responsible. Within limits, we can encourage the formation of the one at the expense of the other, and so achieve a balance suitable to the impersonal requirements of a social and political situation. Ideally the two types of attachment should reinforce one another in promoting the growth of responsible attitudes. In practice, at any given time and place we have a choice as to which we shall further and emphasize. And it is this question with which the idea of metropolitan citizenship confronts the institutional engineer.

Two currents, in particular, of modern political theory are relevant to the problem of developing and sustaining responsible citizenship. The first of these has its origin in the work of Hobbes, though some might wish to refer in this connection to Aristotle's emphasis upon the importance of the habitual in human behavior. I have in mind the Hobbes who recommended his *Leviathan* to the "potent" and who urged the sovereign to teach "justice" to the common people, whose minds he likened to "clean sheets of paper." The essence of the Hobbesian formula for responsible citizenship is to enlighten the élite and to condition the masses. In his view human dynamics are such that men respond favorably to direct and systematic indoctrination. In this way Hobbes thought human energies may be released while social frictions are minimized and security effectively sustained.

The evolution of Hobbes' basic prescription for responsibility may be traced through the work of eighteenth-century writers such as Helvetius and nineteenth-century utilitarians such as James Mill. The prescription is based on the psycho-

logical theory of associationism, indeed it relies almost entirely
on this theory of human dynamics to provide a basis for social
and political reconstruction. David Hume made notorious
use of this theory in both his philosophical and political
works. Given an historical flavor, it underlies the thought of
Burke, uniting him ironically with French theorists whom he
despised. To some extent, at least, the principle of association
helps to account for Marx's belief that man's environment
shapes his mind, a belief which finds both pessimistic and
utopian applications in Marxist ideology. Even Rousseau,
despite his reluctance to tamper with the human mind, has
one foot in this tradition. Believing, as he did, that productive forces are spontaneously released only within the small
group, when confronted with the task of building responsible
citizenship in the nation state, Rousseau turned to a civil religion as the means by which to reinforce men's social spirit.
For the Poles Rousseau prescribed nothing less than systematic
civic indoctrination. More recently the techniques of indoctrination have been tirelessly and ingeniously elaborated by
B. F. Skinner to create the social nightmare of *Walden II*.

The distinction between persons and things appears to be
a basic feature of the structure of human thought and discourse. Perhaps these writers blur this distinction to a degree
which falsifies experience. Certainly the existentialist would
say so. But clearly it would be unwise to neglect so steady a
current of thought about how to deal with human recalci-
trance in ways that are consistent with some sort of happiness.
A view to which so many powerful minds have subscribed in
one form or another, and which also finds so many contemporary applications, ranging from the techniques of advertising to those of brain-washing, demands consideration on its
own merits. I shall not attempt this, for such a task goes well
beyond the limits of this paper. Rather I merely wish to point
out that today we move still, perhaps far too much, within
the Hobbesian framework of thought about political responsibility.

Fear that modern populations are not equal to the responsibilities imposed upon them now reinforces the original scientific impulse to explain human behavior and thought in terms of a few simple laws which may be used to engineer consent, security, happiness, or whatever else the thinker judges valuable. Hobbes' formula, with nuances in statement and application, has come to seem to many minds more appropriate and relevant than ever before. I refer to the common conceptual structure behind the writings of Harold D. Lasswell, Walter Lippmann, C. Wright Mills, Philip Selznick, and Andrew Hacker—to mention only the more vocal and striking representatives of this tradition. No matter whether their orientation be judged conservative or liberal, to these writers it makes good sense to think of modern societies as composed of élites and masses. As H. Stuart Hughes has recently demonstrated, other strands of thought, including romanticism and Freudianism, converge on this dichotomy. Recent European history seems to support this outlook and sociological analysis tends to confirm it—a fact which ought not to surprise since Durkheim was an adherent to the psychological doctrine of associationism. Behind the American writings are the impressive analyses of Pareto, Mosca, Weber, Wallas, and Mannheim. These men thought society to be polarized, and what may well have been the truth about nineteenth-century European society is now being applied to the mid-twentieth-century American scene. Indeed for distinction of ideological ancestry, for apparent possession of explanatory and prescriptive power, and for hard-headedness and realism, it would be difficult to find a competitor to these contemporary American forms of Hobbism. Even the late Lord Lindsay, for all his contempt for Hobbistic and Freudian accounts of the human mind, was inclined to think that industrialization inevitably divided society between those who manage and those who get managed.

There are significant differences among the American authors mentioned, and in other contexts I should not wish to minimize these. For present purposes what is important is that all think it appropriate and illuminating to view our society through the concepts of élite and mass. Consider this aspect of Lasswell's work! He would enlighten the élite as to the nature of their task, the navigation of the tides of insecurity to which the masses are exposed. In addition, he would protect the mass against warped candidates for political leadership through such devices as personnel boards, the purpose of which is to assess the psychological health of individuals. To these prescriptions for increasing political responsibility there is a directness which is fully in accord with the Hobbesian tradition. Compare also Lasswell's concern with the early years of life and James Mill's insistence upon the crucial role of education in the formation of human utilitarians. In both cases, the indirect influence of political institutions upon the formation of character tends to disappear.

Walter Lippmann in his *The Public Philosophy* is concerned to protect and to insulate élites against the pressures of the short-sighted electorate. Having abandoned hope that the people can ever face the "hard" decisions, Lippmann would have leaderships more responsive to standards embalmed in natural laws. His views find an echo in George Kennan's desire to have our foreign policy conducted by the uncommonly able, unhindered by the waves of emotion which sweep through a less astute public. Again there is a willingness to rely upon the impact of expertise and personality rather than to explore the popular educational possibilities of institutional reform.

C. Wright Mills thinks *The Power Elite* real, cohesive, and irresponsible, and despairs of the effectiveness of organizations that serve to link interests and national power. He, too, would appear to underestimate human institutional sensitivities and to exaggerate our responsiveness to the more direct stimuli of personality and the word, spoken or written. Such is the case also in the work of Selznick and Hacker. The former fears the institutional vulnerability of mass society and looks to leaderships, essentially administrative in their composition, to preserve its institutional integrity through a process which he calls "value infusion." The latter places his hopes on the mellowing of the new men of power, the successful manipulators of memberships and publics, dependent though they may be upon the mass responses which they engineer.

There runs through this body of analysis and recommendation a simplistic polarization of modern society into the leaders and the led, a dramatic dichotomy of manipulators and manipulated. The result of this drastic assumption is a directness of analysis and prescription which depreciates the more subtle, and perhaps more pervasive, influences of institutions upon human character and motivation. In this perspective human behavior appears responsive mainly to the personalized stimuli of career patterns and direct controls based on the cultivation and exploitation of attitudes, often infantile in their origins. To the extent that highly mobile, possibly atomized and anomic, urban populations find a basis of solidarity in metropolitan loyalties and aspirations, the Hobbesian approach to responsible citizenship should become both less plausible and less relevant. There would be less temptation to condition, to manipulate, to indoctrinate potentially dangerous masses should their desire for significance find satisfaction in the social and cultural achievements of the new metropolis. Wider and better informed concern for the less obvious consequences of policies within metropolitan "conurbations" should render less attractive the idea of treating urban populations as masses, either dangerous to or dependent upon élites. This is one of the promises held out by an enlarging sense of metropolitan citizenship. Political responsibility would become, within significant though restricted areas, more the outcome of spontaneous developments within the human psyche, and less the deliberate objective of a battery of forms of indoctrination. New forms of metropolitan government, more comprehensive and more effective in their intent, could be devised to encourage the development of this spirit, to mobilize energies now dispersed in flight from the decaying central cities, and to evoke loyalties now dormant in financially insulated suburbs. And these reorientations on the part of metropolitan populations would accord well with an ethic in which both the idea of moral freedom and the idea of the free acceptance of responsibilities are central. The ideal of spontaneously assumed responsibilities need not prevent one from dealing harshly with inherited institutional invitations to evasion, among which the political "Balkanization" of our metropolitan areas is outstanding.

The other current of psychological theory relevant to an appraisal of the idea of metropolitan citizenship has its source in the work of the classical Greek thinkers and finds its most powerful modern statement in the writings of Rousseau, in particular in his *Émile* and *Discourses*. Now neither Plato nor Aristotle were above indoctrinating the citizens of their projected societies. But they never treat man simply as a bundle of habits or conditioned reflexes. For them, he is also a cluster of potentialities, both moral and social, which require for their realization an appropriate social and political environment. By way of contrast to the Hobbesian mechanical outlook, this kind of psychology may be designated developmental. John Stuart Mill had this contrast in mind when he asserted that man is not a machine to be constructed after a certain model, but rather more like a tree, which is not built but grows. For a time the developmental outlook was eclipsed by the work of Hobbes and his successors, but it reemerges, lacking the inequalitarian presuppositions of the Greeks, in the thought of Rousseau. The élitist implications of this psychology, so vividly portrayed by Plato, are dissolved by Rousseau's analysis of the unfortunate moral consequences generated by differences in status, both social and political. Indeed, so far as modern political thought is concerned, this developmental psychology has its founder in Rousseau, the Rousseau who saw moral freedom and responsibility, the productive forces in man, released by direct participation in the political activity of a small society. Without this opportunity, Rousseau thinks that man would become alienated both from himself and from his fellows. All forms of inequality are dangerous to man's moral development. Citizenship for Rousseau, as it was for Aristotle in a more limited way, is essentially an active business. There is not a place in his thought for a distinction between an active minority and an inactive, passive majority. Such a division would be incompatible with social spirit and responsible attitudes. All must participate if the laws are to embody the rational principles which each would freely choose to apply to himself as a social being. Men's achievement of rational standards of morality is made directly dependent upon personal participation. The only alternative which Rousseau recognizes to this active citizenship is personal alienation and distortion, followed ultimately by general dissatisfaction with social life and moral disappointment bitterly apparent to all.

No doubt Rousseau exaggerates the extent to which human development is directly dependent on individual performance of political roles. Either he does this, or he holds to a view of freedom to which few are prepared to give serious consideration because its implications are inconsistent with the material achievements of an advanced society. Assuming that the flaw in his theory is psychological rather than moral, it must be granted that his exaggeration is of the kind that has both fruitful and harmful consequences, not the latter alone. Rousseau's ideas about human development have been fruitful because they have helped to keep alive the idea that men require neighborhoods as well as nations in which to mature. Perhaps his most influential intellectual descendant is Mary Parker Follett, who gave so powerful a statement to the developmental principle in psychology. Still her work itself shows how difficult it is to provide an appropriate institutionalization of this principle. Eloquent though she may have been about the neighborhood group, a glaring weakness mars her thought: The lack of institutions and arrangements effectively to link neighborhood and nation. And it may be added that Lewis Mumford's ventures into regionalism have hardly filled this gap, although it would be unwise entirely to discount the efforts toward regional planning. Rousseau's ideas have been fruitful again in helping to maintain the ideal of

an integrated personality, recently so attractively restated in
the work of Erich Fromm. In this connection, the writings of
others should be mentioned, such as Solomon E. Asch, Gardner
Murphy, and Gordon Allport. These theorists have weakened
the prestige of the mechanical psychology by exploring its
weaknesses and revealing its inadequacies.

Still Rousseau's conception of human growth has been a
force for harm, for like the Hobbesian tradition it can, if
accepted, lead to dismay about the possibility of joining the
smaller communities of neighborhood and city with the
national centers of authority. He toyed with federalism as the
device by which one could retain the moral value of the
directly participating group and also have the advantages be-
longing to membership in the great society. But he did not
really care to face this problem, for his psychological presuppositions precluded him from any solution he would have
thought morally acceptable. If you think that human character is distorted by any political system other than direct
democracy, then you will necessarily despair of the quality of
life achieved in modern societies. Norton Long strikes an
authentically Rousseauistic note when he says that "the problem of mass democracy is its almost inevitable deficiency of
institutions for vital participation in the community's public
life." Thinkers in the Rousseauistic tradition have never convincingly met the challenge of combining intense participation in the affairs of a locale with significant contributions to
the politics of the nation.

Follett's notion of delegates from the neighborhood groups
to the national groupings is the most vague and least satisfactory part of her theory. Even the pluralists, whose debt to
Rousseau is manifest, never succeeded in making clear their
ideas about the integration of society. Negotiation and mutual good-will, as G. D. H. Cole in his guild socialist writings
seemed all too often to think, are no substitutes for institutional arrangements, hierarchical and ultimately coercive in
their effect. The institutional residue of pluralism would appear to be lavish use of advisory groups attached to an ad-

ministrative structure, very much sovereign in its backing. After a brave start in the politics of pluralism, Harold Laski condemned the separation of powers, declared federalism obsolete, and placed all his hopes in the basket of concentrated authority sensitive to a postulated popular will. It would be a mistake to regard pluralism as quite bankrupt, for its spirit, at least, lives on in various forms, some less odd than others. I note that Erich Fromm's institutional prescriptions, as displayed in his *Sane Society,* concern the creation of the good life on an almost neighborhood scale of existence, too primitive and inward-turning for the tastes of many. But we do have many new forms of democratic participation, as John D. Lewis has pointed out. And indeed a kind of *de facto* pluralism permeates our society because of the potential veto powers possessed by so many groups. Industrial pluralism in the shape of syndicalism and the doctrine of workers' control appears to have been by-passed, with the exception of co-determination in Western Germany, by reliance on less direct instrumentalities of control such as party, parliament, and minister. The pluralists never liked the party. It always seemed to them too much an instrument of compromise and not enough of integration. But it has been the party which has filled that gap between the locality and the nation. It has done the double job of unifying and responding to the people in a way that no pluralist invention ever could. This suggests that no form of direct participation at a local level, whether it be geographical or functional, can be a substitute for institutions to occupy effectively the intermediate spaces of society, whether they be political, regional, or corporate.

The difficulty is that excessive reliance on the developmental principle in psychology in the shape given it by Rousseau, Follett, and Fromm may lead to a perverse kind of Rousseauistic pessimism. If it is impossible to elicit men's productive potentialities in the great society, then Hobbism, in the shape of the élite-mass dichotomy, may seem to be the only realistic stance. In his later works Rousseau went down this road himself. He insidiously suggests that moral freedom and responsibility are not to be had once we leave the intimate world of the city-state. The covert implication is that we are doomed to move in a stultifying society composed of mutually antipathetic élites and masses. The scale on which we must live if we are to have our material advantages precludes our being genuinely morally free creatures, united by mutual affections and responsibilities. The inequalities generated by bureaucracy and hierarchy are bound to impair our moral development. We purchase material satisfaction at the price of the only right that counts, the right to determine who we are and who we shall become. We acquire characters with built-in disappointments. "Other-directed," "automatons," "sheep," "cheerless robots," are among the phrases currently used to describe man in the modern age. From an Aristotelian standpoint, Hannah Arendt now offers a dreary future in which even the narcotic of work shall be denied, thus mercilessly exposing our lack of inner resources. It seems that the implications of the Aristotelian psychology, when elaborated by Rousseau and his successors, are no less foreboding than those of the contemporary forms of Hobbism.

Here, I think, is the second promise contained in the idea of metropolitan citizenship. It offers us the chance of having our things and our souls, and each in greater measure than ever before. For it projects a grouping sufficiently large for the purposes of production, and yet not so large as to weaken our sense of identity and responsibility. The metropolitan entity promises an outlet for what William Ernest Hocking calls man's commotive impulse, the desire to do grand things together, a sort of overflow of the will to create. If the metropolis can become a point of attachment and unity, this should mitigate the corrosive resentments and discouragements that functional inequalities are said to generate. New dispositions and attitudes, more civil than those of localism and nationalism, should emerge in man and prove that he need not be debased by the expansion of life.

For these reasons the rebuilding of the metropolitan areas is a highly desirable thing to accomplish. Institutional inventiveness can alter the shape and the significance of urban politics still further in the direction of human welfare. Already American cities have moved from machine dominance to a more benign multi-centered pattern of pressure politics. It is still the case, however, that cultural, ethnic, and status cleavages strain the urban fabric. As Coleman Woodbury has so eloquently stated in *The Future of Cities and Urban Redevelopment,* one of the prime tasks of this generation is the recreation of an urban consensus. For upon this depends the texture of civic life, the quality of education, and more effective use of the technology at our command. Fortunately the prospect of financial disaster may be expected to reinforce, not to counteract, these considerations.

It would be a mistake to regard a resurgence of metropolitan feeling as a manifestation of the "self-reference effect," far less irrational than McCarthyism, but still a turning inward and away from national and international sources of irritation. Mumford reminds us that the city, properly designed, can be an environment both stimulating and educating, which prepares persons to meet the requirements of justice on a world scale. It would be unfortunate if our core cities are allowed to become islands of segregation surrounded by defensive suburbs. This would stamp upon the metropolitan area those class divisions which blemish the face of London and Paris and so defeat Mumford's vision. More recently Frederick Watkins has argued that the path to international unity lies through the neighborhood and its potential contribution to psychological health. Again this hope depends upon the formation of neighborhoods which integrate, not separate. It would be irresponsible to leave the pattern of metropolitan life at the mercy of market pressures and human evasiveness. And the growing sense of metropolitan citizenship indicates that the atomistic disposition to go-it-alone is weakening. Concern for the metropolis is rooted in genuine problems, not only financial, and carries implications more broad than is immediately apparent. Little more can be asked of a new ethical idea, especially one which refuses to be cowed by the underestimations of human capacity implicit in both the Hobbesian and Rousseauistic currents of psychology. On these grounds alone the spirit of metropolitan citizenship deserves encouragement in forms as diverse as federal financial assistance and distinctive architectures. Perhaps the metropolis will become the ethical idea which can link neighborhood and nation, a territorial corporation, which is more vital than the inherited structure of states, and yet avoids the divisiveness inherent in corporativism. If to all this should be added deeper appreciation of cultures, both western and non-western, and greater confidence in the viability of liberal democratic ways of life, one could hardly ask for more. It is worth recalling that one of the heresies recently denounced in the Soviet Union was that of "cosmopolitanism."

Despite these imposing credentials, there are limitations to the metropolis conceived as the prime source of a new sense of unity and responsibility. These limitations are, I think, inherent in the Aristotelian-Rousseauistic conception of citizenship itself. For we are now in an era in which no form of emotional insulation against ethical and technical pressures can long endure. In some degree the cultivation of geographical loyalty attempts to establish barriers against the world outside, even as it releases energies and generates satisfactions within. No doubt great disparities in income help to sustain nationalistic feelings. This generalization appears to apply within metropolitan areas as well as between nations. But the striking fact about our world is that claims for support and help based on considerations of justice are mingled with nationalistic aspirations. And it is also noteworthy that many are responsive to these claims. This suggests that we may be entering an era in which ethical considerations will gradually supplant geographically oriented dispositions as the major bases of human unity. If this be so, then Aristotelian attitudes will become increasingly regressive.

Lindsay used to argue that the decisively dangerous fact about western civilization was that economic and technical interdependencies had outstripped political will and capacity. It was easier, he thought, for men to form economic ties than enduring political relationships. The result is an explosive situation. Now this is precisely what has happened in the metropolitan areas of this country. People have become interdependent in ways with which neither their attitudes nor the political machinery at their disposal equip them to deal. In many cases the result is competitive planning by core cities in financial distress, planning the purpose of which is to improve tax bases by attracting industry and exporting low income groups to the suburbs to which the well-to-do had already fled. This warfare spreads into city-state relationships and even on to the highways where the commuters frustrate one another to the dismay of their high-powered cars. The lack of a sense of common destiny reveals itself in the general reluctance to provide a standard of education consistent with both needs and resources. Essentially the spirit of metropolitan citizenship is a rational response to the tensions aroused by the disparity between an increasingly intense interdependence on the part of rapidly urbanized populations and the attitudes supported by a structure of political boundaries inherited from a rural age. The emergence of the metropolitan spirit represents an effort to bring obviously inappropriate attitudes into line with economic and sociological interdependencies. An enlarged sense of unity and responsibility is the natural and appropriate response to a maze of irrationalities which many deplore and for which no one can be held accountable. In time it should make our cities far more attractive and psychologically healthful places in which to live. An improvement in the quality of urban living is much to be desired, but it will not of itself develop responsible citizens of the kind that our international responsibilities require. Indeed, it is even possible that mere material improvements would intensify divisive feelings. Some sociologists argue that material improvement was an important factor in the outbreak of the McCarthyite irrationalism. In other words, enlarged and intensified geographical loyalties may be an appropriate response to a situation shot through with material and social frustrations. But appropriateness on this level does not guarantee the absence of unanticipated and unfortunate consequences in other areas of concern.

Reason and past experience suggest that the contribution of metropolitan citizenship to political responsibility is likely to be both distinctive and partial. Geographical attachments, especially those of a limited kind, are a powerful stimulant, perhaps more powerful than any ethic can hope to provide. The restrictive impact of nationalism on liberalism is a case in point. But today surely it is geographical loyalties that most seriously weaken men's sense of responsibility. Certainly McCarthyism, despite its ideological overtones, represented or triggered an outbreak of intense national feeling. These considerations suggest that responsible citizenship requires foundations of a more institutional and less geographical kind. The quality of modern citizenship is more to be judged in terms of standards possessed than in terms of opportunities for participation exercised.

Hence it is in order to explore still a third current of political theory to determine its bearing on the development of responsible citizenship. Perhaps this current may be called Hegelian by way of contrast to the Aristotelian emphasis on devotion to the affairs of a limited group. I have in mind, of course, not the Hegel who is said to have made the nineteenth-century Prussian monarchy an ultimate, but rather the Hegel for whom this stopping-point was a betrayal of his own principles, the one who saw the human spirit at home in nothing short of a world-embracing culture. Not the *Politics* or the *Social Contract,* but the *Philosophy of Right* may turn out to be relevant to the problems created by an increasing scale of society. For Hegel, and the English Hegelian, Bosanquet, at least faced and attempted to deal with the discouragements of size. Hegel tried to explain how an interlocking set of institutions running from the family through the corporations of civil society could provide an environment in which human freedom and responsibility could thrive. It is to Hegel's endeavor and not to his results that I desire to direct attention. For some such comprehensive conception of a web of institutions, combined with genuine knowledge about human institutional sensitivities, is the real challenge to political thought today.

Some years ago John Gaus tried to explain British success in developing responsible citizens in just these terms. More recently Talcott Parsons and other sociological theorists have attempted to present maps of institutional relationships and their dependence upon human dynamics. The political scientist who distrusts Hegel and finds his descendants obscure may find in John Stuart Mill's concept of the "spirit of political institutions" a more congenial way of approaching the question of institutional structures and their impact upon their human components.

Mill said that it was the "spirit of political institutions" that old-style utilitarians such as his father were most prone to disregard. Their methods for developing political responsibility were too direct and relied too heavily upon the formation of indissoluble associations through what they chose to call education. Their psychology, inherited from Hobbes and Hume, did not reveal to them the ways in which political institutions can indirectly shape men's outlook and impart to them standards of behavior and performance. It is implicit in Mill's concept of "spirit" that political institutions set the very tone and atmosphere of society. This they do not only through their direct influence upon our ways of thinking and evaluating, but also indirectly by their pervasive influence upon relationships within the family, school, and factory. Note in this connection Mill's argument for giving women the vote—without it they would regard themselves, and so would their husbands, as not fully human and deserving of respect. Note also that Mill's theory is not vitiated by modern findings that many significant political attitudes are acquired early in life through the mediums of the family and school.

The "spirit of political institutions" may be expected to permeate these agencies of transmission and also to sustain the attitudes formed thereby.

I suggest that we enlarge Mill's concept of "spirit" to include the dispositions and standards which exposure to and use of institutions encourage people to adopt for evaluating the performance of various leaderships. To be sure, political institutions are not the only influences operative in so complex a process as that of attitude formation, and I should not wish to assert that they are. But they are a significant influence and perhaps decisive, unless there is present in a society a historical residue of alienation and intransigeance, a consideration which would appear to account for the French workers' attachment to Communism. Even so the French political system probably worsened matters. France, as D. W. Brogan says, has never had the kind of government to which her people are entitled. These considerations suggest that in the absence of countervailing historical factors the single most important source of influence on citizen responsibility is the responsibility displayed by the government itself. Aristotelian opportunities for significant participation based on the decentralization of authority, both political and administrative, are not to be denigrated. But even more important for responsibility in the modern state is the performance of the central authorities. As John Plamenatz says, "Local autonomies ought to be preserved so far as they can be, but it matters even more that those who hold power at the center should be quickly responsive to the many demands and needs of the people, and should deal justly between them." [1] Where government fails to operate in a responsible fashion, it cannot be reasonably expected that citizens will behave responsibly, either. The force of example, the effectiveness of a continuing symbolism, all of which government can provide, the mutual expectations aroused and sustained by governmental perform-

[1] Ernest S. Griffith, John Plamenatz, and J. Roland Pennock, "Cultural Prerequisites to a Successfully Functioning Democracy: A Symposium," *The American Political Science Review*, L (1956), 101-37.

ance, these are the relationships to which Mill's concept of "spirit" should direct our attention. The outlook of a people is to a very great extent dependent upon the kind of government to which it is exposed.

It is noteworthy, I think, that the major examples of public irresponsibility are to be drawn from the field of foreign policy. Popular pressure for withdrawal of our armies from the continent at the close of the second World War is a case in point. Here simple lack of experience combined with inadequate preparation of the public by the political leadership, rather than metaphysical depravities of the kind thought important by Eric Voegelin, would appear to account for failure. Much of the force of Walter Lippmann's indictment of public opinion depends on his failure to distinguish sharply between performances in the national and international arenas.

Political scientists do differ on what kinds of alterations in going political institutions will effect the changes deemed desirable in order to enhance men's sense of responsibility. Probably there is substantial agreement that it is unwise to expose people to politicians whose tenure of office encourages emphasis on short-run results. It is apparent, as Arthur MacMahon has pointed out, that the will of the people is very different when projected through the House, the Senate, and the Presidency. A pattern of responsiveness that maximizes responsibility is that at which we ought to aim. The objective is relatively easy to define as compared with its achievement.

Likely there is less agreement on the proposal that a more disciplined party system would promote responsibility. It probably weakens the people's sense of responsibility to have a security program carelessly administered and to watch government agencies compete for their support with weapons that include financial benefits. No doubt many technical issues are not subject to rational popular appraisal, but a sense of bewilderment may be the lasting outcome of the recurring spectacle of struggle over military appropriations. Perhaps greater organizational sophistication will in time offset some of these technical limitations on the scope of rational judgment. In any event, drastic changes do not appear to be in order in this country. A series of small changes should achieve important results if these are made at strategic points in the institutional fabric. Here, of course, the question arises as to where to concentrate one's efforts. In the recent past, we have expended ex-Presidential prestige and professional resources on the restructuring of the executive branch. Perhaps the time has arrived when we should give serious attention to the improvement of the legislature.

I raise these issues not in order to present solutions, but rather to indicate the directions in which thinking is required in order to increase political responsibility. The acquisition of a "public philosophy" that is genuinely public, and not merely a set of standards for the guidance of insulated élites, depends upon the general improvement of our political institutions. This may well be a slower process than many would like, but it would appear to be the only one consistent with the values of a liberal democratic society, utilitarian in its commitment to the public interest. The public interest is a standard difficult to define with precision and perhaps it functions best as a negative standard. It is easier to say what violates it than it is to specify what the public interest demands. Certainly we all have a stake in the efficient exploitation of the technology at our command. Also we have a stake in the justice of policies, their implications for moral freedom, and the like. Further development of these standards and their use in the evaluation of leadership performances can find support from sources of influence other than political institutions. The schools, the family, work relationships—all affect our political orientation. In areas of policy where scientific and technical considerations are important, professional organizations are a source of standards and their enforcement. But if Mill is right, the role of political institutions is decisive in the long run. For upon these depend the ways in which people define the utilitarian and moral components of the public interest and the strength of the people's attachment to this standard.

Temporarily high mobility and heterogeneity on the part of urban populations may weaken responsibility. But these characteristics are perhaps viewed best either as transient aspects of the urban scene, or features of it to which people will become accomodated. Indeed, one should be cautious in estimating the ultimate consequences of mobility, for the impact of inter-urban mobility on a continental basis may be quite different from that of the rural-urban mobility in the recent past. At least there is no firm empirical basis for characterological pessimism on this score. Inter-urban continental mobility, combined with greater exposure to European environments, may produce not a mass society but rather one of the most politically sophisticated populations in history, more fully aware of its responsibilities than any people the world has seen. In short, the mass characteristics of our society, which many find so threatening to liberal values, may be a passing phase of adjustment to an increasingly urbanized way of life.

Should these possibilities, to which I only allude, materialize, then we may anticipate the emergence of a "national" citizenship. And it would appear that such a form of citizenship accords better with the requirements of a technical civilization than does either "corporate" or "metropolitan" citizenship. Geographical and functional loyalties would gradually decrease in saliency and be replaced by attitudes more cosmopolitan and ethical in their composition. The Aristotelian ideal of citizenship is not entirely obsolete, but it is becoming increasingly inappropriate. The great society requires a public philosophy, but not one medieval in its inspiration and hierarchical in its application. The only standards that count are those reflected by the people and embodied in their institutions.

HUMAN NATURE AND PARTICIPATORY
DEMOCRACY

ARNOLD S. KAUFMAN

SOME THEORISTS have argued that because man's nature is what it is a democracy of participation is undesirable. Others have held that man's nature, together with certain sociological truths, makes a democracy of participation, or even of majority rule, impossible. I will examine the way in which various conceptions of human nature are related to participatory democracy; for the actual relevance of conceptions of human nature to participatory democracy is not usually shown clearly. Consequently, fundamental problems of democratic theory are not formulated precisely enough. My aim is to weaken the hold that certain sceptical dogmas have on the minds of those who might otherwise be inclined to take more seriously the task of increasing the participatory element in modern industrial societies.

Pessimistic conceptions of man on the basis of which social philosophies are reared fall into two classes. There are those who, while arguing that human weaknesses are statistically inevitable, nevertheless believe that any particular person's weaknesses are largely remediable. Then there are those who believe that, for the most part, human weaknesses are not remediable.

Walter Lippmann has provided us with a good example of the first type of theory. His book, *The Public Philosophy*,[1] consists of diagnosis and remedy. In the diagnostic portion Lippmann describes the decline of Western democracies, ultimately attributing the deterioration that has taken place dur-

[1] Walter Lippmann, *The Public Philosophy* (New York, 1955).

ing the last half century to men's acquisitiveness, their lack of basic self-discipline and of intellectual attainment. Though he does not oppose political democracy (he thinks that unless responsive government exists there is bound to be disorder, and in modern industrial societies adequate responsiveness can only be achieved through political democracy, that is, a relatively free opposition and relatively free elections), he maintains that a democracy will only function well if these defects of human character are considerably remedied. Thus, Lippmann pleads for renewal of what he calls "the traditions of civility"; of those traits of character and those beliefs which among other things incline men to choose the best possible representatives. Only if the electorate chooses well, and then permits those elected to govern, will the decline of Western liberal democracy be halted.

What institutional remedies does Lippmann propose for the ills he so eloquently diagnoses? His only practical suggestion is that educational practices be transformed. Otherwise he suggests only that through moral suasion men may be led to discover for themselves the general guides to conduct which should govern their lives. This discovery will be achieved by being "coolly and lucidly rational."

Lippmann's remedies are inadequate. Traditionally, liberal theorists have required that educational institutions carry an intolerable share of the burden of the civilizing process. In fact, performance of an educational task the size of that required is bound to reflect the defects of the surrounding community. Education cannot escape being corrupted by what is evil in its social context. The alternative, education for an élite, is not just nor can it serve the function Lippmann would require of it.

The very framework of commitment within which Lippmann poses the issues rules out the one condition which, more than any other institutional arrangement, is capable of producing widespread distribution of those traits of character and capabilities desired—direct participation. He wills the end, but not the means. For he is caught up in a conflict of his own construction. On the one hand he believes that men ought to acquire certain traits of character, on the other he is too pessimistic about human capabilities to consider empowering the mass in a way which is indispensable to the development of those traits. In practice, Lippmann's position reduces to a variant of the view that human weaknesses are not ultimately remediable. Collectively society should not act; individually they cannot act effectively.

The view that institutional remedies for defects of human character are impossible has taken two forms: psychological and religious. But the religious position entails psychological claims. For, suppose man has all the defects attributed to him by, say, Reinhold Niebuhr; then whether or not this is due to God's intention, the pernicious attributes must exist psychologically. So we must first ask the psychological question, "Do men have certain ineradicable traits which are bad?" and seek the empirical answer.[2]

It should be noted that the question is not "Are men constitutionally wicked?" The argument which links the undesirability of participatory democracy to man's essential nature presupposes only that men cannot be trusted. It does not follow that they ought to be blamed (or punished) for the harmful things they do.

Among contemporary psychologists, psychoanalytic theorists alone have addressed themselves to the problem which interests us. They base their conclusions on a mass of clinical data. The difficulty is that they do not speak with one voice.

This is partly due to Freud's uncertainty. He was very tentative in his conclusions about man's constitutional destructiveness. He originally held that all our thoughts and activities are governed by what he called "the pleasure principle," by which he meant the tendency to diminish unpleasurable tension by lowering that tension. Pleasure is due

---

[2] This, of course, presupposes criteria of badness which need not themselves be empirically determined.

to an economic reaction of the organism to stress. Thus, dreams are wish-fulfilling because the organism reduces unpleasurable tension by expending in dream-phantasies the energy which induces the tension. But, Freud pointed out, certain phenomena do not seem to be explainable on this basis; in particular, various tendencies to repeat painful experiences. Thus children often repeat a painful pattern of separation from parents, soldiers who suffer war trauma relive in dreams the experience which causes their great pain, and persons who have married unhappily, in certain circumstances, repeat the pattern on other occasions. In all these instances the repetition seems to serve no economic purpose; it is not governed by the pleasure principle. The pain inflicted on oneself seems to be pointlessly masochistic.

Freud tried to deal with the problem these clinical findings generated in a monograph entitled *Beyond the Pleasure Principle*. There he suggests the existence of an instinct which lies, so to speak, beyond the pleasure principle. This he called "the death instinct." This is not the place to describe the argument in detail. Suffice it to say that, proceeding with great ingenuity, Freud makes a very convincing case for the supposition that masochistic repetition reflects a tendency to return to an original state of quiescence, or death. But if masochism can be partly explained on this basis, so can certain forms of sadism which are simply the projection on to others of qualities hated and punished in oneself. Thus Freud very tentatively concludes that men are by nature potentially destructive. Only repression and other defenses prevent them from giving their instinctual destructiveness completely free reign.

I emphasize the tentativeness of Freud's conclusion because he himself insists on it. In a passage near the end of his monograph he writes:

It is true that my assertion of the regressive character of instincts (the death instinct) . . . rests upon observed material—namely on the facts of the compulsion to repeat. It may be, however, that I have overestimated their significance. . . . Unfortunately, people are seldom impartial where ultimate things, the great problems of science and life, are concerned. *Each of us is governed in such cases by deep-rooted internal prejudices, into whose hands our speculation unwittingly plays.* Since we have such good grounds for being distrustful, our attitude towards the results of our own deliberations cannot well be other than one of cool benevolence.[3]

Freud himself must thus have anticipated the fact that his followers would differ about his quite fundamental conclusion. There are those who agree with Freud's postulating of a death instinct, pushing the implications even further than he did himself. Thus Melanie Klein writes,

I consider that envy is an oral-sadistic and anal-sadistic expression of destructive impulses, operative from the beginning of life, and that it has a constitutional basis.[4]

She expresses her indebtedness to Freud's formulation in *Beyond the Pleasure Principle,* but believes she and others have found independent and decisive confirmation of his hypothesis in clinical observations, especially of children. Moreover, she believes she can describe the actual mechanisms through which destructive impulses manifest themselves from earliest infancy onwards.

On the other hand, she cautiously insists that these destructive impulses may not decisively determine subsequent development. In particular, constitutional variations exist which enable some persons to be more, some less successful in taming these hostile impulses. But these constitutional limits can only be discovered in the case of any specific individual after extensive psychoanalytic therapy. Finally, she emphasizes the extent to which external experience may influence the development and expression of hostile tendencies.[5]

3 Sigmund Freud, *Beyond the Pleasure Principle* (1950), p. 82. Italics added for emphasis.

4 Melanie Klein, *Envy and Gratitude* (1957), p. ix.

5 Melanie Klein writes (*ibid.,* pp. 81-83) "Freud early accepted that some individual variations in development are due to constitutional factors. . . . I have previously suggested that greed, hate and persecutory anxieties in relation to the primal object, the mother's breast, have an innate basis. In this book I have added that envy, as a powerful expres-

Thus, though certain of the existence of the death instinct and its destructive by-products, Freud's tentativeness and doubt is transposed in Melanie Klein's thinking to the level of doubt about the constitutional strength of the impulse in the case of any particular person, and the consequent variation in the possibility of therapeutic aid.

Erich Fromm is probably the best known spokesman for that psychoanalytic school of thought which rejects Freud's hypothesis of a death instinct. In the course of expounding his "humanistic ethics," Fromm argues that Freud's theory is "dualistic," emphasizing the forces that make both for good and for evil in man's nature. Fromm then asks, "Are we to understand this dualism to mean that both the drive to live and the drive to destroy are innate and equally strong capacities in man?" His answer is an emphatic "No." [6] He argues that all tendencies to human destructiveness are due to blocked development of potentialities, and are thus "secondary." Unfortunately, the conditions which block personal development occur all too often in the lives of everyone. Thus the impulses to destroy are universal. But the strength of these impulses varies widely according to the occurrence of unfavorable conditions. Nevertheless Fromm confidently concludes that clinical observations "have shown that man is not necessarily evil but becomes evil only if the proper conditions for his growth and development are lacking." [7] Though he

---

sion of oral- and anal-sadistic impulses is also constitutional. The variations in the intensity of these constitutional factors are in my view linked with the preponderance of the one or the other instinct in the fusion of the life and death instincts postulated by Freud. . . . Another factor that influences development from the beginning is the variety of external experiences through which the infant goes. . . . The existence of the innate factors referred to above points to the limitations of psychoanalytic therapy. While I fully realize this, my experience has taught me that nevertheless we are able in a number of cases to produce fundamental and positive changes, even where the constitutional basis was unfavorable."

[6] Erich Fromm, *Man For Himself* (1947), p. 214.

[7] *Ibid.*, p. 218.

denies the existence of the sort of constitutional limits which
Klein and, more tentatively, Freud believed existed, he does
emphasize how widespread are the conditions which cause
men to become destructive. "Indeed," he writes, "there is less
reason to be puzzled by the fact there are so many neurotic
people than by the phenomenon that most people are relatively healthy in spite of the many adverse influences they are
exposed to." [8]

I do not want to argue for one position or the other, nor do
I want to deny the important implications the differences may
have for other policy considerations, or for therapeutic practice. What I do maintain is that as far as the problems of
democracy are concerned, the views of Freud, Klein, and
Fromm have substantially the same implications. Moreover,
these implications, while they support the case for a form of
democratic organization which protects and stabilizes, in no
way rule out the case for a democracy of participation, though
they surely weaken some of the power for good which some
may be inclined to attribute to it.

A democracy of participation may have many beneficial
consequences, but its main justifying function is and always
has been, not the extent to which it protects or stabilizes a
community, but the contribution it can make to the development of human powers of thought, feeling, and action. In this
respect it differs, and differs quite fundamentally, from a
representative system incorporating all sorts of institutional
features designed to safeguard human rights and ensure social
order. *This distinction is all-important.* The fundamental
error many critics of democracy make consists in failure to
recognize that different institutional forms of democracy may
be and are defended on the basis of different functional consequences.

Clearly, the three views considered all support the position
of those who insist that a representative system of some sort

8 *Ibid.,* p. x.

is desirable. Whether one agrees with Klein in maintaining that there are instinctual destructive impulses, or with Fromm who denies this, all would agree that the conditions which make for and support the growth of destructive tendencies are very widespread. The Platonic-Calvinist belief that there is a class of men, the philosopher kings or the elect, who can early and easily be identified as possessing special exemption from destructive urges, has been shattered once and for all by Freudian discoveries. Surely Freudianism does weaken the case for aristocratic theories (though Freud himself tended to be an élitist, a fact which is admirably discussed and analysed by Fromm).[9]

On the other hand, while Fromm and Klein disagree about man's native constitution, they would agree that the possibilities of personal development are difficult to determine, and, in any case, generally great. Nothing in what either of them says precludes the possibility that participatory democracy may play an important role in enabling a person to develop his constructive and creative powers and achieve greater happiness. True, we can no longer accept the buoyant optimism of the Enlightenment concerning the potentialities for purely social reform. And assuredly underlying Rousseau's classical defense was a very great faith in the power participation has to effect personal development. We must admit that these institutions are not quite as important as Rousseau himself supposed, but this does not imply that they are not vitally important. The issue must be decided independently of Freudian theories of human nature, on the basis of the relevant evidence.

Participatory democracy has also been attacked on the grounds that most men are constitutionally lacking in intelligence. The scientific evidence for this claim is based primarily on the cumulative record of intelligence testing. A

[9] Erich Fromm, *Sigmund Freud's Mission* (1959).

very able criticism of the anti-democratic conclusions sometimes drawn from these results has been given by David Spitz.[10]
I will restrict myself to a few observations.

First, the score of 100 I.Q. has come to represent the thresh-
old of adequate intelligence in the popular imagination. It is
too often forgotten that this score is a relative figure, and implies little about the basic capacity to exercise political responsibility. Second, I.Q.'s are not irrevocably determined by
inheritance. There is much evidence for the view that whatever it is that intelligence tests test may be greatly affected by
environmental changes. The more we learn, the more does
nature seem to give way to nurture as a determining influence
in human affairs.[11] Third, participation may be an important
if not an indispensable condition of a person's fully developing his inherent powers of intelligent thought and action.
Fourth, the suffrage in advanced industrial democracies is, in
any event, going to be almost universal. It may well be that
participation is one of the most important ways of ensuring
that those who vote will make their decisions intelligently. In
a political democracy the important thing is not that the voter
always vote for the best man, but that he never votes for a
stupid, irrationally bigoted, or demagogic person.

Which brings us to the fifth point. No one has ever demonstrated a connection between virtue and intelligence. As Carl
Friedrich has put it, "In the forming of political judgments,
character is more important than intellect." [12] And, as one
psychoanalyst has written, "Undoubtedly there are children
and adults with a defective guilt sense, and such defect is not
specifically linked with intellectual capacity or incapacity." [13]

The results of intelligence testing, while they may induce
more realistic expectations, do not seriously harm the case for

10 David Spitz, *Patterns of Anti-Democratic Thought* (1949), pp. 163-90.
11 Spitz summarizes the evidence for this conclusion in *op. cit.,* chap. 7.
12 Carl J. Friedrich, *The New Image of the Common Man* (1950), p. 16.
13 D. W. Winnicott, "Psychoanalysis and the Sense of Guilt," in *Psychoanalysis and Contemporary Thought* (1958), p. 16.

participation. Nor does the fact, and I accept it as a fact, that all men are irrational a good deal of the time.

Joseph Schumpeter has argued that what he calls the "classical doctrine of democracy" (by which he seems to mean a rather vague synthesis of Rousseau's views and the naive utilitarianism of the worst classical economists) is untenable because men are demonstrably irrational. In defending his conclusion he mentions the theories of many men, Freud among them, as well as the results of contemporary empirical economics. All of these sources, he argues, tend to confirm his belief that men are very irrational, much more so than classical democratic theorists ever suspected. Schumpeter's argument has greatly influenced prominent intellectuals (e.g. Seymour Lipset and Kenneth Galbraith), so one approaches it respectfully. But in the final analysis his argument against participatory democracy is puzzling and incoherent, especially those parts which bear on man's irrationality. Yet it is sophisticated and entirely representative, so I will use it as a peg on which to hang criticism which I believe to have more general validity.

I must abbreviate Schumpeter's argument, but that part which is relevant can be sketched easily enough. Schumpeter wants to disprove the fundamental assumptions on which "the classical doctrine of democracy" rests. That doctrine affirms that—

The democratic method is that institutional arrangement for arriving at political decisions which realizes the common good by making the people itself decide issues through the election of individuals who are to assemble in order to carry out its will.[14]

The psychological presupposition of this doctrine is, according to Schumpeter, the belief that "every normal person can be made to see (the common good) by means of rational argu-

[14] J. Schumpeter, *Capitalism, Socialism and Democracy* (3rd ed.; New York, 1950), p. 250.

ment," and that, therefore, only ignorance, stupidity, and anti-social interest prevent the common good from being realized. The classical democrat is thus placed "under the practical necessity of attributing to the will of the *individual* an independence and rational quality that are altogether unrealistic." [15] For, even supposing there are no widespread anti-social interests, the argument presupposes that everyone knows exactly what he wants to stand for, has the ability to sift information and, in so doing, to select the most rational means to an end. But, says Schumpeter, the evidence against these assumptions is overwhelming.

It is at this point in his argument that Schumpeter invokes the testimony of Freud and others. His detailed criticism is, however, restricted to mention of the results of investigations of crowd behavior and of economic behavior.

Le Bon and others, in their studies of crowd behavior, have learned that "under the influence of agglomeration," and particularly under the stress of excitement, civilized modes of thinking and feeling break down. There is "sudden eruption of primitive impulses, infantilisms, and criminal propensities." [16] The economists have demonstrated the same curious break-down of rational intelligence in consumer behavior. Through careful observation they have begun to discover that the wants of consumers "are nothing like as definite and their actions upon those wants nothing like as rational and prompt" as utilitarian economists had supposed. People are so easily influenced and persuaded by appeals unrelated to the nature of the commodity that the economist is forced by the facts to give up his belief that humans decide rationally in an enormously wide range of economic choice.

Schumpeter refrains from pushing his criticisms of the classical assumption to an untenable extreme. He insists, for example, that within limits the consumer does know precisely what he desires, as well as how to select what he wants from among existing alternatives. And, more generally, those "de-

---

[15] *Ibid.*, p. 253.   [16] *Ibid.*, p. 257.

cisions which lie within the little field which the individual citizen's mind encompasses with a full sense of its reality" are often made with definiteness and rationality. Nor does this field suddenly vanish as we move away from purely personal concerns. "In the realm of public affairs there are sectors that are more within the reach of the citizen's mind than others." [17] In his consideration of such municipal and national issues the average citizen's degree of interest and realistic assessment may be great. But the number of such issues is much smaller than classical democratic theorists supposed. As the issues grow more remote, a person is more likely to give in to "dark urges," and the group will is more easily "manufactured." Schumpeter concludes,

All of this goes to show that without the initiative that comes from immediate responsibility, ignorance will persist in the face of masses of information, however complete and correct.[18]

Though Schumpeter fails to do so, in order to complete the picture we must again refer to Freudian theory. For Freud and his followers have given the most detailed account of the way in which an individual's desires are confused, and what he thinks are good means to given ends are dictated, not by rational thought, but by irrational rationalization.

What Schumpeter has written does indeed appear to be a powerful indictment of traditional democratic attitudes—the attitudes reflected most concisely in the motto *Vos populi, vox dei*. Nevertheless, Schumpeter, far from repudiating the essential elements of the classical doctrine he attacks, actually supports what is central to it; moreover, his general line of argument *cannot* weaken that doctrine.

To begin with, Schumpeter commits what I have already suggested is the fundamental error of all such critiques; he confuses the functions of direct participation with the functions of a representative system within a framework of countervailing institutional power. The first has more to do with what can be done *to* men, with the development of distinc-

[17] *Ibid.*, p. 260.   [18] *Ibid.*, p. 262.

tively human powers; the second with what can be done *for* men, with protection against tyranny and establishment of social order. *This distinction is absolutely essential to any clear thought about democracy and its implementing institutions.* For corresponding to the distinction are two different, though overlapping, sets of institutions. Differences between institutions are inevitable when we are trying to implement different and possibly incompatible general aims. In the course of making his case for democratic processes of one sort, Schumpeter has inadvertently suggested the case for institutions of the other sort.

Schumpeter also seriously confuses popular rhetoric and popular beliefs. Primarily preoccupied with the economic theories with which he is familiar, his description of what he calls the "classical doctrine" is a caricature. But, for the purposes of discussion, let us assume that he has accurately described what the classical democrats believed.

Does Schumpeter's argument weaken the case for extension of participatory institutions? In a passage already quoted Schumpeter writes, "without the initiative that comes from immediate responsibility, ignorance will persist." If we admit that participatory institutions ought not to be extended to embrace all social decisions, then the question becomes, how much should they cover in order to make democracy, in the sense of free competition for leadership, function well? For, as Schumpeter himself admits, it is only when men acquire direct responsibility for a certain range of decisions that social imagination breaks through its parochial barriers and envisages larger possibilities. Where Schumpeter errs, or where he at least does not even begin to prove his case, is in supposing that a man's sphere of direct responsibility must be confined to the rearing of children, the purchase of butter, and the construction of sewer systems.

Let me put the points that emerge in the form of two hypotheses. In modern industrial societies men can successfully assume responsibility for the direction of many affairs which today they regard as largely irrelevant to their lives because these affairs seem so remote. Moreover, in the case of those types of decision which it is best, for other reasons, to put into the hands of delegated agents, the best agents will be selected when those who make the selection have direct responsibility for decisions which are similar to those with which the agent will be entrusted.

Schumpeter insists upon the role of leadership in modern industrial societies. "Collectives," he writes, "act almost exclusively by accepting leadership—this is the dominant mechanism of practically any collective action which is more than a reflex." [19] Assuming this assessment of the role of leadership is sound, Schumpeter gives us no hint as to how good leadership is to be ensured. The only aspect of his analysis which suggests what those mechanisms might be is what he says about direct responsibility. I wish simply to state more explicitly and emphatically what Schumpeter very reluctantly suggests even though his suggestion conflicts with the main thrust of his analysis. The most important condition of the emergence of good leadership in modern industrial societies is, for the great mass of human beings, direct responsibility through participation. A nation can be lucky. Perhaps France has been lucky in its choice of a strong man. But a nation can be unlucky. Germany was. The stakes are too important to trust to luck. If this is true of the nation, it is no less true of all the collectives within the nation. Like Lippmann, Schumpeter wills the end, but not the indispensable means.

If what I have been arguing is sound, it is because an empirical case can be made for participatory institutions. That is why I have put my main points in the form of hypotheses, unexamined hypotheses up to this point. For this reason it is important to emphasize that I have shown only that Schum-

[19] Schumpeter, *op. cit.*, p. 270. I agree entirely with the following description of Schumpeter's position by James Meisel *The Myth of the Ruling Class* (1958), p. 353: "Essentially, Schumpeter's reappraisal amounts to an integration of élitist elements into a democratic framework which is much more modest than the structure built two hundred years ago, more diffident and more complex, but basically still within the classical tradition."

peter, rather than ruling out an extension of participatory institutions, has by implication suggested that direct participation is essential for the proper functioning of democracy in
his restricted sense. What remains to be shown is that direct
participation is an effective and indispensable condition of
diminishing the extent to which men think irrationally about
all things.

   Can an empirical case be made for participation? This is
not a question which the great advocates of participatory democracy have ever faced seriously enough. Usually they have
simply assumed that participation will make a vital contribution to the development of human personality.
   In this connection, it is interesting to note a change in the
tactics of participatory democracy's critics. The heart of Plato's
attack on democratic participation was the claim that it
turned men into beasts, incapable of restraining the pull of
either appetite or passion. In short, Plato thought that democracy makes monsters of men. Echoes of the Platonic critique persist, e.g., in the writings of Russell Kirk. But the
most effective critiques are today tinged with a sad "would
that it could be" reluctance to draw the awful conclusion.
Those who base their rejection on a pessimistic conception of
human nature do not deny that participation can be, in itself, beneficial; it is simply that in balance it is pernicious. We
cannot take the chance of permitting men to devour or injure
each other through stupidity, however much it might contribute to personal development. Others, shortly to be considered, reluctantly conclude that participation is impossible
in advanced industrial societies. The point is that, whereas
Plato met the democratic case head-on, simply contradicting
Pericles' famous defense, today critics try rather to outflank
the advocates of participatory democracy.
   Thus, though there is general agreement with the proposition that participation contributes to personal development,
it is both valuable and necessary to make the empirical case.

This has never really been done adequately. Neither G. D. H. Cole nor John Dewey, for example, ever developed an empirical defense. An adequate philosophy of participatory democracy demands a more systematic approach to the problem. But in this paper I can make only a few suggestions.

The first step in the fulfillment of an empirical program must be a much more precise definition of participation than theorists usually work with. In a recent symposium which dealt with Workers' Participation in Management, the symposiasts were able to agree that at least three different forms of participation had to be distinguished: formalized direct participation, formalized indirect participation, and informal participation.[20] But what is essential to all these forms of participation? The suggestion I should like to make, though not argue for in detail, is that participation essentially involves actual preliminary deliberation (conversations, debate, discussion) and that in the final decision each participant has a roughly equal formal say. While this does not imply majority rule, it does preclude rule by a minority of those sufficiently interested to participate. Nor does it imply that each person has influence equal to that of those who have the equal power of formal decision. The distinction between power and influence is vitally important. If someone is specially influential because he has special knowledge about a problem or because he thinks more clearly or more imaginatively about certain issues, his influence is compatible with equal participation in the sense intended. (This is the confusion on which Schumpeter's conclusion about the inevitability of leadership in collectives is based.)

If we have an adequate conception of participation to work with, we can then proceed to examine the evidence for the key hypothesis—that in advanced industrial societies participation is, in balance, beneficial because of the contribution

[20] Most of the papers read at this symposium, which was held at the 1957 meeting of the International Sociological Association, are reprinted in the *International Archives of the Sociology of Cooperation*, 2 (1957), 106-82.

it makes to individual personal development. This implies that side effects do not have long term detrimental consequences which more than outweigh momentary benefits. Empirical investigation thus gets very complicated. But concern with empirical complexity is all the more necessary. It is necessary not only in terms of justifying participation, but, just as important, it is by acquiring this kind of systematic knowledge that we will be able to implement participation in a way which minimizes harmful consequences. The results of participation are not the same in very different situations.

I will give only one example of the sort of investigation I have in mind. The syndicalists have traditionally supposed that workers could assume managerial functions with good results both for the workers themselves and for the larger society. But careful sociological analysis of the results of experiments in Germany, Yugoslavia, Poland, and elsewhere seem to indicate that this optimism is not justified. One symposiast concludes, "Any form of participation that is based on the appointment of workers to managerial or quasi-managerial positions is bound to defeat its own ends." [21] Another, more optimistically, considers the possibility of eliminating conflict through an extensive rotation of managerial jobs. All agree that the issue is fundamental for the future of workers' participation.

There are many problems that the *symposiasts* do not go into. For example, one difficulty seems to be due to the jump in income enjoyed by workers' managerial representatives. This tends to destroy their ability to represent their rank and file in a mutually satisfactory fashion. The differences between modes of selecting workers' representatives, the way in which their accountability is ensured, and so on—in short, the truly participatory element in the whole business—is extremely influential in determining the outcome. My point is simply that these are the concrete details of various types of participation which must be seriously considered by those who advocate

[21] R. Dahrendorf, *op. cit.*, p. 163.

its implementation in different spheres. The unargued presupposition of this paper is that participation is immensely beneficial. The burden of my argument to this point has simply been to prove first, that what we know about human nature does not force us to conclude that participation is either pernicious or useless. In the last few paragraphs I have indicated that what we know about the effects of participation indicate that it has a role to play in such improvement, but its role is immensely complex. Much empirical study is required both to prove that participation is beneficial and to clarify the way in which it can best be implemented in specific social spheres.

Important as these empirical considerations are, there is more to the perennial debate concerning man's nature and the consequent desirability of participatory democracy than can be embraced by a strictly empirical approach. There is something which Freud hints at in a passage quoted earlier. In thinking about the great problems of man's goodness or evil "each of us is governed . . . by deep-rooted internal prejudices, into whose hands our speculation unwittingly plays." This is profoundly true; and no discussion which ignores it can be adequate. Beliefs concerning man's basic constitution and the consequent possibilities of personal development can not be defended or explained on empirical grounds alone. The *something more* involved concerns the relation between belief and effort.

William James, in his much maligned essay *The Will to Believe,* illustrates one of the dimensions of belief with which he is concerned by describing a lover who wins the one he woos by *believing* that she loves him. James was, I presume, trying to say that often making the effort to achieve a possible good depends on our belief in the possibility of that achievement—that the very nerve of our effort to achieve a good may be cut by premature admission of its impossibility. Surely, the lover who *believes* courts disappointment and defeat—disappointment and defeat which may be all the more disillusioning because he has, so to speak, lowered his defenses in an act of faith. But, and this is James' central point, the defensive posture, while it protects, precludes achievement.

James goes on to misuse this point about the relation between belief and effort in discussing the existence of God. But it does have relevance to our problem. For surely the belief in the possibility of personal development is an important condition of its achievement.

All-or-nothing conceptions of human endowment are definitely disconfirmed by the relevant evidence. That which is most certain about our knowledge of human nature is the extent of the variation over which a person's destructiveness, irrationality, and stupidity may range. It is impossible for anyone to know the upper limit of potentiality for any human being with much accuracy unless he has a good deal more knowledge than is available even to a parent, an intimate friend, or an intimate enemy. It is, in general, a supreme conceit to think that one has the intellectual power or the moral justification to describe the fixed frame of human potentiality for any individual. It is desirable, without blinding oneself to existing defects, to assume that remedial action is always possible. This is the essence of the optimistic conception of human nature. Far from being "naive" or "unrealistic," it is the only assumption that makes realistic sense in an imperfect world whose inhabitants' will to perfect themselves is so easily undermined by pessimistic beliefs that are not justified on the evidence.

It has been argued that Condorcet is misinterpreted if we regard his doctrine of the perfectibility of man as implying that man is or ever can be perfect.[22] Condorcet meant only that one cannot at any given time say with reasonable certainty that the upper level of possible achievement has been reached. Given any level of development, through effort more can be achieved. With the sobering empirical qualifications

22 Cf. Charles Frankel, *The Case for Modern Man* (New York, 1955).

already described, this faith of the Enlightenment is sound today. In the final analysis pessimism, while it protects us from disappointment, blinds the individual to possible lines of advance. It is necessary to encourage and renew man's efforts to improve himself and his world, not wither the will to try, by subjecting it to a bombardment of sophisticated and somewhat cynical arguments which never actually prove the extreme conclusion they either affirm or, more likely, insinuate.

Of all that has gone before a critic might remark, "What you have written is infused with commendable moral concern. If the world were the kind of place in which participatory democracy could exist on any substantial scale, I would be all for it. Unfortunately we must face hard facts. And the hard facts are that participatory democracy, and even majority rule, are not possible in modern industrial societies, however desirable theoretically. If you want to avoid wasting your time, bend your efforts to the achievement of possibilities, not ideal impossibilities." The view that democracy is impossible is identified with the names of Mosca, Pareto, Michels, and in the United States, James Burnham. *The Iron Law of Oligarchy* is its slogan.

Many have criticized important claims made by these élite theorists.[23] But few of the élitists' critics have tried to defend the position these men were actually attacking. For it is clear that it was against Rousseau that they aimed their sociological darts. For example, Mosca wrote:

. . . the modern democratic theory, which had its source in Rousseau, took its stand upon the concept that the majority of the citizens in any state can participate and in fact *ought* to participate, in its political life . . . We shall not stop to refute this democratic theory here, since that is the task of the work as a whole.[24]

[23] E.g., C. J. Friedrich, *op. cit.;* D. Spitz, *op. cit.;* J. Meisel, *op. cit.*
[24] G. Mosca, *The Ruling Class* (New York, 1939), p. 52. In another place Mosca wrote, "If by democracy is meant, as Rousseau believed, that the state must be governed by a majority of the citizens, then let us say at

The most systematic and empirical sociological case against the possibility of participatory democracy and majority rule is made by Robert Michels. That it is against Rousseau's views rather, say, than those held by James Madison or even John Stuart Mill, that Michels directs his argument in the book, *Political Parties,* is most clearly revealed in a chapter entitled, "Mechanical and Technical Impossibility of Direct Government by the Masses." There Michels writes:

A mass which delegates its sovereignty, that is to say transfers its sovereignty to the hands of a few individuals, abdicates its sovereign functions. For the will of the people is not transferable, nor even the will of the single individual.[25]

This passage is almost a paraphrase of a basic passage in Rousseau's *Social Contract.*[26] But, unlike Rousseau, Michels goes on to argue that only representative democracy is possible in mass organizations. That proposition is the essence of his *Iron Law of Oligarchy.*

The first thing one should note about Michels' book is that his desire to debunk socialist pretensions permeates the whole. He wants to prove that socialist organizations can be neither democratic nor revolutionary. A sense of passionate disillusionment leads Michels, like so many contemporary sociologists, to see in sociological analysis a way of purging himself of his earlier socialistic commitment, now felt to be naively optimistic.

---

once that the new anti-Aristotelian doctrine does not find it necessary to give battle—it simply denies the democratic principle on the ground that it cannot be realized in practice." (In J. Meisel, *op. cit.,* p. 166.)

[25] Failure to recognize that this is the position against which Michels' argument is directed has resulted in some misapplications of it, e.g., P. Magrath, "Democracy in Overalls: The Futile Quest for Union Democracy," *Industrial and Labor Relations Review,* 12 (1959), 504ff. See also Part II, chaps. 6 and 7 of *Political Parties* (New York, 1949). There Michels describes the fierce struggle that goes on among leaders in socialist parties and trade unions; how, for example, they reflect important regional differences (hence, corresponding regional majorities). Yet he considers all of this competition for leadership proof of his own basic thesis!

[26] Rousseau, *Social Contract,* Book III, chap. 15.

The actual argument must here be pared down to its barest essentials. Political effort based on mass discontent must, he contends, be organized if it is to be effective. Organization implies specialization of function, which implies the existence of leadership. The imperatives of technical expertise together with the imperatives of leadership in a situation of deep social conflict inevitably increase the remoteness of the relationship between membership and officials. Reinforcing these sociological forces are certain basic psychological tendencies. Custom, apathy, the primary need for authoritative direction, political gratitude, ignorance, and deficient intellect all reinforce the drift toward oligarchical domination. Moreover, officials have a basic desire for power as well as a great tendency to satisfy their self-interest. These sociological and psychological forces give rise to a generalization which holds universally—the iron law of oligarchy. "Thus the majority of human beings, in a condition of eternal tutelage, are predestined by tragic necessity to submit to the dominion of a small minority, and must be content to constitute the pedestal of an oligarchy." [27]

Now the argument I wish to suggest, but cannot fully defend, is that the organizational imperatives to which Michels attributes such importance must control organizational development only at a certain stage in the development of industrial societies. The relevance of Michels' psychological assumptions to democracy have already been considered. Therefore, the impossibility of participatory democracy or of majority rule is not proved by his argument. Michels' claim that organization implies specialization of function and leadership need not be disputed, for it is tautological. The question is, does specialization and leadership imply minority rule and the impossibility of participatory institutions on any substantial scale? Does it imply oligarchy, in Michels' sense?

At this point it is necessary to emphasize that Michels is primarily concerned with political parties and trade unions, both of which have been traditionally engaged in fierce competition

[27] Michels, *op. cit.*, p. 407.

for power. It is this element of unceasing and deep conflict which gives Michels' sociological hypotheses their basic credibility. *To the extent that conflict abates or does not run so deep, participation and majority determination of basic policy becomes possible.* But I believe that long-term social tendency both within and among societies is toward harmonization. Social harmony is not inevitable, but it is possible and there are forces which powerfully support this tendency. The basic instrument of harmonization is law. Through law the resolution of the major forms of conflict are regularized. It seems quite likely that in the not too distant future industrial relations in advanced industrial societies will be entirely governed by law. As regards political conflict, through affluence the main causes of deep conflict, *though not of personal discontent,* can be progressively eliminated. This development is not inevitable, but it is possible. The historical epoch through which we are passing, an epoch which has been marked by such deep social division, is not necessarily a permanent thing, though man could conceivably perpetuate it through stupidity and bad will. And so we return to our starting point. At the base of the sociological pessimisim to which Michels and the other élite theorists subscribe, is a pessimistic assessment of man's nature. As James Meisel has written:

Élitism is a defensive doctrine, a new Dismal Science aimed at the naive optimist of eighteenth-century enlightenment . . . Confidence in the wisdom of the common man was misplaced; therefore its rationale, the doctrine of popular sovereignty, had to be expunged from the middle-class canon.[28]

But, for reasons already given, the psychological pessimism which lies at the root of the élitist doctrine is an inadequate ground on which to base rejection of either the possibility or the desirability of participatory institutions.

The main justifying functions of free competition for leadership are maintenance of order, protection against the tyran-

28 Meisel, *op. cit.,* pp. 10-11.

nical exercise of power, and fulfillment of actual human preferences without unduly sacrificing the values of efficient decision and expert opinion. The main justifying function of participation is development of man's essential powers—inducing human dignity and respect, and making men responsible by developing their powers of deliberate action.

How can both sets of aims be achieved? By developing two sets of institutions which are able to coexist. This cannot be done without conflict or sacrifice. But rather than focusing exclusively on the drawbacks, the social cost of permitting a greater degree of participation must continually be weighed against the human cost of denying such extension. Obviously, no precise quantitative judgments are possible. These are decisions which are at best based on reasoned hunches.

But to destroy the nerve of effort by preaching psychological and sociological despair when remedies are at least possible is unrealistic folly. If the possible remedies are never employed, then these doctrines will themselves be an important cause of their own fulfillment. For the persistent truth is that participation is an essential condition of the good society and the good life.

RESPONSIBILITY AND THE GOAL
OF SURVIVAL

HERBERT J. SPIRO

I F WE LOOK on politics as the process by which a community deals with its problems, and on problems as obstacles between men and their goals, then we may state the task of political philosophy as follows: To define the goals toward which a community is or should be striving, in a clear way that makes possible a systematic understanding of the concrete conditions of human existence so as to be of help in solving the problems to which these conditions give rise. This is the task to which those philosophers who have been judged great in the light of hindsight addressed themselves. The goals or values which they formulated have in every case been related to the most crucial problem of the age and area in which a philosophy wielded its greatest influence: survival of the *polis;* relations between *civitas Dei* and *civitas humana* and between spiritual and secular authorities; anarchy before power had been centralized and, following solution of that problem, control of the exercise of centralized power; relations among members of emergent "mass" societies; and the organization of production.

The present poverty of political philosophy has been variously noted and lamented.[1] Self-critical political philosophers admit that they are living off the capital of ideas and ideals one or two centuries old. They work with conventional analytical concepts, like state, power, war, and peace. When they are not writing the history of political thought, they are

---

[1] E.g., by Alfred Cobban, "The Decline of Political Theory," *The Political Science Quarterly,* LXVIII (1953), 321-37.

elaborating values, like liberty and equality, which are so well worn by use that they mean all things to all men, and certainly incompatible things to antagonistic groups of men. This evaluation of contemporary political philosophy may sound too harsh—but where is the Mill or the Marx of our time? The answer seems harder to find than would have been an answer to the question, raised in the nineteenth century, about its Rousseau or its Locke.

The relative failure of political philosophy in our age cannot be attributed to the absence of, or to our inability to recognize, one crucial problem of overriding importance on whose solution everything depends. Quite the contrary, the existence of only one such problem appears much more clearly today than it could have to any generation of our forefathers at least since the Reformation. For us, *the* problem is how to prevent the extermination of mankind. Perhaps the fearful dimensions of this problem, and the possibility that it may be the last problem about which men make decisions, explains the reluctance of political philosophers to come to grips with it. The concrete nature of the threat to survival is becoming ever more evident almost daily. It involves the destructiveness of nuclear weapons, the speed with which these can be released, dangers of radio-active fall-out, and the like. But the problem presented by threats to survival cannot be solved, unless the goal of survival—on the road to which these threats are our obstacles—can be defined in a way which commands nearly global consensus.

For this purpose the concept of responsibility may be of help.

A community may be said to exist among those who are aware of problems which they are facing in common. In this sense, awareness of the possible extinction of human life as it has been known is bringing a world-wide community of mankind into being. This community will be based upon the belief of men that all of them together are facing the alternatives of extinction or survival. A community can be confirmed and stabilized, and it can achieve success in dealing with its common problems only by becoming a political system, that is, by using more or less stable procedures for the resolution of issues arising out of its problems. Political procedures of this kind can become established most easily where those who use them agree on the ultimate goals of politics. These final goals may have a relatively negative content, as was true in the international political system of the nineteenth century, which resolved its issues by means of fairly stable procedures of both diplomacy and warfare. Or the content of the ultimate goals of a political system may be more positive, as were those set forth in the Preamble to the Constitution of the United States.

Whatever the content of the goals, their definition and elaboration, or even their creation, is the task of political philosophy. Values or goals should be stated with reference to the concrete problems of the community for which the philosopher is working. In order to be effective, the goals contained in a political philosophy should be capable of eliciting the agreement of all those members of the community whose disagreement could prevent achievement of the goals. In the past, philosophers were able to satisfy this requirement by securing the agreement only of the strongest part of the community. This is no longer true for the world community, because any nuclear power acting in it could set off a train of events which would culminate in general extermination. (Conceivably this might be done even by a State not possessing nuclear weapons, through interference with the attack-detection system of nuclear powers.)

The political philosopher who identifies himself with the global community of mankind must, therefore, seek to find and define goals that can command the widest possible consensus, at least among those men who can start a nuclear holocaust. This kind of search may be condemned as immoral ("Why should we seek to find a basis for agreement with the evil Soviet Communists?"), or rejected as futile ("Nothing will

keep the Russians from pursuing their goal of world domination!") The burden of proving either immorality or futility
rests with the critics. If they should turn out to be right,
chances are that they will not be alive to tell us, "We told
you so"—nor we to concede the point.

The crucial problem is the threat to survival, and the task
of political philosophy is the search for goals commanding
enough agreement. Until now, most political philosophers
have concentrated on defining differences between the values
of the "Free World" and the "Communist World." The wide
currency of these phrases, or their Communist counter-slogans,
shows the strength of emphasis on differentiation. This emphasis has been so successful that Americans found it very
difficult to visualize life behind the "Iron Curtain" in terms
other than those which would be used to describe a vast
concentration camp. This explains the over-reaction of many
when, during the "thawing" years of the "Cold War," they
discovered that Russians were human beings like themselves,
with families, loves, worries, jobs, and ambitions. Political
philosophy which concentrated on differences between the
goals pursued by the two great camps served the useful purpose of strengthening the will to resist—on "the other side,"
perhaps, to commit—aggression. But such philosophy stood in
the service of, at best, one of the two great camps, at worst,
only a national community or less. Neither this kind of
philosophy nor those committed to it can be expected to
provide much help in solving the present problem.

Still, the study of such philosophies may be helpful in the
search for a common denominator of ultimate goals capable
of securing support from both sides of the Iron Curtain and
the "uncommitted" areas of the world as well. But this kind
of comparative study of philosophies and ideologies presents
several difficulties. Among these is the loose use of words,
another their mobilization for propaganda. There are few
political philosophies left in the world, and fewer politicians,

that do not advocate freedom, equality, democracy, constitutionalism, international harmony, reduction of the incidence of violence, and similar causes. The trouble is that it is hard to tell whether they do this because they want to win friends and influence peoples, or because they actually believe in these goals.

Even where real commitment can be established, how do we know the content of the goals to which a philosophy is committed? The meaning of goals is obscure, not only because they have been used for so many, often contradictory, purposes. Terms like freedom or democracy are obscure also, because they were given their original modern meanings in response to the distinctive problems of earlier ages. This applies alike to normative and analytical concepts. For example, power was defined at a time when its consolidation was a major problem. To use the term in its conventional meaning for an analysis of current relations between the United States and the Soviet Union is, therefore, not likely to be very helpful (especially when power is thought of in the old-fashioned mechanical sense instead of, say, an electrical or electronic sense). The goal of equality was filled with its modern content at a time and in places where tremendous economic, social, and political inequalities constituted the single most important problem. Such inequalities no longer exist in the United States, Europe, or the Soviet Union. But since the Industrial Revolution, equality has been put to so many different uses and in so many different contexts that it would be very hard to redefine it in a way designed to overcome contradictory prevailing stereotypes of equality. To get agreement on the desirability of a redefined notion of equality as a goal would probably prove impossible. The same seems true of similar other concepts.

If the conventional values of political philosophy are inadequate to serve as goals commanding enough agreement to prevent extermination, where else should we turn in our search? Perhaps the two great camps are so fundamentally opposed to each other in their ultimate goals that they could agree, if at all, only at the level of temporary and expedient policies, that is, of immediate goals. This attitude has been taken by those, on both sides, who favor "co-existence" only as a transient measure, e.g., on the issue of the Austrian peace treaty.

Those, again on both sides, who assert that negotiations can do no harm and may do some good go a little farther, when they hope that negotiations about minor issues may produce experience with, and agreement on, procedures for negotiating which could later be used for the resolution of major issues. Such hopes may or may not be warranted. In either case, resignation to finding agreement only at the pragmatic level of immediate goals implies a much wider resignation. It contributes nothing to the solution of the central problem. Moreover, since such resignation means failure to live up to the task of clarifying ultimate goals, it may involve either side in the first step on the road toward concessions which might end in surrender of its ultimate goals. (From a Western point of view, such concessions from the Soviets would, of course, appear desirable. They are in fact much more likely to be made by pragmatic Americans than by ideological Communists.)

Could agreement on matters lying beyond politics proper reduce the threat to the continued existence of humanity? Since the beginning of cultural, technical, and scientific exchanges with the Soviet Union, the similarity of problems faced by members of various professions on both sides has often been remarked upon. Pianists and poets, farmers and pharmacists, architects and astronomers are all members of communities based on a commonality of problems, knowledge, and experience, and on the use of the same methods, techniques, or procedures for dealing with their problems. Except for differences in the standard of living, auto workers in Detroit and Leningrad or subway workers in New York and Moscow lead very similar lives—more similar, at any rate, than any of their lives are to those of a Chinese peasant or an African tribal chief.

These kinds of agreement explain why it has been so much easier for scientific and technical experts to resolve issues about the control of nuclear tests, than it has been for politicians to arrive at agreement on the same issues. This fact suggests that issues about ultimate goals will always be raised, and that consensus on the level of every-day solutions to every-day problems is not enough.

If neither lip service to old values, nor pragmatic agreement on temporary policies and procedures for their negotiation, nor finally consensus on professional methods seems designed to help solve the problem of the threat to human survival, how can we hope for such aid from the concept of responsibility, at the level of ultimate goals?

Is it not the ultimate goal of the Soviet Communists to dominate the world, and of the West to resist any extension of Soviet rule or even to expand the area of the Free World? The first glimmer of hope comes from assertions made by both sides to the effect that rule by itself is not the ultimate goal but envisaged rather as means toward some further end: establishment of the global classless society for the Communists, establishment of conditions favorable to the self-realization of the individual human being in the West. True, each side casts doubts upon, or rejects the credibility of, the other's protestations to this effect. But each side at the same time also indoctrinates its own youth—and especially its future leadership—with these ultimate goals.

The contents of these two sets of final goals are rather similar, for the obvious reason of their common roots in the values of the eighteenth and nineteenth centuries. The forms of their statement also bear a great deal of resemblance, e.g., in their indefiniteness about the future. Just how wise this vagueness in the statement of ultimate goals is, is shown by the rapid and radical changes in the content of human problems, brought about by the expansion of human knowledge about and human control over nature and even the universe.

It is virtually impossible to project goals in definite and substantive terms when one does not know what vast new possibilities of human achievement the future (if any) may bring.

"From each according to his ability, to each according to his need," in "an association in which the free development of each is the condition for the free development of all," after execution of the "leap from the realm of necessity into the realm of freedom"—these are ultimate goals not fully accepted in either the Soviet Union or the United States today. Their emphasis on the individual, on equality, freedom, and reason are derived from the common sources of Marxian and non-Marxian philosophy. As interpreted on each side, goals such as these might be mutually acceptable, but interpretations of the current problem derived from them would hardly be in sufficient agreement to produce compromise in the resolution of issues generated by that problem. The reason is twofold: first, the vagueness of terms like equality and freedom, along with the propaganda use to which they have been put, as mentioned above; and second, possibilities like the conceivable future solution of problems of production and the consequent irrelevance, in a world of plenty, of both productive abilities and material needs—possibilities that make the forecast of substantive goals very nearly impossible.

Does responsibility, as an ultimate goal, suffer from the same handicaps? Except for an unfortunate legal encumbrance,[2] there is hope that it might not. The legal encumbrance comes from the claim staked by lawyers and legal philosophers to

[2] The legal encumbrance, of which this volume contains illustrations, is considered unfortunate for the following reasons: Legal philosophy in the Common Law world has a retrospective temporal orientation. Legal philosophy in the Civil Law world has a passion for the systematic which often leads it to unrealism and lack of concreteness. The nature of politics as the "master science" demands that political philosophy look to the future, propose and define goals for it, and do so in a way that makes reference to concrete problems easy.

the concept of responsibility, in the sense of answerability, accountability, or liability. This is undoubtedly the sense in which it was used by Alexander Hamilton, James Madison, and others in the eighteenth century. Since then, the emphasis of common usage has shifted to responsibility in the sense of "capacity to cause," i.e., to choose in the light of knowledge about consequences and with resources for implementation. Even in the early legalistic days of responsibility, there was a clear desire to bring a man's accountability into proportion with his capacity to bring about the events for which he had to answer. Hamilton wrote, in *The Federalist*, No. 70:

Responsibility is of two kinds—to censure and to punishment. The first is the more important of the two. . . .

And Madison, in *The Federalist*, No. 63:

Responsibility, in order to be reasonable, must be limited to objects within the power of the responsible party, and in order to be effectual, must be related to operations of that power, of which a ready and proper judgment can be formed by the constituents.

In the course of the democratization of constitutional governments and the opening of many and intricate new channels through which citizens can contribute to central decisions, responsibility in this sense has been extended to ever more, and eventually to all, citizens. In the course of scientific and technological progress, human responsibility has been extended to realms previously wholly beyond its scope—like private and public health, aerial and space flight, before long the control of weather, and already the survival or destruction of responsible human beings as a species. Individuals can now become responsible, to an extent unthought of a hundred or even fifty years ago, for such matters as education, career, mate, residence, or the looks of one's face. There are differences in this regard in different areas of the world, but everywhere the trend is toward the extension of responsibility. Usually, the capacity of the community to become responsible for its future precedes the capacity of its individual members to become responsible for theirs and to contribute to central decisions about their common fate. But increases in communal responsibility have usually been justified as serving the ultimate goal of increased individual responsibility.[3] The norm of individual responsibility has been and is being advocated by a large number of prominent thinkers from different fields of learning and activity and with widely differing ideological convictions.[4] If properly defined, the value of responsibility might serve as a lowest common denominator of normative agreement.

An individual is in a sound "situation of responsibility," [5] when he can become responsible for those matters for which he is accountable, in the sense in which Madison used the term; that is, when he can contribute to those decisions whose consequences will in turn affect him. He can do this to the extent that three conditions are met: Alternatives must be available with which to implement the choice; resources must be available with which to implement the choice; and knowledge must be available about the probable consequences of the decision. On the goal of improving situations of responsibility, in this sense, it may be feasible to elicit the kind of consensus needed for solving the problem of the threat to the survival of mankind.

Such agreement could be reached most easily with regard to improvements in resources as a desideratum, especially resources for increasing human control over non-human parts of nature and the universe, for with respect to nature and

[3] Except in a few cases which may be considered abortive or aberrant, like a few remaining absolute monarchies and the racialist and other élitist movements associated with Fascism.

[4] See the author's "Responsibility in Citizenship, Government and Administration," *Public Policy: Yearbook of the Graduate School of Public Administration*, IV (1953), 116-33.

[5] For an attempt to apply this concept systematically to the comparative study of government, see the author's *Government by Constitution: The Political Systems of Democracy* (1959).

cosmos men come closest to forming a true community. Collaboration for the achievement of intermediate goals, as in the case of the International Geophysical Year, may serve as an illustration. Agreement should also be easy to obtain with regard to the desirability of improving foreknowledge of the consequences of decisions. Even if it were not "in the nature" of knowledge to become common property, increasing communication among all scientific workers in the world makes the prolonged restriction of improvements in knowledge very difficult. At least no one of influence on either side of the cold war today would make a statement like the following, made in 1938 by an official of the Spanish Ministry of Education:

All the misfortunes of Spain come from the stupid desire of the governments to teach Spaniards to read. Teaching a man to read is only to oblige him to assume a position that will cause misfortune for himself and for his motherland.[6]

It would be much harder to get agreement on the kind of alternatives that could or should be made available for choice. Because they deny that persistent limits are set to all human foreknowledge, adherents of necessitarian ideologies like Marxism-Leninism often refuse to admit the existence of any alternatives but those of accepting, either cheerfully or reluctantly, that which is inevitable: *Volentem fata ducunt, nolentem trahunt.* By contrast, constitutional democrats usually want to offer alternatives even to those people whose choice is likely to lead them to disaster. Nevertheless, Soviet Marxists would agree with them that, at least ultimately, each should have opportunities to make contributions to decisions made about the future of all, that is, to central decisions whose consequences will affect himself, and to the extent that this will be true. The Communists, after all, criticize "bourgeois democracy" because they believe that under it the working class, a majority of the population, are denied meaningful opportunities to make such contributions. Communist propa-

---

[6] The Marques de Lozoya, quoted by Howard K. Smith, *The State of Europe* (1949), p. 241.

ganda designed to stir up sentiment on behalf of cessation of nuclear tests also implies the belief that alternatives are available with regard to the most crucial problem.

Political philosophies in the Free World and the Soviet World are in agreement that the extermination of mankind is not necessary and that its prevention is desirable. They are in disagreement in their answers to this question: What is the best solution to the problem posed by this threat? This disagreement is due to the fact that the two sides hold different visions of the content of the goal of survival. This goal is not really ultimate—it is a penultimate goal. Neither camp stops short of wanting to prevent the outbreak of a nuclear war. The West is very unlikely to resign itself to maintenance of the status quo. Even if it wanted to do so, technological change would make such an attitude untenable. There are people on both sides of the Iron Curtain, political philosophers among them, who would prefer universal death to survival under domination of the victorious other side.

How can this preference be explained? [7] Partly in terms of poor information on each side about life in the other camp, and of the projection into the future of this information. No regime has ever been able to eliminate completely all hope on the part of its subjects. There are reasons to expect that a world-wide Communist regime would find it impossible to eliminate hope for its own improvement—enough reasons to warrant the prediction that "this, too, shall pass." Marxist ideology, on the other hand, predicts the necessary collapse of capitalism, whether it be world-wide or not. But there is another explanation, besides poor information and forecasts based on it, for this preference of universal suicide to domination by the enemy of the Cold War: refusal to face up to the likelihood that universal suicide is one of the two alternatives. The attempt to construct additional alternatives, like limited nuclear war, is an example of this refusal.

[7] We are not asking how this preference can be justified.

Both the refusal to accept the extermination of human life as one of two alternatives, and the implicit or explicit preference for general suicide, are related to thought—again on both sides—in terms of goals about the solution of problems which are no longer crucial, many of which have in fact come close to being solved. Among these goals are equality, security, welfare, and democracy. The degree to which political systems have approached realization of these goals differs, between the Free World and the Soviet World, and within each camp. But the problems, in response to which these goals were given the content which they still hold today, are no longer the most serious problems faced by the citizens of these countries (though perhaps of the "underdeveloped areas" of the world).

The most serious problem for men living in the two great hostile camps is that presented by the threats to human survival. In order to be able to solve it, we need clarity about the nature of the ultimate goal, next to which survival itself is penultimate. The purpose of this essay has been to show that this final goal can no longer usefully be defined in terms of the conventional values of contemporary political philosophy. The frequent and unpredictable changes in the substance of the problems confronted by mankind suggest that a definition of ultimate goals in substantive terms would also be of little help. The value of responsibility, as here conceived, is procedural: It defines how communities should go about the solution of their problems, not what the solution should be in any particular case.[8] This is another aspect of the goal of responsibility, which commends it as a common denominator capable of commanding sufficient agreement for solving the problem of the threat to survival.

If political philosophers work on behalf of the emerging global community of mankind, the path toward making their contribution to the solution of the crucial problem of our time may be similar to the one outlined here. In any case,

---

[8] For the distinction between substantive and procedural values, see the author's "Authority, Values, and Policy," *Nomos I*, pp. 49-57; and "Consensus," in *Government by Constitution*, chap. 22.

that path must be quite different from the one which influential political philosophy on both sides of the Iron Curtain (though not in countries like India) is traveling today. If we continue to follow that path, chances are that all our paths will come to an abrupt and permanent end. Prevention or postponement of such an end cannot be guaranteed by concentration on the formulation of ultimate goals capable of eliciting the needed consensus. But if political philosophy were to address itself to this great task, responsible human beings will at least have the consolation, if worse comes to worst, of having brought about their own demise in a responsible manner.

APPENDIX

THREE WAYS OF SPILLING INK

JOHN AUSTIN

IN CONSIDERING RESPONSIBILITY, we often need to decide whether someone did something *intentionally* or not, whether he *intended* to do this or that or not, whether this or that was his *intention*.

Compare *intentionally* with *deliberately* and *on purpose*. A schoolteacher may ask a child who has spilled ink: Did you do that *intentionally? Deliberately? On Purpose?* These may appear to mean the same (or to come down to the same). But do they?

By using various dodges, to be sampled rather than fully exploited here, we may persuade "ordinary language" to yield us information. Generally, we may (1) examine what we should say in different specified cases, (2) probe the backstage phenomena of grammar and philology.

I

[Justification for examining cases: a datum: which should enshrine something which makes good sense]

(1) Cases of intention or purpose:

—I stretch a string across the stairhead for my aunt to trip over.

—I dip into the till to get money to play the ponies, but of course I was going to put it back.

—I throw broken glass off the pavement onto the sidewalk.

—I feed the penguins peanuts.

(2) Cliché cases:

—Wounding with intent to kill) (for the purpose of.
—Declaring your honorable intentions) (purposes.
—Deliberate intention) (intentional deliberation.
—Deliberate decision, choice) (intentional.

(3) Cases of dissociation and opposition:

—Intentionally and on purpose but not deliberately:
on impulse, spontaneously (?), agony of mind (?).
—Deliberately and intentionally but not on purpose:
wantonly.
—Deliberately but not intentionally (nor unintentionally): incidental obstacles.
—"Accidentally done on purpose."

II

Hints from grammar and philology:

(1) *Deliberate* and *deliberation,* verb and noun, are
quite different from *intend, intention* and *purpose,
purpose.* Cf. *am deliberating*) (*am intending* (*purposing*): former a process, latter not. *Protracted deliberations* but not *protracted intentions.*

(1a) *I intend* (*I purpose;* too) quite different from, in this
sort of sense non-existent, *I deliberate.* "I *intend to*
X" has vector, future, committal, effect: cf. "I *shall*
X." Might be called an auxiliary (cf. also "I promise
to X"): no standard future "I shall intend."

(2) Adjective terminations: *-ate, -al, -ful* or *-ive.* Meanings of. Comparison with conside*rate,* precipit*ate,*
thought*ful.*

(2a) Adjectives, negative forms of: , *un-, -less.* Significance of. Comparison with *careful, careless.* [Justification for "superstition" about language: the origins of
speech.]

(3) Phrases, prepositional etc.
On purpose (to); *for* (the) purpose of
With the intention of
After or *with* deliberation
To some purpose
No part of my intention.

(4) *Deliberately, purposefully* used to describe overt manner of executing some action; *intentionally* never so used.

(5) Etymologies. In *deliberate,* metaphor from weighing up. In *intend,* metaphor from bending, straining towards (cf. *intent, intense*). In *purpose,* setting up before oneself.

III

Suggestions about the meanings of the three words:

Intention. My idea, picture, notion, conception of what I'm up to, doing. I don't "know what, I'm doing" by looking to observe (= realizing what I am or have been doing, in odd cases); but by knowing the plan being acted on. Thus conduct describable by active, non-behavioristic verbs. Carrying out my intention in action.

[Not a case where the negative word, *un*intentional, wears the trousers]

The miner's lamp lighting our way ahead. Arbitrariness of its range ahead and around, of the detail it takes in. Our action carved out of background of *circumstances, incidentals, consequences.*

Phrases of a campaign: structuring. The bracketing effect of *intention*—my action to be judged *as a whole* (cf. the till-dipper).

Contrast with *purpose* to be effected or achieved as result of what I'm doing. My action to be judged in the light of end, aim, object, purpose (cf. the string-stretcher). May be *no* purpose (a circumstance); cf. care. *On*) (*with*.

Deliberately, deliberate. I stopped to ask myself "shall I or shan't I?" (and decided for X, which I did). Weighed up the pros and cons: there must be some cons. Need not decide in favor of it; need not carry out what I decide to do: deliberation not about means to ends. *Command* matter, not staff (planning) matter.

[Overriding considerations: interference by outside agents, etc.]

So it does make a difference in the spilled ink case too?

But of course other words needed in connection with each of our three to get full story: e.g. motive) (intention and purpose: premeditation) (deliberation, mean) (intend. Suggestion on this last.